Bathroom Remodeling For Dummies®

Tackling Tile

Ceramic tile calculator: Determine how many ceramic tiles y[...] to cover and dividing that number by the tile factor for each s[...]

Total area (floor, wall, countertop): Length (feet) x width (feet) = total area (square feet)

Tile to order: Use the following formulas to figure out how much tile to order:

- ✔ **For 4-inch tiles:** Total area divided by 0.1089 = number of 4-inch tiles needed
- ✔ **For 6-inch tiles:** Total area divided by 0.25 = number of 6-inch tiles needed
- ✔ **For 9-inch tiles:** Total area divided by 0.5625 = number of 9-inch tiles needed
- ✔ **For 12-inch tiles:** Total area divided by 1 = number of 12-inch tiles needed
- ✔ **For 18-inch tiles:** Total area divided by 2.25 = number of 18-inch tiles needed

Very Vinyl

Use the information in the following sections to determine how much vinyl to order.

Working with sheet vinyl

Sheet vinyl flooring calculator: Determine how much vinyl flooring to purchase by calculating the square footage of floor you plan to cover and dividing that number by 9 to get the number of square yards of flooring you need.

Floor area: Length of floor (feet) x width of floor (feet) = floor area (square feet)

Sheet vinyl to order: Floor area divided by 9 = number of square yards of floor covering needed

Note: Sheet vinyl comes in rolls up to 12 feet in width. Room dimensions over 12 feet require a seam.

Working with vinyl floor tile

Vinyl floor tile calculator: Determine how many vinyl tiles to purchase by calculating the area of floor you plan to cover and dividing that number by the tile factor for each size of tile.

Floor area: Length of floor (feet) x width of floor (feet) = floor area (square feet)

Tile to order: Use the following formulas to figure out how much vinyl tile to order:

- ✔ **For 9-inch tiles:** Floor area divided by 0.5625 = number of 9-inch tiles needed
- ✔ **For 12-inch tiles:** Floor area divided by 1 = number of 12-inch tiles needed

BESTSELLING
BOOK SERIES

Bathroom Remodeling For Dummies®

Cheat Sheet

Wild about Wallpaper

Wallpaper calculator: Determine how much wallpaper to purchase by calculating the area you plan to paper and dividing that number by the usable yield per roll of paper.

Wall area: Total length of all walls x wall height = wall area

Unpapered areas: Use the following formulas:

- ✔ Window area = window height x window width x number of windows
- ✔ Door area = door height x door width x number of doors

Wallpapering area: Wall area – unpapered area = wallpapering area

Wallpaper to order: Number of single rolls needed = wallpapering area ÷ usable yield

Usable yield charts: Wallpaper rolls come in two sizes: American and European. The drop of a wallpaper pattern refers to how much the pattern drops from top left to bottom right to match the adjacent strip.

Pattern Repeat (Drop)	Usable Yield (American Rolls)	Usable Yield (European Rolls)
0 to 6 inches	32 square feet	25 square feet
7 to 12 inches	30 square feet	22 square feet
13 to 18 inches	27 square feet	20 square feet
19 to 23 inches	25 square feet	18 square feet

Pretty in Paint

Wall paint calculator: To determine how much paint to buy, find the square footage of the area that you plan to paint, and divide by the number of square feet covered by a gallon of paint.

Total ceiling area: Wall length x wall width = paintable area

Total wall area: Total length of all walls x wall height = total wall area

Unpainted areas:

- ✔ Window area = window height x window width x number of windows
- ✔ Door area = door height x door width x number of doors

Paintable area: Paintable area = total wall area – window area – door area

Paint to order: Use the following formulas to figure out how much paint you need:

- ✔ Number of gallons needed for smooth walls = paintable area ÷ 350
- ✔ Number of gallons needed for rough, textured walls or unpainted wallboard = paintable area ÷ 300

Note: Round off any fraction of a gallon over 0.5 to the next gallon. It's usually cheaper to purchase a gallon of paint than 3 quarts.

For Dummies: Bestselling Book Series for Beginners

Bathroom Remodeling

FOR

DUMMIES®

Bathroom Remodeling FOR DUMMIES®

by Gene and Katie Hamilton

WILEY

Wiley Publishing, Inc.

Bathroom Remodeling For Dummies®

Published by
Wiley Publishing, Inc.
111 River St.
Hoboken, NJ 07030
www.wiley.com

Library of Congress Cataloging-in-Publication Data:

Library of Congress Control Number: 2003105848

ISBN: 0-7645-2552-2

Manufactured in the United States of America

10 9 8 7 6 5 4 3 2 1

 is a trademark of Wiley Publishing, Inc.

About the Authors

Gene and Katie Hamilton have been working on houses and writing about home improvements for over 30 years. They have remodeled 14 houses and write a weekly newspaper column entitled "Do It Yourself . . . Or Not?" which appears in newspapers across the country and on Web sites.

The Hamiltons are authors of 16 home improvement books, including *Home Improvement For Dummies, Carpentry For Dummies,* and *Painting and Wallpapering For Dummies.*

They are the founders of HouseNet.com, the first home improvement site on the Internet and America Online.

You've seen these veteran do-it-yourselfers appear as home improvement experts on CNN, *Dateline,* the *Today* show, *Home Matters, Today at Home,* and *Our Home.*

They live on the eastern shore of Maryland.

Author's Acknowledgments

Over the years, we've tapped the expertise of countless professionals in the home improvement industry, and although we've thanked them individually, we've never acknowledged how much we appreciate their help. We began writing about home improvements some 30-odd years ago while we were working on our first fixer-upper house. We've been doing it ever since, and as our career continues to evolve, we keep on learning from a cadre of people in the home improvement industry.

We want to thank all the knowledgeable salespeople in hardware stores and home centers who have helped us and so many other customers with questions and concerns.

For many years, we've tapped the expertise of design professionals, contractors, and tradespeople, and they've always been generous in sharing their experience and knowledge with us.

We always appreciate the information and support we receive from manufacturers of home improvement products. The communication folks and their public relations comrades keep us informed of the latest and greatest new innovations. The product managers are always quick to respond to our questions and observations.

We are fortunate indeed to be part of this vital and growing home improvement industry.

Publisher's Acknowledgments

We're proud of this book; please send us your comments through our Dummies online registration form located at www.dummies.com/register/.

Some of the people who helped bring this book to market include the following:

Acquisitions, Editorial, and Media Development

Project Editor: Marcia L. Johnson

Acquisitions Editor: Tracy Boggier

Senior Copy Editor: Tina Sims

Editorial Program Assistant: Holly Gastineau-Grimes

Technical Editor: Pam Price

Senior Permissions Editor: Carmen Krikorian

Editorial Manager: Jennifer Ehrlich

Editorial Assistant: Elizabeth Rea

Cover Photo: ©Corbis

Cartoons: Rich Tennant, www.the5thwave.com

Production

Project Coordinator: Erin Smith

Layout and Graphics: Seth Conley, Stephanie D. Jumper, Linsey Osborn, Mary Gillot Virgin

Special Art: Lisa Reed

Proofreaders: TECHBOOKS Production Services, Brian H. Walls

Indexer: TECHBOOKS Production Services

Special Help:
Jill Burke, Traci Cumbay, E. Neil Johnson, Heather Ryan, Alissa Schwipps

Publishing and Editorial for Consumer Dummies

Diane Graves Steele, Vice President and Publisher, Consumer Dummies

Joyce Pepple, Acquisitions Director, Consumer Dummies

Kristin A. Cocks, Product Development Director, Consumer Dummies

Michael Spring, Vice President and Publisher, Travel

Brice Gosnell, Associate Publisher, Travel

Kelly Regan, Editorial Director, Travel

Publishing for Technology Dummies

Andy Cummings, Vice President and Publisher, Dummies Technology/General User

Composition Services

Gerry Fahey, Vice President of Production Services

Debbie Stailey, Director of Composition Services

Contents at a Glance

Table of Contents

Introduction

We're a nation of countless bathrooms that are on the brink of being torn apart, redesigned, and remodeled. Bathrooms are big! The bathroom has gone from being a convenience to a luxury, and everyone wants one of his or her own, even in the most modest of homes. Welcome to Bathroom Remodeling For Dummies, where we tell you how to transform your air-conditioned bathroom from blah to beautiful and inefficient to well designed.

Now we realize all bathrooms are not created equal, and some folks want to create their ultimate home spa, while others just want to replace their old fixtures with new ones. Some bathrooms will be gutted and pillaged and totally transformed, but others will be given a kinder, gentler makeover. Whatever the status and condition of your bathroom, we explain how to plan its design, how to manage the remodeling process, how to do the work yourself, and when to hire a professional.

You may be asking yourself, "Can I remodel my bathroom without spending every penny I have, destroying the harmony and balance of my happy household, and breaking the spirit of everyone involved?" The answer is yes, but it's a qualified yes that hinges on how you plan the project and prepare for the inconvenience and invasion. Sure, a sense of humor is a big help, but remodeling the most important room in the house is not a cakewalk, and don't let anyone tell you it is. But is it worth it? You bet, because every time you walk into your newly remodeled bathroom, the adversity and adventure fade further into memory. Like a woman we met online once told us, remodeling her bathroom was like having her first child. It seemed to take forever, she couldn't imagine the pain she endured, but the end result was truly worth it.

Undoubtedly, you'll enjoy the immediate payback and pleasure of using a sparkling new shower valve with body-tingling spray heads, but you'll also raise the resale value of your house. Even a modest makeover in a bathroom adds value, but an honest-to-goodness remodeled bathroom is an investment worth making. Every survey we see puts a remodeled bathroom at the top of the list of payback improvements, so you can justify the investment and enjoy using it.

Bathroom Remodeling For Dummies provides you with suggestions to guide you through the maze of decisions and options and helps you design a new bathroom that's right for you. Whether you're sprucing up a powder room, making over the kid's bathroom, or creating your ultimate spa and retreat, turn the pages for help.

About This Book

This book isn't a novel, so you don't have to read the pages in order. It's designed so that you can flip through the book and start wherever you like. Don't think about this for your book club, because while we think the content is tantalizing, it's probably not a good choice for a discussion group. Unless, of course, the members are all tired of their old bathrooms and want to remodel them. Then this book will be a winner.

The Table of Contents at the front of the book is useful to find the topic that interests you, whether it's about demolishing the old bathroom to make room for a new one, or finding a reliable and skilled contractor to do the job. Or, you can search the Index for a particular topic or phase of remodeling a bathroom that interests you. Maybe you like to jump around and discover how to install ceramic tile one day and tune into carving out storage space the next day. No matter how you find the information, you can read it and weep (just kidding) or read it and put the book back on the shelf. We wrote it so that you can move around and start and stop wherever you like.

You can find a lot of information within the pages of the book, from advice about specific clearance space around a toilet, to guidelines for choosing cabinets and countertops, to an overview perspective so you understand the scope and breadth of the job. You can read a lot of nuts-and-bolts instructions about removing a toilet and installing a new one or use the advice about hiring a professional to do the job.

Here are some other things you can find in this book:

- Key points to think about before you decide to do the work yourself or hire a remodeling contractor
- What's involved in laying out cabinets and fixtures
- What you need to create a floor plan that works for you
- Key features for an accessible bathroom using universal design concepts
- What's involved in installing different kinds of faucets and valves
- The various options for bathroom fittings and accessories

- ✔ The best way to plan lighting for different size bathrooms
- ✔ Guidelines for creating the correct amount of ventilation in different size bathrooms
- ✔ How to use Web sites to plan and design your bathroom

Conventions Used in This Book

The following conventions are used throughout the text to make things consistent and easy to understand:

- ✔ New terms appear in *italic* and are closely followed by an easy-to-understand definition.
- ✔ **Bold** is used to highlight the action parts of numbered steps or the keywords in bulleted lists.
- ✔ All Web addresses appear in `mono font`.

Foolish Assumptions

In this book we make several assumptions about you, the reader. You want to make your home more livable and enjoyable by updating, expanding, or improving the bathroom. You're interested in finding out how to begin the process of appraising your present bathroom so you can create a new and improved one. You don't want to be pressured into selecting materials and fixtures, because you want to see everything that's available and know all your options. You want to know what's involved in demolishing the walls and removing the fixtures and cabinets and how to install new ones so you can decide whether you want to do some of the work yourself. You're ready to act, move, and make things happen.

Remodeling a bathroom is not for the faint of heart. It's action oriented and requires extra energy and stamina. You realize it's a challenge and are willing to take it on.

How This Book Is Organized

Like all the Dummies books that have come before it, *Bathroom Remodeling For Dummies* is organized to provide lots of useful information that is easily accessible. We divided the book into five main parts.

Part I: Bathroom Spaces: Ahhh, the Possibilities

Remodeling a bathroom didn't used to be so complicated. The plumbing lines in the floor and electrical wires behind the walls have always been there, but the choices in fixtures, faucets, and materials were never so daunting. Part I lays out an overview of remodeling a bathroom to give you the big picture of what's involved. This section explains the different types of bathrooms to help you define what your bathroom project will involve. Whether you're doing some easy-on-the budget fix-ups or a blow-out-the-room transformation, we help you define what's right for you.

This section explains the step-by-step process of remodeling a bathroom so you're prepared for what to expect — physically, emotionally, and financially — and provides guidelines for designing a floor plan to take advantage of every inch of space. Use it as a road map for overall guidance and as a reference for making the details count.

Part II: Taking Control: Planning the Project

Part II deals with being in control of the project from the initial conception of the plan to the day you walk into the completed new bathroom. Many behind-the-scene decisions are needed to pull off a perfect bathroom, and knowing them in advance gives you an advantage.

In this part we explain how to estimate how much it costs and how to budget your funds. One of the first decisions you make when remodeling a bathroom (or any room) is whether you should do the work yourself or hire a contractor, and we give you the knowledge to make the call. We explain how to find a good contractor to do some or all the work, depending on the complexity of the project and your level of skills and time commitment. In this part, you find out the basics of the mechanical, electrical, and plumbing systems so that you can manage the project or do the work yourself, or a little of both.

Part III: Fabulous Fixtures, Vanities, and Faucets

Part III takes you into the wonderful world of the stuff bathrooms are made of — toilets, bathtubs, whirlpools, showers, sinks, faucets, cabinets, and countertops — with advice about choosing, finding, and installing them. You may be stymied by the choices, but with knowledge comes wisdom to choose them with confidence and insight. The more you know about fixtures and materials, the more informed your decisions will be.

And don't forget the new status you'll achieve with that knowledge. At cocktail parties, you'll be sought after as an expert on solid surfaces and sink installations. At Little League games, you'll be the resource who people turn to for advice about what toilet to buy. The knowledge you acquire may be the first step into a career as a bathroom consultant. It could happen.

Part IV: Winning Ways with Walls, Windows, and More

Part IV takes you through the process of simple decorating techniques to more complicated installations, all using strategies to help you determine what's best for your bathroom. The walls and floors are the largest surfaces in a bathroom, so covering and finishing them are important. In this part, we explain how to install floors — ceramic tile, vinyls, and laminate — and suggest a variety of windows and wall coverings for any style room. We explain the importance of lighting and ventilation in a bathroom and suggest specialty doors to save floor space.

Part V: The Part of Tens

The famous Part of Tens unique to *For Dummies* books is designed for finding useful information fast. Read these "quick hits" about remodeling a bathroom and apply them to your room: how to create storage space in any bathroom, some really inexpensive and easy decorating ideas, and a list of really useful Web sites for remodeling a bathroom. If you like good ideas laid out in a fast format, you'll like the Part of Tens.

Icons Used in This Book

This icon marks the parts of the bathroom remodeling project that you really should leave to the professionals.

This icon sits next to key details you need to keep in mind in order to design and create the best bathroom you can. It's a helpful reminder to do certain things we think are important.

If you're the kind of person who always asks, "Why?" you'll like these icons because they point out how something works.

Text marked with this bull's-eye icon gives a helpful pointer, a shortcut, or a timesaving secret.

This is an icon to watch out for. It means to really pay attention to what you're doing so you don't do more damage than good. Heads up when you see this one.

Part I
Bathroom Spaces: Ahhh, the Possibilities

The 5th Wave   By Rich Tennant

"I like the marble vanity and the wall sconces, but I think the Eurostyle fixtures on the whirlpool take away some of its simple country charm."

In this part . . .

Remodeling a bathroom can be daunting and demanding, but the end game is a well-designed room that's comfortable and convenient to use. In this part, we tell you how to be in the driver's seat from day one and plan and design a bathroom that suits your needs and your budget. You can find out what features and fixtures to look for to make your dream bathroom come true. We discuss the types of bathrooms to consider so you approach the project with an overview and then bring it closer to home (yours) with details and design concepts.

You find out how to come up with a new floor plan and what to expect during the remodeling process. You also get a list of tools you'll need to make the work go smoother. Finally, we tell you about the floor and wall materials that you can choose from.

Chapter 1

Reinventing Your Bathroom with a Splash

*O*n emotional, practical, spiritual, and financial levels, a remodeled bathroom can be a very good thing. Maybe you're thinking that colorful new wall tiles will lift your spirits when you walk in there each morning or after a hard day at the office. Perhaps that shiny, new shower will recharge you, or a relaxing whirlpool bath in the new tub will wash away the day's problems. And the improvements are sure to enhance the value of your house. You'll probably appreciate your brand-new bathroom for years to come. You have to spend time there anyway, so you may as well surround yourself in beauty and luxury.

If that idea appeals to you, welcome to the world of bathroom remodeling. We hold your hand, nudge you along, and help you make good choices as you rethink and design your new bathroom. At first, you spend a lot of time just noodling, or thinking about how to reinvent an old bathroom to create a new and improved one. But all that brainpower won't go to waste. You'll receive an immediate payback every time you use the new accoutrements in your bathroom and a long-term payback when you sell your house. You can't ask for more than that.

Everybody's Doing It in the Bathroom

Everybody's doing it. Remodeling their bathroom, that is. Really, there's never been a hotter market for the bathroom remodeling industry. Empty nesters are gutting their kid's bedroom to create their ultimate bathroom spa, and parents in need of pampering are remaking their master bath as an in-house oasis, strictly off limits to the kids. The family bathroom is being redesigned and updated with functional shared spaces for kids of all ages. Even the powder room is getting a makeover with showoff fixtures and fittings.

Homeowners of all ages want to make their bathroom more user-friendly and accessible. In years past, universal design concepts that encouraged wider door openings and low thresholds for a wheelchair were a tough sell. Today, however, with aging baby boomers and transgenerational households on the rise, high-style fixtures and fittings that are easy and convenient to operate have universal appeal. People of all ages are realizing that wider doorways and continuous floor surfaces make spaces feel larger and more open, and they're using universal design concepts to create functional and aesthetically pleasing bathrooms.

Whatever you have in mind for your bathroom, — a simple spruce up or a total redesign — you're not alone. The 2003 Kitchen and Bathroom Industry trade show attracted record-breaking numbers of exhibitors and attendance. Bathrooms are hot. Just look in any magazine or watch any home improvement show. Bathrooms are being face-lifted, made over, and completely rebuilt from the bottom up.

And because of the interest in bathrooms, remodeling has never been easier. If you're ready to attack your bathroom, you have an army of services and suppliers at your disposal. And if you want to do it yourself, you have an array of products and materials designed for you to install.

Receiving Your Just Reward

While you will most definitely enjoy using your new bathroom, you'll also reap a financial reward. If you're looking for a way to rationalize the investment, consider this: Real estate professionals predict you will earn back almost 100 percent of your investment.

Every year, Remodeling Online does a cost versus value report that compares the estimated cost of professionally installed renovations with the value it is likely to add to the home a year later. The value numbers are based on the opinions of 200-plus real estate agents and appraisers located in the 35 metro markets.

The 2002 report says that adding a bathroom costing $15,058 to a house with one or one and a half baths recoups 94 percent of that investment. This particular project is an addition of a full 6-by-8-foot bath within the existing footprint of the home near the bedrooms.

To update an existing bathroom with new fixtures, flooring, and everything else at a cost of $9,720 recoups 88 percent of the investment. Not a bad return on your money either.

If you're still having a hard time rationalizing the initial expense, turn to Chapter 6 to find out how to estimate your budget and find the money you need for your project. You'll also get advice about financing the project with everything from traditional home equity loans and lines of credit to the latest trend of using a credit card with reward points. It's a new twist on double dipping.

Planning the Perfect Bathroom

Everyone knows that you need a game plan to take a remodeling project from wish list to completion, but not everyone gives homage to the organizational skills required. In Chapter 2, you can use a handy checklist to rate your present bathroom. It's an easy way to start you thinking about what you like and don't like about it and can help you fine-tune your list of gotta-have features in your next bathroom.

The length of time it takes to remodel your bathroom depends on the scope of the project, but the pleasantness of the process is all in the planning. Whether you envision a magical makeover with new wallpaper and floor or a complete rehab, you can make your bathroom go from bad to beautiful with a plan of attack and strategy to keep the work progress on track.

Obsessing over bathrooms

Bathroom remodeling starts with simple steps — deciding how much you're ready to do and what shape those plans will take — and it quickly moves to near obsession with everything from tile to toilet paper holders.

Start by thinking of your bathroom as a shell of a room with floors, walls, ceiling, and windows. Then focus on the fixtures and fittings. By going from the broad to the specific, you'll define the space and the functions it needs to perform. You may find that you need to take space from an adjacent room to make a new larger bathroom. Losing a hall bedroom closet that backs up to a bathroom is a tactic that remodelers often use.

After you get started, it's hard not to fixate on your bathroom. Go into a friend's home and you're immediately drawn to their bathroom. You begin snooping around under their vanity, wondering how it's attached to the wall. For the first time in your life, you become enchanted with towel bars and tissue holders. You begin spouting the recommended CFM (cubic feet per minute of air) requirements for bathroom ventilation at chic cocktail parties, and you know that you're ready to begin planning your bathroom. You are armed with information and ready to go forth and fix.

Remodeling: It's all in the plan, Stan

The actual remodeling process uses your plan as a starting point and proceeds through a series of grunts and moans and oh-my-goshes. And of course, there's always the case of the best laid plan that ran amuck when a hidden copper water pipe in a wall gets severed by a saw and springs a leak.

The journey can be a smooth one with careful planning, which we discuss in Chapter 3. From start (tearing the old stuff out) to finish (getting approval from the local building department), the whole process is laid out for your remodeling enjoyment.

No matter whether you hire a contractor or do it yourself, someone has to manage the project and make sure that the flow of work continues in order and on schedule. If the drywall contractor hangs the wallboard before the building inspector looks at the electrical wiring and plumbing work, there's trouble. The wallboard has to come down so the inspector can do his job. One person — a contractor, designer, or homeowner — needs to wear the manager hat to keep tabs of tradespeople showing up, doing their work, doing it correctly, and coordinating all the jobs.

Getting the right person for the job

We're big fans of doing it yourself if you have the time, the talent, and the temperament, but not everyone does. In Chapter 7, we share what we've learned about making the decision. Sometimes a work plan is devised to combine both, which is ideal if you enjoy working with your hands and want to take part in the process. For those projects you know are beyond your capabilities (or patience), we guarantee that someone somewhere has the know-how to get the job done. (See Chapter 7 for a list of specialty contractors.) You just have to know where to look.

Who would have guessed that the Internet would become a good place to find a contractor to remodel your bathroom? Not us, that's for sure. But there are also plenty of traditional sources to find a contractor, designer, or tradesperson. When you make contact, be able to explain your plans for your bathroom, have pictures from magazines or books to illustrate what you want, and know much money you have budgeted for the project.

Most contractors and the growing number of specialty tradespeople work in specific areas or counties and are familiar with the local building codes and requirements. For example, a plumber knows what diameter of copper or plastic pipes will pass code in his area. An electrician knows the specifications for exhaust vents and GFCI (ground-fault circuit interrupters) required in bathrooms. To expand your knowledge of what's required, ask your local building department and contractors as you interview them.

It saves you work in the long run, but hiring a contractor is a job in itself, and a very important one. We offer guidelines for conducting an effective interview in Chapter 7, which also gives advice about drafting a solid contract.

Shopping for sinks and so on

When you begin shopping for bathroom materials and fixtures, you'll discover from the get-go that you have way too many choices. There's no easy way to escape this except to dive in, swim around, and come up for air as you peruse the aisles of home and bathroom design centers. And don't forget to push back from your computer screen every so often to take a breather from crawling from Web site to Web site while looking for materials and ideas.

Where can you find the best selection of bathroom fixtures and materials? They're everywhere. But unless you live near a bathroom design center or large home center, the materials usually aren't in one place. Kitchen and bath design centers and the big-box home improvement stores have the lion's share of bathroom components. And they offer design services that are hard to beat.

Flooring retailers, ceramic tile, and lighting centers have the largest selection of specialty materials, and they offer installation services for their products. The staff members tend to be well versed in their subject and can offer suggestions or a creative solution to a problem. They usually have more time to spend with customers, so they're a good starting point.

Bathroom remodeling involves more than just choosing a bathtub and toilet. The behind-the-walls and under-the-flooring materials are casts of characters all to themselves. But they're important for you to know about because they provide the smooth surface and foundation for the fixtures and finishing materials. Eventually, you'll become comfortable citing the difference between green board and cement board, two materials of considerable importance. You can find all this and more in Chapter 5.

And speaking of things behind the walls, wait until you get up close and personal with the mechanical systems of your new bathroom. Chapter 8 takes you behind the walls to discover how the plumbing, electrical, and ventilation systems work so you can make prudent choices and understand what changes you can make and those you can't. Even the more mundane chore of spotting electrical outlets in the new bathroom takes on new meaning when you create a wiring plan to locate outlets for everyone's personal electronics.

Finding your style

Are you high style or low country? Do you know the difference? Do you care? The major manufacturers of plumbing fixtures have coordinated their products in eye-catching suites and collections of styles to take the guesswork out of knowing what style toilet looks best with what style of bathtub. These collections include toilets, bidets, sinks, and bathtubs, with faucets and fittings that complement each other. The styles range from contemporary to traditional and country to Victorian, just to name a few.

Getting Started

Take your time going through the process of planning your new bathroom. The choices are many, and the decisions aren't trivial. Spend as much time as you can afford planning and refining your ideas. If you're in doubt about the fixture style you like, double back to others you once considered. Take a fresh look at the tiles you like. You should absolutely love everything going into your new bathroom. Unless someone has a gun to your head, don't be pressured by the idea you have to do it now. It's your bathroom. You want to make it the best it can be. Devote time to looking at as many choices as you can. And when you know what you want, strike! Go for it! Just do it! And enjoy your new bathroom.

Chapter 2

Designing the Bathroom That's Right for You

In This Chapter

▶ Defining the features in different types of bathrooms

▶ Making a bathroom functional and comfortable to use

▶ Laying out a bathroom design like a pro

▶ Creating a floor plan to scale

According to the National Kitchen & Bath Association (NKBA), the average cost of remodeling a bathroom is $14,600, which includes the design, appliances, fixtures, materials, and installation. So before you plunk down the big bucks, spend some time planning its design. Start a list of your likes and dislikes to create a wish list for your new bathroom so you'll know the must-have features to include and those to omit. Notice what works and what doesn't in your current bathroom. Pay attention to features in bathrooms you use at work and at play and even those you use when traveling.

Whether your new bathroom is strictly for taking care of business or for pampering yourself after a long, hard day at the office, focus on the elements in a bathroom that's right for you. This process may be time consuming, but you'll find that it pays off in the end by giving you the bathroom that you've always dreamed of.

Get a notebook, preferably one with pockets, and designate it as the "bathroom notebook." That's where you'll record facts, figures, measurements, and phone numbers. In the pockets, tuck samples of wallpaper, paint color cards, fabrics, and other small items you come across and like; magazine clippings; and other reference materials. Create columns labeled "never again" and "must have." If your current bathroom has tile grout and you're tired of cleaning it, add ceramic tile to the "never again" side of the list. If you stay at a fancy-schmancy hotel and savor the luxury of soaking in the whirlpool tub or the convenience of having a telephone in the bathroom, add those features to the "must-have" side. Use all your bathroom encounters to hone the list and help you define desired features.

Do your homework by browsing the pages of home decorating and remodeling magazines for ideas. Tear out articles and ads with ideas and products you like and put them in your notebook. Use decorating books as references. When you see a bathroom design you like, make a copy of it — don't tear out the pages.

After you read this chapter, you'll have a good idea of the different types of bathrooms and what goes into each of them. With this basic knowledge, visit a design center that specializes in bathrooms, like those found at kitchen and bathroom showrooms or large home improvement stores. Here, you can get a close-up look at a dizzying array of bathroom settings and touch a large assortment of fixtures, materials, and furnishings to see whether you like how they feel against your skin.

Bathrooms for All Seasons and Reasons

Bathrooms can be categorized into several different types based on their size and function, who uses them, and their location in the house. The smallest footprint for a bathroom is usually the powder room and the half bath. Bedrooms with nearby or attached bathrooms include the guest bathroom, a kids' bathroom, and the master bathroom. Variations of them include a bathroom with laundry facilities, a basement bathroom, a bathroom with fixtures and features that are accessible to the physically challenged, and a luxury master bathroom suite with whirlpool or sauna, workout equipment, and dressing room.

It's a small world: Powder room or half bath

A powder room is a small bathroom on the first floor of a home, usually located off a hallway or the main living area. It has a small vanity or sink, mirror, and toilet and is designed to accommodate guests, as well as family members. You can make a powder room complement your living-area decorating style by choosing compatible colors and furnishings.

In many older homes, the closet or space under the stairway was drafted as a powder room so visitors didn't have to go upstairs to use the main bathroom. These bathrooms have just enough space for the essentials: a toilet tucked under the stairway, and a tiny corner sink with a mirror.

Wall-mounted light sconces are a good way to provide adequate lighting without overwhelming a small space, so they're a good choice in a powder room.

Going up a size: Three-quarter bath

A three-quarter bath, a term created by home builders and realtors, is also usually small, but large enough to include a shower with the vanity and toilet, and often features storage shelves.

The small space of a half or three-quarter bath may be the place to splurge on materials. You can rationalize purchasing high-end tiles because so few are needed; the same holds true for wallcovering. When shopping for material, know exactly how much you need so that you can take advantage of leftover bargain-priced materials that will fit in your small space.

Welcoming visitors: The guest bathroom

A guest bathroom is a full or three-quarter bath and is usually adjacent to a guest bedroom or a room used for occasional visitors. In the home of empty nesters, a guest bathroom is often a reincarnation of the kids' bathroom. Plenty of counter space is a plus so that visitors have room for travel shaving kits and toiletry cases.

Because the guest room isn't used on a full-time basis, many people make the adjoining bathroom do double duty by also using it as a laundry room. Many people also borrow an idea from condominiums and vacation time-share units and make good use of a small area (such as a closet area) by incorporating a stacked or side-by-side washer and dryer. See Chapter 8 for the electrical and plumbing requirements for what's behind the wall.

In many homes, the lower level or basement serves as the place for a guest room, so the addition of a bathroom is convenient not only for visitors but for family members, too. An ejector pump, described in Chapter 9, grinds up waste and pumps it uphill, so it's a key solution for a basement bathroom in which the main drain exits above the slab. The ejector pump can also handle water from the shower and sink, making it the ideal solution for a basement installation.

Just for kids

The ages and numbers of kids should determine the design of a kids' bathroom. For young children, a bathroom with accessible fixtures and reachable faucets is important. For teenagers, privacy is at the top of the list. A shared bathroom that serves both young and old or several children becomes multipurpose and needs functional shared spaces. This type of bathroom is most accommodating when it has partitioned areas for a tub and shower and a toilet compartment for privacy. For school-age kids all leaving the house at the same time in the morning, a large vanity with double sinks eliminates congestion during the morning rush. Materials and fixtures that are easy to clean is a high priority for high-use bathrooms for kids of any age.

For a kid-friendly bathroom, choose shower faucets and body sprays that can be lowered and raised to adjust to the size of the family member.

If little children will be using the bathroom, consider choosing child-size fixtures that you can easily replace with full-sized models later on. For example, a two-piece child-size toilet with a rim height of 10¼ inches is perfect for toddlers and grade-school-aged kids, and you can easily replace it with a full-size unit later. Many sinks can be installed in an adjustable countertop that is mounted on the wall at a lower height for little ones and then raised later on. You need flexible piping for the drain, and the faucet may be mounted on the sink or the deck behind it as long as the spout is long enough to extend over the sink.

Those electronic faucets that are used in public places, such as airports, are now available for home use. These make a lot of sense in a kids' bathroom because the temperature can be preset, making it a great safety feature. You don't have to reach the faucet to start the water flow, so the little ones find it easier to use the sink. In addition, the water turns off when the kids are finished, so you'll never have to hear, "But Mom, Mary was the last to use the bathroom. She left the water running, not me!"

To take advantage of every inch of floor space in any bathroom, consider replacing a hinged door, which takes up floor space as it swings open and closed, with a pocket door that slides into the wall. See more about pocket doors in Chapter 15.

Retreating to luxury: The master bathroom

A master bathroom is a welcome respite for weary and time-challenged workers, empty nesters, and parents in need of pampering. It's a retreat where you

Childproofing a bathroom

The slippery surfaces and hot water in a bathroom can make it a not-so-safe place for little ones. With a little bit of thought and planning, you can make your bathroom a safe and sudsy room for kids.

✔ Use only a bathmat or rug that has a rubber backing so it won't slide across the floor.

✔ Choose a countertop with rounded edges and no sharp corners that can hurt little ones.

✔ Install antiscalding devices on faucets and shower heads that have a maximum hot water setting (120 degrees is a safe setting) and are pressure balanced. That way, when it is turned on and adjusted, the ratio of hot and cold water remains the same (even if somewhere in the house someone flushes a toilet or starts the dishwasher at the same time).

✔ Avoid a platform tub with steps that can be slippery when wet.

✔ When bathing little ones, install faucets where you can comfortably reach and control the water level and temperature from outside the tub.

✔ Install grab bars at a lower level in tub and shower areas so that a child can safely reach them.

✔ Choose a shower or tub doors made of safety glass.

✔ Keep cleaning chemicals and medicines in a locked cabinet.

can soak and steam or just sneak away to an in-house oasis that's off limits to everyone else. As a companion to the master bedroom, the bath creates a private suite for relaxing, sleeping, dressing, and bathing. This is the room to indulge yourself with high-style fixtures, a whirlpool tub, or sauna and steam jets, and — with space permitting — a dressing area and fitness gear (if you're so inclined).

When a master bathroom is for a couple, it's a luxury version of a shared bathroom. For an individual, it's a private space with amenities that make it a comfortable sanctuary. Your lifestyle, your budget, and the amount of space you have to work with will determine how luxurious your bathroom can be.

Some of the most popular features in today's master bathrooms include these amenities:

✔ Universal design features (see the following section)

✔ Toilet in a semiprivate compartment

✔ Double vanities with sinks and a mirror

- ✔ Sauna or steam shower or a walk-in shower with double shower heads installed at levels for each user
- ✔ Soaking or whirlpool tub
- ✔ Radiant floor heating (see Chapter 14)
- ✔ Adjacent bedroom and dressing areas that include walk-in closets and full-length mirrors
- ✔ Laundry centers
- ✔ Storage for linens and personal items
- ✔ Clothes hooks
- ✔ Chair or bench
- ✔ Towel warmer
- ✔ Telephone
- ✔ Television

Gaining Easy Accesses: Universal Design

Not so long ago, universal design was associated with physical disabilities, but today it means a home design philosophy that is user-friendly, regardless of a person's age or limitations. Really savvy homeowners are remodeling their homes, especially the kitchen and bathrooms, with an eye to the future.

An accessible bathroom has increased lighting for more visibility when grooming, reading, and bathing. The materials used are safe and not slippery, and all surfaces are easy to clean. The room design should anticipate what you need, whether it's conveniently located clothes hooks or a grab bar for safety.

Remodeling a bathroom, and a whole house, for that matter, with universal design concepts in mind makes sense for all homeowners. Replacing that old shower stall with one that does not have a threshold to step over makes life easier for you today, especially if a family member has a knee or hip injury, and in the future should anyone in your household ever use a wheelchair.

The following list tells you what to keep in mind as you plan your accessible bathroom — feature by feature:

✔ **General room features:** These overall elements of an accessible bathroom make it comfortable and convenient:

- Nonslip flooring

- Ample natural and glare-free lighting

- Motion-sensing light

- Easy-to-reach open storage shelves and hooks

- Telephone and intercom system by the toilet

- Lever door handles

✔ **Bathtubs and showers:** For bathing and showering, choose features that make the experience enjoyable, invigorating, and easy to use:

- Lighted compartment

- Slip-resistant surface

- Adjustable height shower head with extendable hose

- Scald-guard tub and shower controls offset from the shower spray for easy access should the water need to be turned off in an emergency

- Removable transfer seat into a bathtub

✔ **Shower stall:** Stepping into and out of a shower stall should be safe and comforting, so include these features:

- Low or curbless threshold

- Molded-in or fold-down seat

- 36-inch-wide entrance

- Grab bars, grips, or safety bars

✔ **Toilet and toilet paper holder:** The height of a toilet seat is key to comfort and convenient use. A spring-free toilet tissue holder makes changing the paper easy. Also consider adding these features:

- Elevated toilet or adjustable toilet seat convenient for anyone who is physically challenged and has difficulty sitting down or rising

- Auto-flush mechanism

- A toilet paper holder with an open-end design featuring a single post that's easy to change with one hand, or a new design toilet paper holder with a pivot bar that you lift to reload

- **Sink:** Consider the following sinks or sink fixtures:

  - A wall-mounted sink, which is convenient to use and operate, especially for people in wheelchairs

  - Height-adjustable or English style roll-under sink

  - Wall-hung sink with knee space and panel to protect user from pipes

  - Lever handle faucets with temperature control

- **Vanities and faucets:** Make a vanity cabinet more user-friendly with hardware and faucetry that's easy to use.

  - Cabinets with pulls instead of knobs

  - Countertop height at a comfortable level that eliminates bending over

  - Countertop with an edge in a contrasting color to create a visual clue

  - Electronic motion-sensing faucets for convenience

  - Faucets with lever

  - Tilting mirrors to improve visibility

If the bathroom includes a laundry, choose a washer and dryer with front-loading doors, which make them easy to load and unload. Choose a model with tilted tubs that improve access and visibility.

Reviewing NKBA Planning Guidelines

The National Kitchen & Bath Association (NKBA), a trade group of design professionals, suggests these planning guidelines for a safe and functional room for all to enjoy. When these people refer to "clearance space" around a fixture, it means the space required so that the fixture can be used with comfort and ease. Note that these clearance spaces in front of or around fixtures can overlap.

The following list gives you some basic clearance guidelines:

- **Bathtub:** It's the biggest fixture in most bathrooms, so determining its location is key to good use of space.

  - For a standard tub, plan on a space 30 to 32 inches wide and 54, 60, or 72 inches long.

  - For a standard whirlpool tub, plan a space that is 36 inches wide by 72 inches long. Many shapes and sizes are available.

  - For clearance space in front of a tub, allow at least 30 inches.

✔ **Sink:** Customize the height of a vanity to suit the people who use it and allow for plenty of space around it.

- A standard vanity is 30 to 32 inches high, but many people prefer it higher to eliminate bending down. Depending on the height of the user, anywhere from 34 to 42 inches is comfortable.

- Allow for 30 inches between a double vanity, measuring from the center of one basin to the center of the other. However, if the sinks are wider than 30 inches, the minimum distance between them should be increased.

- For clearance space in front of a vanity and sink, allow at least 30 by 48 inches of clear space.

- The bottom edge of a mirror over the sink should be a maximum of 40 inches above the floor or a maximum of 48 inches above the floor if the mirror is tilted.

- The minimum clearance from the centerline of the sink to any side wall is 15 inches.

✔ **Shower stall:** Make the shower experience enjoyable by sizing it to fit the bather and allowing floor space outside it for drying and dressing.

- For the minimal size shower stall enclosure, allow a space at least 34 inches square.

- For clearance space in front of the shower stall, allow a minimum of 30 inches.

- Install shower heads at a height that is comfortable for the users. For example, for someone who is 5 feet 4 inches tall, the height of the shower head should be 72 inches; for a taller person, it should be higher. When one shower serves different height users, consider mounting two shower heads (at different heights), a hand-held shower head, or an adjustable shower head.

- Install shower benches 17 to 19 inches high and at least 15 inches deep. If they're built in, the shower must be large enough so the bench doesn't encroach on the minimum 34-x-34-inch floor space.

✔ **Toilet and bidet:** Whether enclosed in a compartment or open in the room, consider their location in relation to the doors and other fixtures.

- An enclosure for a toilet should be at least 36 inches wide and 66 inches deep and have a pocket or outward opening door. A door that opens into the toilet area isn't recommended because the door can't be opened in an emergency should the occupant faint or fall on the floor.

- For clearance space in front of a toilet or bidet, which you'll find out more about in Chapter 9, allow at least 48 inches by 48 inches, and 16 inches from the center of the fixture to the wall or other fixtures.

✔ **Door openings:** The all-important bathroom door takes up considerable space, so spend time considering the options.

- The clear space at a doorway (measured at the narrowest point) should be at least 32 inches wide.

- A clear floor space at least the width of the door on the push side and larger clear floor space on the pull side should be planned at doors for maneuvering to open, close, and pass through the doorway.

- A minimum clear floor space of 30 inches by 48 inches is required beyond the door swing in a bathroom.

Looking at some basic bathroom layouts

No two bathrooms are alike, but the layouts in Figure 2-1 are good examples of well-designed, functional, comfortable bathrooms. In Figure 2-1a, the bathtub and shower borrow space from an adjacent bedroom closet. Figure 2-1b shows a 16-x-17-foot bathroom with two separate vanities, a whirlpool, shower compartment, enclosed toilet room, and linen storage. Figure 2-1c shows a bathroom with separate entrances and double vanities, and the floor plan does a good job serving two kids' bedrooms on either side of it. It features a bathtub storage in a linen closet, and toilet in a space partitioned with a door for privacy. Figure 2-1d shows how two bathrooms back to back can take advantage of having bathtub and shower plumbing lines on a common wall. Use these ideas for positioning fixtures and spacing to create a design that will suit your needs.

Rating your present bathroom

Here's more help from NKBA — a handy checklist to help you find out just how functional and fashionable your present bathroom is . . . or isn't! There are no right or wrong answers, just thought-provoking questions to help you make meaningful improvements in your next bathroom. Answer yes or no to the following questions:

Fixtures

___ Is the shower head at a comfortable height for all users?

___ Is the shower safe (equipped with nonslip floor, grab bars, a bench seat, and temperature controls)?

___ Is the bathtub big enough?

___ Is the bathtub safe (easy to get into and equipped with faucets within reach and a nonslip bottom)?

___ Is the sink at a comfortable height to wash your face?

___ Is the toilet in a good location (that is, away from swinging doors)?

___ Are the fixtures an attractive color?

___ Are all the fixtures easy to clean?

___ Do shower doors have tempered safety glass?

Storage systems

___ Is the cabinet door style and finish up-to-date?

___ Is the cabinet finish in good shape?

___ Is there enough storage space for your grooming equipment?

___ Do cabinets include a well-organized storage system?

___ Is there a convenient spot for soaps and shampoos in the shower area?

___ Are there enough towel bars?

___ Is there space for towel storage in or near the bathroom?

Mechanical systems

___ Is there an efficient ventilation system in the room?

___ Is the bathroom comfortably warm (in the morning) and after a shower or bath?

___ Is there adequate lighting for your bathroom activities?

___ Are all the electrical outlets protected with ground-fault circuit interrupters to prevent electric shock?

___ Are the plumbing pipes free from leaks?

Major surfaces

___ Are all the surfaces easy to keep clean?

___ Are the walls in the shower or tub free from mildew or dry-rot damage?

___ Is the room aesthetically pleasing?

Room orientation

___ Is the existing bathroom big enough?

___ Does the bathroom relate to adjacent rooms the way you would like?

___ Can two people use the bathroom comfortably and conveniently at the same time?

___ Do entry, closet, or cabinet doors interrupt walkways or block fixture use?

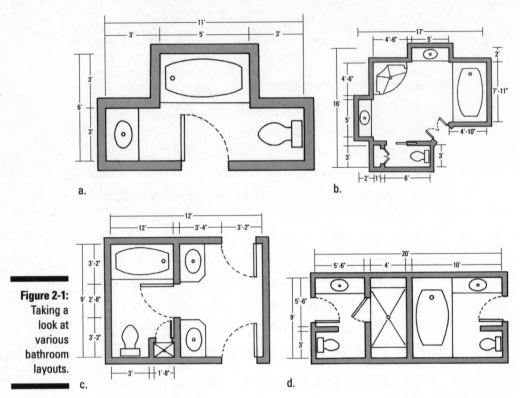

Figure 2-1:
Taking a
look at
various
bathroom
layouts.

Planning Your New Bathroom

While you're bursting with ideas and inspiration, it's time to take the next step and find the exact amount of space you have to deal with. If you're remodeling within the walls of the existing bathroom, take measurements of the space within the walls, which can vary from 6 to 10 inches thick. Many bathroom remodeling projects involve expanding the space by borrowing it from an adjacent room or closet. You can remove a wall between rooms, assuming that the wall is not a bearing wall and a structural part of the building. If expansion is your plan, measure the floor space, including any walls or partitions, and add it to the existing bathroom dimensions. You may want to make two plans, to see just how much more space you gain by incorporating an adjacent room or part of it in your redesigned bathroom.

To determine whether a wall is nonbearing, look for exposed joists (in the attic) or rafters (in the basement). If they run parallel to the wall you plan to remove, it's not a bearing wall.

Taking advantage of existing fixtures

Whenever fixtures share the same plumbing on a wall, the wall is called a "wet wall." Because the plumbing lines servicing the fixtures are on the same wall, the cost of the plumbing job is reduced. Consider this factor in your design.

Also avoid changing the location of the toilet, because it's directly connected to the main plumbing pipe, called the soil pipe or stack. You can rotate the toilet to face another direction without much fuss, but to totally relocate a toilet requires altering the drainage and possible the soil stack. This process gets expensive because the soil stack and the 3- or 4-inch-diameter drain leading from the toilet to the soil stack are difficult to relocate without getting into the structure of the house.

Talk to any plumber and he'll tell you that just about anything is possible. But unless you plan to fully fund a retirement plan for the guy or gal, think twice before you relocate the toilet or any other fixture for that matter. Don't rule this relocation out; just work out all the details and expense beforehand.

The same is true for other plumbing lines that run into the bathroom. But new lines can more easily be run for a vanity and bathtub or shower. You can read more about this in Chapter 8, but as you plan your new bathroom, remember that running new plumbing lines means a more expensive job.

Drawing up a floor plan

The best way to help you visualize the remodeling possibilities is to do what the professionals do: Make a scale drawing of the space. The process of creating a scale drawing forces you to take careful note of the existing room and everything in it. And it gives you a concise record of the key dimensions of the area you plan to change. As you work through the design with a contractor or designer, or if you do the work yourself, a scaled drawing gives you information to carry on an informed discussion, ask questions, and choose materials and fixtures more confidently.

Using design software tools

To design your bathroom, you can use graph paper, buy inexpensive software, such as Broderbund's 3D Home Architect (about $30), or use the online tools available on the Internet at manufacturer Web sites such as Kohler.com. If you don't have a computer, go to your public library, where you can get access to the Internet.

The real advantage to the high-tech approach is that after you create the basic floor plan, the computer can render a virtual bathroom from the floor plan that lets you see what the bathroom might look like in a three-dimensional image. These tools also can generate a shopping list of all the fixtures and cabinets you need.

Expect a learning curve when using design software for the first time, but you can figure out most simpler house design programs without too much anguish.

Even if you use a computer to create your design, you still need to do some low-tech tasks with a tape measure, paper, and pencil because any computer software you use is based on the data or dimensions you put in it. Spend the time and effort to get accurate measurements and preliminary drawings of the existing bathroom or area you want to remodel because any new designs depend on the accuracy of this initial information.

Designing the old-fashioned way

The pencil-and-paper approach is less expensive than computer-based design and will certainly get the job done. To make a scaled drawing of the existing bathroom, you need the following:

- ¼-inch-square graph paper
- 16-foot (or longer) steel measuring tape
- Art gum eraser
- Masking tape
- Pencil
- Ruler
- Tracing paper
- Unlined paper

Even if you hated art class in school, this is going to be fun because no drawing is required. Sit on the floor or the toilet or in the tub and make Leonardo da Vinci proud.

1. **Sketch it out.**

    Make a rough paper sketch of the room on unlined paper. This sketch should have all openings, including doors and windows; the location of the existing plumbing fixtures (toilet, bathtub, shower, and vanity); the location of all electrical lines, including outlets and receptacles, light fixtures, and fans; heating and cooling pipes and heating ducts; and walls and partitions.

    If you're considering borrowing space from an adjacent room, make a sketch of it, too. You may want to use space from a closet in the room next to it, a linen closet in the hall nearby, or an adjacent bathroom.

2. **Add dimensions to the sketch.**

   Next, with the help of a friend, use the tape measure to take measurements of the bathroom. Hold the tape tightly at both ends to get exact dimensions. Measure the length of the walls, windows, and fixtures and mark them on the rough sketch. Go back and double-check the measurements for accuracy.

3. **Transfer the room dimensions to a sheet of graph paper.**

   Each ¼-inch square on the graph paper is equal to 6 inches, or ½ foot.

   For example, a 6-foot-long wall will be 12 squares long in the drawing. First, draw the bathroom walls and partitions and then the surrounding areas. Include the doors and the direction they swing open and, of course, any windows. Then draw in the fixtures to complete the floor plan.

You now have the basic layout of the existing bathroom and its adjacent areas. If you plan an addition to expand the size of the bathroom, the scaled drawing should include the exterior wall you plan to open.

Don't lose your original sketch. Keep it safely tucked in your bathroom notebook so it's safe and you won't lose it. Some people like to keep it on a clipboard so it's easy to work on. Whatever you decide, don't misplace it.

Making an overlay

The scaled graph paper floor plan becomes the background that you can use with several different designs on tracing paper. To make your first one, place a piece of tracing paper over the sketch on the graph paper and hold it in place with a piece of masking tape. Then trace over the floor plan with a sharp pencil to transfer the floor plan to the tracing paper, as shown in Figure 2-2. Voilà — you have an accurate rendition of the existing floor plan as a starting point for your new design.

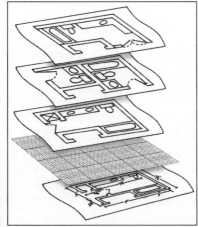

Figure 2-2:
Use tracing paper to create different room designs.

Lift the tracing paper up off the graph paper, and you'll see you've created the basic layout of the bathroom. You can have several versions going at the same time; just tape additional sheets of tracing paper over one another. Each version can be a variation of the other, but they're all based on the existing location of the walls, doors, and windows. Make design changes to the tracing paper.

If the new bathroom will take space from an adjacent room, note any walls or partitions that will be removed. If the new bathroom will be bumped out onto cantilevered floor joists, make note of the foundation and ground space below it.

Making templates

Place Figure 2-3 on a photocopier and make a copy of it. Then cut out the shapes of the basic fixtures and use them on the scaled drawing.

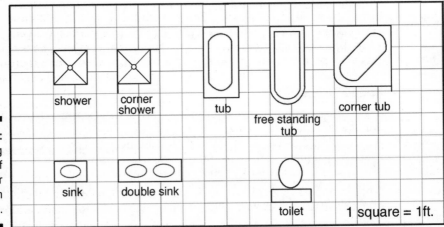

Figure 2-3:
Creating templates of your bathroom floor plan.

shower   corner shower   tub   free standing tub   corner tub

sink   double sink   toilet   1 square = 1ft.

Alternatively, you can purchase a plumbing fixture template from your local drafting supply or art store. Most house plans use a scale of ¼ inch to a foot, but because the bathroom is a smaller area than a house, a scale of ½ inch to a foot is easier to work with. If you can't find a template of ½ inch to the foot, purchase the ¼-inch-scale template and make each square on the graph paper equal a foot.

Being creative with design tools on the Internet

If you're using design software or a design tool at a manufacturer's Web site, use the dimensions from the sketch you made. In general, you follow a sequence of inputting or filling in the size of the room and the location and length of walls, windows, and doors. When completed, the software generates a design. This can be a time-intensive exercise depending on how user-friendly the software or design tool is and how easily you can input the data. But tough it out, be patient, and let the computer do the work and churn out different designs.

Choosing an accessory collection

You'll find collections of stylish bathroom fittings and accessories — both wall-mounted and free-standing items — that blend seamlessly with the decorating style of your house. Finding tasteful, functional accessories that match your personal taste has never been easier.

To choose a design and pattern that enhances the bathroom fixtures and furnishings, think of accessories as jewelry for the bathroom and use them to complete the look you want to achieve. Basic brass can be beautiful in any setting, and so can simple but stylish chrome. If you're remodeling a Craftsman bungalow bathroom, consider carrying out the design with Mission-inspired accessories to complement the architecture and style of the house. To create a Victorian motif, consider using accessories that combine brass and crystal, reminiscent of the luxury and splendor of a bygone era. For a thoroughly modern home, choose the clean lines of a sophisticated and minimalist look with chrome fittings.

Not sure of the style of your house? Go to the Baldwin Web site (www.baldwin hardware.com) and use the Architectural Style Online Guide to help you recognize and match your home's styles with hardware and accessories that will look just right.

If you can feel the weight of the accessory, you'll understand the difference in quality and price. Lift two different towel rings or soap dishes, and you'll find that the weight of the accessory is a tip-off to its quality. The heavier pieces are made from solid brass and have durable finishes that require less maintenance. Buy the best quality you can afford.

Jazzing up your hardware

To personalize ordinary but nice cabinets and doors in a bathroom, replace the existing hardware with new decorative knobs, pulls, and handles. You'll find complete suites of hardware, including coordinated cabinet hinges and switch plate covers, to transform a bathroom.

Decorative cabinet hardware is a growing segment of the home decor industry, meaning that consumers have many more options. By adding customized cabinet hardware, you're adding your personal signature with style.

Playing with the possibilities

After you have the basic floor plan, you can start playing with the possibilities. People in the remodeling industry like the saying "Anything is possible, given enough time and cash," and the operative word here is *cash*! In Chapter 6, you face the reality of your budget. Forget about that for a while (of course, you really can't forget your budget forever) and explore what you can do in the existing space. Consult your wish list and notebook clipping file for inspiration.

Even an unlimited budget can't overcome the problems of a bad design. Remember to pay attention to the recommendations about the minimum clearance space needed for fixtures from the NKBA (discussed in the section "Reviewing NKBA Planning Guidelines," earlier in this chapter).

To help you visualize these minimum guidelines, use your tracing paper to draw up a template for each type fixture. For example, the minimum open space in front of a toilet should be 48 inches square. Draw the outline of a toilet on your graph paper and then draw a 48-inch box in front of the toilet. Do the same with a standard bathtub outline, but place a 30-inch-deep box in front of the bathtub. Follow the NKBA recommendations and include the free space in front of all the fixture templates you created. Then in your new design, arrange the fixtures so that no fixture is located in the free space of another fixture. The free space area of each fixture may overlap, however. You may discover that you have lots of possibilities.

Creating positive forces by using feng shui

Want to include some feng shui when designing your new bathroom? The main problem with incorporating this ancient Chinese art into your bathroom is that a bathroom has drains, the largest being a toilet, which eliminates energy (along with wastewater). The solution is to make sure that the toilet isn't visible when entering because it drains the room of energy. A better choice is to locate a toilet behind the door or a wall so that you can't see it from the doorway.

In general, eliminate the draining effect of any bathroom by always keeping the bathroom door closed. To find out more about this topic, read *Feng Shui For Dummies*, by David Daniel Kennedy (published by Wiley).

Chapter 3

Warning: Bathroom Work Zone Ahead

· ·

In This Chapter

▶ Going through the stages of a remodeling project

▶ Mentally and physically gearing up for the work

▶ Estimating the length of the project

· ·

*A*ll remodeling projects have key elements or processes, and knowing what they are prepares you for the adventure. And that's a good way to look at remodeling. The experience consumes your life for a period of time, but when it's over, you'll have created a new and improved home and you'll have learned something. Maybe you'll decide you never want to do it again, but just maybe it'll entice you to remodel another part of your house.

The old saying "a little knowledge goes a long way" certainly applies to a bathroom remodeling project, or any other remodeling project for that matter. You can't be too informed about what to expect and how the work is planned and carried out. Understanding the process is important because, although some phases of a job can be performed independently of the others, many depend on other tasks being completed first.

Think of these stages like dominos because they're all interrelated. Now every bathroom is different, but here we include just about every scenario we can imagine. It will help if you make a list of the elements of your own bathroom — for example, what you're going to replace and anything you plan to reposition — so that you can create a custom list of phases for your particular project. The more time you spend noodling the process, the less time you'll waste after you begin the actual remodeling.

Walking Through the Stages of a Typical Bathroom Remodeling Project

Remodeling (any room or rooms) involves a lot of individual processes and projects that have to be completed in sequential and workmanlike order. When you understand the process of remodeling, you're better prepared to know what to anticipate. From start to finish, the following sections give you a breakdown of the ten stages of remodeling a bathroom.

Getting the permit

So you have your plan, got bids for the project, and selected a contractor or are confident you can handle the project yourself. You're ready to roll. Stop! Don't even think of lifting a hammer until you have the building permit in hand. And don't contemplate doing the job without one, or some bright, sunny day (building inspectors don't go out in the rain), someone will knock on your door and ask to see the permit. If you think the building inspector can be a bit cranky on a good day, just try to deal with one after you're caught red-handed without a permit.

Most building departments are helpful and will make suggestions to get the plan approved. If you're hiring a contractor to do the work, he'll deal with getting the permit, but you should insist on seeing it before the work starts. In most towns, the permit must be displayed on the job before the work starts.

Creating the work zone

When the bathroom is the construction site, you must remove all furnishings and personal belongings so work can proceed. This is the time when you shift toiletries, cleaning supplies, medicines, and all personal bathroom stuff to (hopefully) another bathroom to keep the household running as smoothly as possible. Don't underestimate the time it takes to do this. You'll be amazed at all the stuff you'll find stashed away behind the towels in the cabinet.

After you have pried all the old stuff out from the back of drawers and under the counter, go through all the medicine. Wine and fine whiskey may improve with age, but drugs don't.

All construction creates clouds of dust, and now is the time to take some preventive action. You may think that you won't notice drywall dust in your corn flakes, but you will and the rest of the family will, too. Most dust can be contained by taping heavy plastic dropcloths to the doors. Cut two plastic sheets several feet larger than the door opening. Tape the first to the top of the door molding and to the left jamb molding. Then tape the other sheet to the top and right molding. The overlap seals the door but allows you to enter the room. Commercial door seals complete with zipper doors are also available.

In addition to sealing the doors, don't forget to seal the furnace ducts, especially the cold air returns. The furnace blower can spread dust throughout the house if the ducts aren't carefully sealed.

Finally, place a box fan in the window so it blows air out of the work area. The fan will create a negative pressure in the room and help keep the dust at bay. The air will move into the room and carry the dust out the window. During the winter or hot summer, you can run the fan during the worst of the demolition.

Tearing out the old stuff and taking it away

The size and scope of the project determine how much demolition is required. For a swap job that involves simply replacing fixtures, cabinetry, and flooring, the process is basically remove, replace, and redecorate. But if your project involves replacing windows, framing in a new door, bumping out a wall, or combining two rooms, the job can be much more complicated.

You may need a Dumpster, or what some people call a roll-off container, to haul away the old materials. This large box is delivered on the back of a special truck and dropped in place. After it's full, the truck picks it up and takes it to the landfill. If you need one of these, schedule a delivery date that gives you enough time to fill it up, but not so much time that the item becomes a permanent fixture in the neighborhood. Companies that rent dumpsters are listed in the Yellow Pages under "Rubbish & Garbage Removal." If you're having your regular trash collector remove the materials, check to see whether you need to make special arrangements, pay a fee for pickup of additional material, or require a special permit to leave the container on the street if you can't store it on your property.

If you're enlarging your bathroom, then obviously you must remove the adjacent walls. This, of course, will affect any room that shares the common wall with the bathroom. A closet on a common wall is a natural place to borrow space for a larger bathroom; if that's the case, you must empty the closet.

Removing cabinets and fixtures in a bathroom requires turning off and disrupting the water and electrical services in the house. Careful planning of this phase can assure that the utilities are off for the shortest time possible. You can temporarily cap water lines as you remove the fixtures, and the water can be turned back on. The same is true for the electricity. Remove the electrical fixtures and install wire nuts on the ends of the wires and tape the ends. Push the wires back into the electrical boxes so they're out of the way.

Let your family know as far in advance as possible when the water and electricity may be shut off. Everyone needs to know when they won't be able to flush the toilet or how long the furnace won't be cranking out heat.

Framing and making structural changes

At this phase of the project, the bathroom is empty, the walls and floor are pocked with holes, and the room is ugly. During this period, the new walls are framed in to create the floor plan. Rough framing is installed outlining the new walls, and partitions around tubs and showers are built. Unless you're making major structural changes to the floor or other parts of the bathroom, this phase of the project goes surprisingly fast. The old bathroom begins to be transformed with the smell of lumber outlining new walls, windows, or skylights.

Laying out and roughing in plumbing lines and electrical wires

This phase changes the room with new plumbing supply lines for all the water fixtures (toilet, bidet, sink, shower, tub or whirlpool). If the drain pipes have to be moved to accommodate a new location for a fixture, the floor may have to be cut up and then reinforced after the piping is installed.

The electrician arrives and *roughs in* (does all the behind-the-walls work) new electrical boxes for switches, outlets, light fixtures, venting, and heating and cooling lines. Then electricians run wiring to the boxes and back to the power panel, but they don't turn on the electricity just yet.

Getting code work approved

While the walls are still open and the new plumbing and electrical rough-ins and the wall framing can be seen, your local building inspectors must visit the work site and inspect the job. The inspector may require leak testing of the drainage system if major alterations have been made. Many jurisdictions require you to bring whatever is accessible up to current code. If all the work meets the local building codes, he or she will approve the work, and the next phase of the project can begin. Until the inspection is complete, you can't close up the walls, so scheduling that inspection is key to keeping the remodeling on schedule.

Finishing wall, ceiling, and floor surfaces

After the rough-in plumbing, electrical, and framing work passes code inspection, workers can close up the walls. Standard drywall is applied in adjacent areas. Moisture-resistant drywall called green board is applied to the interior bathroom walls. Waterproof cement board goes on tub and bath enclosures. The walls are taped and finished with several coats of drywall compound to conceal the joints between panels. This phase of the job produces a lot of dust, but the bathroom is taking shape. Next, workers install the flooring and wall tile, paint, and add the wallcoverings.

Setting fixtures and furnishings

The room begins to take on its own new life when the fixtures are put in position. This process involves setting the toilet, tub, shower, and whirlpool in place and hooking up plumbing lines and testing them. Large one-piece showers and whirlpools may be placed in the bathroom before the wall framing is complete. Carpentry work includes installing cabinetry, open or linen closet shelving, and any other built-in furnishings.

Finishing up the electrical and mechanical work

Workers hook up new receptacles and outlets, along with heating and cooling lines and lighting and venting systems. Everything is in place, so you should have a good idea what the project will look like when totally complete. Now is the time to go over the original plan and check that all the fixtures, lights, outlets, and heating and cooling ducts are in place and that nothing is damaged.

Start a notebook with any problems you discover and write down the problem and the date. The building trades call this a *punch list*. At this stage of the project, you need to meet with the builder and work through any problems.

Getting final code approval

The local building department makes a final inspection and signs off on the job. This sign-off usually is in the form of an occupancy certificate. The inspector checks that the wiring is installed correctly and that all the plumbing fixtures work. He notes any problems, which must be corrected before the inspector will issue the final approval.

Because the inspector has already been on the job for the initial inspection and is sure everyone is aware of the code requirements, in most cases this step is a formality. But because your family is probably really, really, ready to put the new bath to use, the inspection can be a bit tense. A cup of coffee and some cookies may make this step go a bit smoother.

Bracing Yourself for the Destruction

The bathroom is only one room, but you'll be amazed at how much material goes into making it fully function as the bathroom of your dreams. So where does all the stuff get stashed when it's delivered prior to installation? You guessed it — wherever there's space in and around your house. Some folks feel that tripping over and living around large boxes and building materials are the worst parts of remodeling because those annoyances discombobulate their daily life. But if you can mentally prepare yourself for being displaced for a while, it's not nearly so bad.

Watching your house turn into a mini-warehouse

Any remodeling project creates stress. To make the job run as smoothly as possible, spend time thinking about the process and how it will affect family members. Also take into account that the house will become a mini-warehouse of materials to be used in the new bathroom. This storage issue may not be much of a problem in a large home, where there's space galore, but it can be a real challenge in a smaller house that's already packed full.

Plan a staging area for the new materials. Make space for all the components of the new bathroom. It's a good bet they'll be delivered at different times, and often the first items to arrive will be the last things to be installed, so be sure not to block access to any of them. Most of these elements are large and bulky. The framing lumber, a whirlpool tub, and cabinets take up a lot of floor space, and you need to provide a clean, dry storage space. An enclosed garage offers the best protection; a porch or breezeway is another possible location. Any wood products, such as framing lumber or flooring, stored outside should be protected from the rain and brought inside for several days before installation to allow them to adjust to the new indoor environment.

As materials and fixtures arrive, open the containers and check to see that what is delivered is what you ordered, that all the parts are included, and that the parts aren't damaged. Check fixtures for the correct color, style, and size. See that the flooring is the correct style and amount, and check the wall-covering to see that it's the correct pattern and that all the rolls came from same dye lot or run.

Making it easy on yourself

During any major remodeling project, the contractors you hire will become part of your family, whether you like it or not. To make it as stress free as possible, take preventive steps to prepare for the increased activity throughout the house.

Decluttering

Get ready for the invasion — no, not of body snatchers, but of contractors, plumbers, carpenters, and electricians working on your project. Before they arrive and during the remodeling, your house will become an open door to tradespeople and inspectors, who are all focused on the bathroom. They want to get in, do their job, and get out, so make it easy for them to do so. Unclutter the hall or area leading to the bathroom by removing any furniture. Lay down a heavy-duty dropcloth to protect the floor or carpeting from foot traffic.

Creating a tool zone

Designate a space near the bathroom where workers can put their tools or gear or where you can store yours if you're doing the work yourself. Some workers tote and store their tools in their truck, and others may leave their large, heavy tools at the job site (your house.) If you do the work, you'll want to designate a place *near* the bathroom to keep your tools and not clutter up the small confines of the work area.

Surrendering to dust

If new wallboard will be hung, prepare for drywall dust, not just once, but several times as installers sand and then resand the seams. Even when contractors hang protective plastic sheeting at the door to seal off the rest of the house, the sanding produces clouds of fine dust throughout the house. Until the walls are painted or finished, plan to get used to a fine white haze that permeates every conceivable surface of your house.

Purchase a shop vac that is designed to pick up dust and debris. A standard vacuum is not designed to pick up this type of material. The fine dust will eventually damage the motor, and the vacuum will just spread the dust around the house. Most shop vacs have an optional bag that installs over the standard filter that is designed to contain fine particles such as drywall dust.

To prevent a nervous breakdown, relax and take major cleaning chores off your schedule during remodeling. Admit that dirt and dust cannot be contained. Concentrate instead on keeping the job site clean, which will reduce the possibility of accidents. This attitude will also send a message to the workers that you expect them to maintain a clean, professional work site.

TIP

Surviving bathroom remodeling in a one-bath house

What if you live in a one-bathroom house, and you want to remodel it, but you have to live in your house while the bathroom is being remodeled? Now that's the challenge that tests the mettle of a family or a relationship.

Work with the contractors to schedule the job so that all necessary inspections can be done soon after the work itself is completed, thus enabling the utilities to be hooked up again for temporary use. This type of living is not for the faint of heart, but if you like to camp, you have the coping skills. (If not, get a hotel room.) The following list offers some survival tips.

✔ You'll be using a bathroom without walls, using nails for hooks. Just bang nails into the studs wherever you need to hang a towel or robe; then pull them out when it's time for the wallboard.

✔ To cover windows, nail up an old towel.

✔ If a new shower stall or tub is installed without its door, jury-rig a curtain with an inexpensive curtain rod.

✔ Cover the floor with a heavy dropcloth and a rug that you can easily remove when the workers return.

While you're functioning in this arrangement, don't forget to treat yourself to expensive chocolate or fine wine — whatever indulges you. You deserve it.

An extreme alternative: Use camping equipment. In a warm climate for a day or two, use a portable toilet and portable shower. This is an especially good idea if you plan to audition for *Survivor.*

It's at times like these that your health club membership comes in handy — showers and a sauna for tired muscles.

Avoiding entertaining

Remodeling a bathroom is stressful enough, so don't plan any other major events while you're living through it. Unless you're Martha Stewart, don't think about entertaining or having a houseguest. Wait until the bathroom is remodeled. That way, you can enjoy your guests *and* show off your new bathroom.

Of course, you may not want to become hermits, so if you give into the temptation and decide to entertain, just be straightforward with your guests. Explain to them that they'll have to run to the gas station down the street when they need to use the facilities . . . just kidding. If you're comfortable having guests, serve wine and cheese in the shell of the bathroom — it's probably the only entertaining you'll ever do there. You may be surprised how many visitors are interested in seeing your bathroom in the making.

Being there 24/7

You need to stick around the house during the remodeling. You may be tempted to avoid the project completely and take off on a vacation. What the heck, hand the house keys to the contractor, hit the road, and return to a perfect new bathroom. Wrong!

You gotta be there. In the first place, someone has to be home to accept the delivery of materials, which come at different times before the project begins.

 In the second place, you have to be available when a snafu comes up. Despite the best-laid plans, any remodeling often involves some on-the-spot decisions and improvisation. When the plumber discovers a water line that can't be rerouted and that affects the position of a pedestal sink, you have to be there to consider the options and make a decision. If you're not available 24/7, you can't expect the workers to make the call for you.

And really, you don't want to miss out on this! Remodeling can be annoying, exhausting, and downright messy, but in the end, you'll look back at the project and marvel at the results.

Beating the Clock: A Timeline of What to Expect

The mini table in this section shows the amount of time involved in remodeling a bathroom. This project involves using the existing space without making any structural changes and replacing the bathtub with shower, sink and vanity cabinet with faucet, toilet, vanity countertop and light, medicine cabinet, sensing light/vent fan in the ceiling, and faucets.

This particular project includes laying ceramic tile on the floor, on the three walls enclosing the bathtub, and on the walls 36 inches high as wainscoting. Finishing the room includes painting the door, window, upper walls, and ceiling and installing a sliding tub/shower door, one towel bar, one towel ring, one toilet paper holder, one wall hook, and one safety grab bar.

Task	*Time Required*
Removing old fixtures, flooring, and vanity	6 to 10 hours
Rebuilding walls around bathtub enclosure	2 to 4 hours
Installing bathtub overflow and drain and rough in new plumbing and electrical	10 to 12 hours

(continued)

Task	Time Required
Installing cement backer board around bathtub enclosure	3 to 6 hours
Installing tile in bathtub enclosure	5 to 7 hours
Installing tile on walls	7 to 8 hours
Laying tile floor	5 to 6 hours
Painting upper walls, window, door, and trim	4 to 5 hours
Installing sink/vanity fittings, cabinet, and countertop	12 to 14 hours
Installing toilet and fixtures	8 to 9 hours
Installing medicine cabinet	2 hours
Installing electrical light switches and ground-fault circuit interrupter (GFCI) outlets	4 to 5 hours
Installing ceiling light/vent, vanity lighting	2 to 3 hours
Installing towel bar, ring, tissue holder, wall hook, and safety bar	3 to 4 hours
Installing sliding tub/shower door	2 to 3 hours

A quick scan of this estimated timeline adds up to 75-plus hours of work. Sure, a couple of workers can probably knock out this job in a week. Well, technically it's possible, but not probable. Even the best-planned projects will run into some delays. A more realistic time frame for this project is two to three weeks. That's starting after all or most of the materials are actually on the job site.

If you hire a contractor, he'll hire a plumber and electrician, so several tradespeople will be involved, which means waiting for their scheduled arrival. If you do the work or part of it, your work schedule can be interrupted by other things that take precedence.

You'll have downtime when the wallboard compound dries and the ceramic tile grout cures. You can also expect unforeseen snafus. All you need to upset a timeline is the plumber not showing up to complete the rough-in work. That delay can push the inspection back, and the project can grind to a halt because the walls and floor can't be closed up until after the inspection.

Will this happen to your project? With good planning, it shouldn't, but it can. The best planning can't foresee every bump in the road. Will knowing that a remodeling project may take longer than planned make it easier for you and you family to put up with? Probably not, but being forewarned is being forearmed. Place the picture of that dream bath on the fridge. Seeing it every morning won't make the drywall dust taste any better, but it will help you keep your goal in mind.

Chapter 4

Tooling Around

• •

• •

*I*f you own a house, you need certain tools. Acquiring tools, especially power tools, has become a national pastime — all right, an obsession for some of us — and there's no limit to the basic and specialty tools available. Tackling a bathroom renovation will require all your basic tools and then some — some you should own and some you should rent or borrow.

Peeking Inside the Well-Stocked Toolbox

If you have owned a house for any length of time, you probably have the basics — a hammer and an assortment of screwdrivers, adjustable wrenches, pliers, and possibly an electric drill. You probably purchased most of them for a particular repair. While this purchase-as-needed strategy may be a good way to build a basic toolbox, you can also end up with too many specialty tools and not enough general tools.

If you're remodeling a bathroom, you have to consider your toolbox an essential investment that will add to your confidence and skill level. Of course, you can take this idea to the extreme and rationalize buying all the latest whiz-bang tools. But don't get carried away. Remember that the cost of specialized tools to complete a project can be a major factor in determining the economics of doing the job yourself or hiring a professional, which we discuss further in Chapter 7.

It's in your hands now: Gotta-have hand tools

A basic toolbox for remodeling should contain the basic hand tools we list in this section. You don't have to purchase all of them at the same time. But before the dust settles, you'll reach into your toolbox for every one of these tools. If you buy good-quality tools, they'll last a lifetime. With hand tools, you really do get what you pay for.

For example, a complete screwdriver set may cost less than a single quality screwdriver. The difference is the steel used to make the quality screwdriver. Its tip is most likely heat treated for strength and coated with a nonslip surface, which helps it grip the screw. If you've ever tried to loosen a stubborn screw with a cheap screwdriver, you know how it strips the slot as you twist it. A quality tool — whether it's a screwdriver, hammer, pliers or drill bit — gets the job done.

You can rent many specialty and costlier tools and equipment at a rental center, which you'll read about later in this chapter. If you're on a tight budget, you can borrow tools from a friend, neighbor, or relative. Just remember to return them in good condition and soon after you've used them.

Purchase the best-grade hand tools and accessories that you can afford. It's money well spent.

The following sections give you a rundown of basic hand tools you'll use for everyday repairs and for remodeling a bathroom.

Adjustable wrench

An adjustable wrench with smooth jaws is the best tool to tighten nuts and bolts without damaging the nut. Because many sizes of nuts and bolts are available, a 10-inch adjustable wrench is a versatile size. If you have that tool, along with 6-inch and 12-inch wrenches, you'll be able to loosen and tighten just about any size fittings.

Basin wrench

Trying to reach up under a vanity sink to tighten the nuts and bolts used to secure sink and plumbing lines can be just about impossible without this handy wrench. This tool prevents skinned knuckles — it's designed so that you can reach up behind the sink and grab the nuts when installing a sink.

Carpenter's level

Fixtures and cabinets must be level to function properly. A 24-inch spirit level is the simplest and most accurate tool to use. An inexpensive 8-inch bullet level comes in handy for small jobs and tight spaces.

Carpenter's square

A carpenter's square is a tool used to mark straight lines on lumber or wallboard (or any surface) so that you can cut it straight and square. It's made of steel or aluminum, with two arms set at a right angle, enabling you to check to see whether the corners are set at 90 degrees.

Caulk gun

Most caulk and construction adhesive is packaged in tubes that require a caulk gun to dispense the material. The gun holds the tube or cartridge in its body, and when you squeeze the trigger, it applies pressure to the tube, forcing the material out of the tip of the tube. Get one with a no-drip feature. It's well worth the money just in terms of aggravation saved!

Closet auger

This specialized tool with a long handle and a short wire coil snake is used to unclog a toilet. It has a larger head due to the larger trap in a toilet and has a sleeve to protect the bowl from scratches. The handle allows you to work the snake into the toilet bowl and through the trap and break through any blockage.

Combo square

This handy tool is great for laying out cut lines on dimensional lumber. It has a movable steel ruler that is held tight in a head that has a 90-degree edge and a 45-degree edge. The ruler can also be used as a depth gauge.

File

Files, used for sharpening tools and shaping metal, come in many shapes and sizes. Two good choices are a 10-inch coarse, flat file and a smaller, medium-coarse file.

Flashlight

Keep a flashlight with fresh batteries in a toolbox to illuminate what you're working on. A head-mounted light is handy because it shines wherever you look and frees up your hands to do the job. You can get them at camping stores.

Hacksaw

This small handsaw has replaceable fine-toothed blades that are designed to cut metal and plastic plumbing pipe.

Hammer

A good-quality 16-ounce claw hammer is one of the most used tools in any toolbox. Sample several of them and choose one with a comfortable handle.

Remember that the speed — and not the weight — of a hammer is important when driving a nail. Don't purchase a heavy framing hammer unless you're used to doing a lot of nail pounding. Swinging this brute will wear your arm out fast.

Handsaw

Today most people do their heavy cutting with a circular saw. But you really need a handsaw for doing small jobs and finishing cuts that a circular saw can't make. Saws are rated by the number of teeth per inch in the blade: The more teeth, the finer the cut. A crosscut saw with 12 teeth per inch is a good all-purpose saw.

Neon circuit tester

Use this tool to make sure that the power is turned off to electrical wires. This simple device (also called a test lamp) works when you touch the two probes to the circuit wires. The neon tube glows if the circuit is hot, warning you that it's not safe to work on the wires.

Painting equipment

You need these tools for interior painting: 1¼-inch nylon brush, a 2-inch nylon brush, a 10-inch roller and handle, a roller pan, a 4-foot extension pole, and canvas dropcloths for the floor. If the dropcloths seem a bit pricey, then get paper-backed plastic dropcloths, which aren't as slippery as the plastic-only versions. Use the plastic drops to cover furniture and other objects left in the room.

For cleaning paintbrushes and rollers, get a paint spinner, which works like a child's toy. When you slip a roller on the spinner and pump the handle up and down, it rotates and spins the water out of the roller. After you clean the brush or roller, place it in the spinner and then pump the handle. This spins the brush or roller, forcing out the remaining water. Be sure to place the spinner in a bucket or wastebasket or spin the brush or roller outside. The spinner throws off water like a shaggy dog that just stepped out of the lake.

Pipe wrench

A 14-inch pipe wrench is used to work with galvanized steel pipe. Because most older bathrooms probably have galvanized pipe, the wrench is used primarily to remove old fixtures and pipes.

Pliers

Pliers come in a wide variety of shapes and sizes. The most useful types are self-adjusting. One of the leading brands, called RoboGrip, adjusts itself to the size of a pipe or bolt as the pliers are squeezed tight. The 10-inch size is the most versatile.

Putty knife

The flexible-blade version is the best tool for spreading wallboard compound, putty, and glazing in small cracks and nail holes. The stiff-bladed version is good for scraping surfaces and light prying.

Safety equipment

Any time you use a striking tool, protect your eyes by wearing a pair of safety glasses. Also, you'll find it easier to use most power tools if you wear them because you can keep your eyes open and not worry about getting sawdust or drill trailings in your eyes. A good dust mask or N95 particulate respirator is a must; purchase a box of them and use them. Protect your ears with a set of earplugs, which are inexpensive enough for you to get a pair for every member of the family.

Screwdrivers

Invest in a set of slotted (also called straight slot) and Phillips screwdrivers of varying sizes. A slotted screwdriver has a flat tip or blade, and a Phillips head has a cross head for screws with two intersecting slots. A quality-grade screwdriver lasts longer and works better because it has strong handles attached to a high-grade steel shaft.

Tongue and groove pliers

Tongue and groove pliers are a gripping tool with adjustable jaws used for tightening pipes, trap nuts, and other large-diameter objects. It can grip a wider range of objects because the jaws of the pliers can be adjusted over a very wide range. The 14-inch size is most useful for plumbing work.

Steel tape measure

A good-quality tape measure has a heavy-duty blade and a strong end hook so that you can extend it without bending it. A 12-foot tape is long enough to measure most things and not too heavy to carry around. The 25-foot tape is larger, but its stiff, wide blade comes in handy when you want to measure something several feet away.

Toilet plunger

This rubber suction cup on a wooden stick is used to force out clogs in plumbing lines. It's an essential tool for all homeowners.

Utility knife

You need at least one of these tools but will probably end up purchasing several because they're so useful and so many variations are available. The tool has replaceable, retractable blades that are stored in the handle. Some have a blade with a break-off feature that keeps a sharp blade always available.

Work light

Also called a drop light or trouble light, this gadget is a light bulb enclosed in a protective cage with a hook and long electrical cord and plug. It's useful when you're working in tight spaces because you can hang it and cast light where you need it.

You've got the power: Gotta-have power tools

The cost of corded power tools has dropped, while the quality has risen. As a result, drills, saws, and sanders that used to cost several hundred dollars are now available for less that a hundred bucks. Cordless tools have developed to a point where they rival corded tools not only in power but also in longevity. The best strategy in purchasing power tools is to buy the tool as you need it. Start off with an electric drill, and then build your power arsenal as needed.

Here are the most useful power tools for remodeling a bathroom or any room in your house. But before you buy one, consider how many times you'll use it. If it's for only one project, keep tool rental in mind.

Heavy-duty extension cord

A 25-foot grounded 16-gauge round cord with a three-prong plug will connect power tools to an electrical outlet as well as power a radio or CD player with

Jimmy Buffett songs to keep you entertained while you work. If you need a longer cord or plan to run heavy-duty tools like circular saws, purchase a 14-gauge cord. For extra safety while working in the bathroom, consider a heavy-duty cord with a built-in ground-fault circuit interrupter (GFCI).

Orbital pad sander

An orbital pad sander, also called a finishing sander, comes in a variety of sizes based on the size of the sandpaper sheet it uses. A quarter-sheet pad sander is the most versatile and comfortable to use because it easily fits in the palm of your hand. It's used for fine finish sanding; the high speed leaves a smooth finish on whatever surface it's working.

Jigsaw

If you're going to purchase one power saw, make it a saber saw, which is extremely versatile. Depending on the blade, it can cut wood, plastic, and metal and at different cutting speeds.

7¼-inch circular saw

The circular saw revolutionized house construction and is the cornerstone of a carpenter's toolbox. A good-quality "circ saw" takes a 7¼-inch diameter blade and has ball bearings rather than sleeve bearings. The motors are rated by horsepower, but the real tip-off to the power of the saw is the motor's amp rating, which is printed on the motor.

If you're going to do rough framing, this saw is a good investment. Otherwise, rent or borrow one.

A sharp saw blade makes an inexpensive saw cut like a gold plater. No matter how powerful the saw is, a cheap blade dulls quickly and causes it to bog down and make an uneven cut. Few saws are sold with top-quality saw blades, so no matter what type of saw you purchase, get several carbide-tipped blades, which stay sharp much longer than a standard steel blade, to go with it.

Shop vacuum

Any type of remodeling makes a mess, so invest in a shop vacuum to clean up. Most models are designed to pick up dry and wet materials. The best ones feature replaceable pleated paper filters that you can remove for easy cleaning. Many versions have an additional bag that is placed over the filter to catch fine dust and other very small particles.

Toolboxes are like chocolate: More is better

You know the story about the guy who built the sandbox in his basement and then couldn't get it up the stairs because it was too big? Well, that's what we did with a toolbox. We built an enormous wooden toolbox that turned out to be so heavy we could barely lift it, let alone move it from one job to another. We quickly learned that more is better when it comes to toolboxes. Even if a large toolbox isn't heavy, it will be when you fill it up with tools. And nothing is more frustrating than digging through a cavern of tools looking for a gotta-have wrench. Fumbling around for tools can be dangerous, too, because many of them have sharp edges.

We have several medium-size toolboxes for electrical, plumbing, and hand carpentry projects. We also have a canvas insert with pockets that sits inside a five-gallon bucket that's a handy place to stash a few power tools and ideal for moving from one job to another.

⅜-inch reversible variable speed drill

The most versatile power tool you can own is a power drill, useful for drilling holes, of course, but also for driving and removing screws. Teamed with an army of adapters and accessories, a basic drill can polish, grind, sand, and probably brush your teeth if you can find the right attachment.

Drills are available in a wide array of sizes and features. Drills are basically categorized by the capacity of the *chuck* (that pointy thing on the end of the drill) that holds the drill bit. The chuck is rated by the largest drill it can hold. They range from light-duty drills with ¼-inch capacity chucks to heavy-duty monsters with ½-inch capacity chucks. The midrange ⅜-inch drill is the most versatile. Most manufacturers refer to the drill capacity without mentioning the chuck, so a drill with a chuck that has a ⅜-inch capacity is called a ⅜-inch drill.

A good-quality cordless drill is reliable and tough running and, with rechargeable batteries, will last as long as a corded drill. That wasn't the case a few years ago, but it's true today. You can't beat a good-quality, variable speed-reversing, 12-volt or 14.4-volt for drilling and driving screws. These units have a gear reduction to increase the torque or power, so they tend to operate at a lower speed than a corded one.

Charge new batteries of a cordless drill overnight because it will take several discharge/charge cycles to get full power from the battery. Before storing them, charge them full, but don't use the charger as a storage case. Read the owner's manual for specifics. Don't charge batteries in extreme temperatures. Allow the battery to cool before charging.

Visiting Your Friendly Rental Center

Rental centers serve small contractors and serious do-it-yourselfers with an array of specialty tools that are available by the hour, half day, full day, or week. If you're tool obsessive, you can get your hands on industrial-strength tools that you could never justify owning. When you need a specific tool for a job and don't have it, consider renting it instead of using the wrong tool.

To bore a large hole in a floor joist, rent a heavy-duty ½-inch drill instead of risking overloading your standard ⅜-inch drill. If you find yourself renting the same tool repeatedly, consider buying one. Better yet, plan your projects to get maximum use of the rental tool when you have it.

For the best selection of specialty tools, find a rental center in your area that caters to contractors. You'll get good advice about using the tool because the tools are workhorses. Check the center's hours. If you're working on weekends, make sure it's open when you need the tool. Walk the aisles and look at all the accessories that go with the tools. These are consumable items like sandpaper belts, masonry drill bits, and saw blades, all designed to make the tool do the job better and faster. Don't be shy about asking questions — the employees have probably heard them all, including the dumb ones. To prevent blowing a fuse or breaker, always ask what electrical service the tool requires.

Checking out specialty rental tools for remodeling

If you like tools, you'll love going to a rental center, a candy store for tool hounds. Even if you don't need the tool when you visit, it's good to know the tools and gear that are available on a rental basis. These specialty tools will help a do-it-yourselfer complete many different projects and phases of remodeling a bathroom.

Airless paint sprayer

An airless sprayer pumps paint through a small hole in the tip of a spray gun at very high pressure. This action breaks the paint up into a fine mist that is then directed at the wall or whatever surface you're painting. Different size tips are available, depending on the surface being painted. Some guns have adjustable tips, which is handy. Make sure that the gun is equipped with the proper tip to spray the type of paint you plan to use. These airless spray rigs can be gas or electric powered; needless to say, a gas sprayer is best used outside.

Spray painting requires a lot of preparation to mask the surfaces you don't want to paint. The sprayer also takes time to clean, so consider the extra preparation and cleanup time required. This work may cancel out the time saved by using the sprayer, but then again, if you've always wanted to use one of these bad boys, go ahead and rent one.

Because of the high pressure, a sprayer can be dangerous if you misuse it. Don't point the spray gun at yourself or anyone else, because the paint can be injected into the skin — no kidding. Protect yourself by wearing a long-sleeve shirt and a good-quality respirator, not just a dust mask.

Belt sander

A belt sander removes material from the surface quickly because it has a large rectangular belt that is in full contact with the surface. This tool is expensive and not as versatile as an orbital pad sander, so it's a good tool to rent instead of own.

Equipped with a coarse sanding belt, this tool can remove just about any finish. You need several belts with different grades of abrasive grit to get a smooth surface because the coarse belts leave sanding marks. Make sure you understand how to change the sanding belt and how to center the belt so it stays on the sander.

The sander should have a dust pickup bag, but you should still wear a respirator and goggles when operating any sander to protect yourself from fine dust particles.

½-inch drill

When it comes to drilling large-diameter (over ⅜-inch) holes, a ½-inch drill is the tool to use. Half-inch drills operate at a lower speed than ¼- and ⅜-inch drills and develop the torque to drill large holes in wood for plumbing pipes and electrical wires. These drills can also be used to drill into masonry with the proper drill bit. If you need to drill large-diameter holes, rent a ½-inch drill and the hole saws designed to work with it. The rental center has special bits used by plumbers to bore holes over 2 inches in diameter, and when teamed with a ½-inch drill, they make this project easier.

If you tell the rental center employee the material you'll be drilling into and the size of the holes you want to make, he can recommend what you need.

Check that all accessories — key chuck, side handles, and depth gauge — are included. The drill has a high-amperage motor and requires a heavy-duty extension cord to run properly, so you'll have to rent one if you don't already have one. The drill spits out small chips of whatever it's going through, so wear safety goggles to protect your eyes.

Heat gun

A heat gun looks like a hair dryer on steroids. Rental heat guns are heavy-duty professional-grade units and work faster than those marketed to consumers. The professional gun is a safe source of concentrated heat when used carefully. Use it with a putty knife and scrapers to soften and remove paint and adhesives. It's also handy to thaw frozen water pipes. A heat gun costs under $75, so if you'll be using one often, buy it instead of renting. Most stripping jobs are time and labor intensive, so the rental fee may add up quickly.

Be careful when operating a heat gun. Don't direct the heat at one area for too long and don't point the gun at glass because the intense heat may crack it. Just because there is no flame doesn't mean you can't start a fire. Wear leather gloves and goggles for protection. And come break time, let the gun cool down before setting it down. Heat guns are not approved for the removal of lead paint.

Long ladders and scaffolding

Owning long ladders and scaffolding is expensive and can be a real storage problem for the average homeowner, so renting them is a smart way to go.

Inside the home, ladders are used primarily for painting and installing fixtures in ceilings or windows. Ladders come in a variety of sizes, ranging from 14 feet and up, and extension ladders can reach even higher — up to 40 feet and more.

Many types of folding ladders are available. One of the most common is the A-frame ladder. This ladder has locking joints between the sections that allow it to be configured into many different shapes.

Reciprocating saw

The reciprocating saw is a saw designed for plumbers who have to work in tight spaces. Many manufacturers make this useful tool today. The corded version is the standard and is available in single- or variable-speed versions. Some versions feature an orbital cutting action that produces a faster cutting speed. Cordless versions are also available with many of the same features as the corded tools. Used with the right blade, the saw can cut through just about anything — wood framing, pipes, and plaster and drywall on walls. It's ideal for removing walls and partitions or doing any kind of demolition work.

Tile saw

A tile saw is designed to cut ceramic tile. Scoring-type cutters can be used on wall tile, but the heavier floor tile requires a tile saw to make clean, accurate cuts. The saw has an abrasive blade designed to cut masonry. The best-grade tile saws are water-cooled (they're also called wet saws) and come with a base that holds the water and catches the tile dust and debris created by the cutting action.

Wallpaper steamer

Wallpaper is popular in bathrooms, and removing layers of heavy vinyl paper can be difficult and tedious. Enter the wallpaper steamer. It uses the heat of steam to force moisture through the heavy paper and loosen the paste so that the paper can be scraped off the wall. The rental unit has a hot plate and water boiler tank connected by a hose. You fill its boiler tank with water, and when the water begins to boil and steam comes out of the plate, it's ready to use. You hold the hot plate in one hand and a wide putty knife or razor scraper in the other to remove the wallpaper.

The steam is very hot and can burn your hand or arm if you're not careful, so wear a heavy pair of gloves and a long-sleeve shirt for protection.

Saving time can save you money

The clock starts ticking when you leave the rental center with the tool, so it pays to have a game plan. Reserve the tool for when you want it and order any accessories or consumables that you'll need. Don't forget related safety gear, such as respirators and safety goggles, too.

If you're renting a large tool like a floor sander, transporting the brute may be the challenge if you don't have a vehicle that's large enough. Don't risk damaging the shocks on your car — avoid this unnecessary expense. Beg or borrow a friend's van or pickup truck if you have to.

Most rental centers require a cash or credit card deposit, plus the rental fee for the tool.

Chapter 5

Selecting Surface Materials 101

· ·

· ·

*B*efore you make any decisions about the design and fixtures in your new bathroom, spend some time thinking about the surface materials you plan to use. Admittedly, musing about wallboard is far from exciting, but the basic materials that make up the surfaces in a bathroom — walls, ceilings, and floors — are important. To create the best new bathroom, take a step back to the basics to discover what makes up the shell of the room. A little knowledge about the different surface materials used in a bathroom goes a long way in guaranteeing surfaces that are sound and durable.

After you've read about the materials here, take a trip to a lumberyard or home center to get a look at all the different materials that you're thinking about using in your new bathroom. The more you know about the choices of materials, the better you'll be able to make good decisions about what to include in your bathroom.

Shopping till You Drop

The mega home improvement stores, home centers, and lumberyards sell a large selection of all the surface materials and fixtures you need to remodel a bathroom. They also sell the tools, fasteners, hardware, and other supplies for major remodeling projects. What they can't offer is an extensive range of materials and fixtures. Even the largest super home store would be hard fixed to offer toilets from all 26 manufacturers.

Another place to shop for these products is design or decorating centers and showrooms. These stores specialize in particular materials, such as ceramic tile and flooring, so they can offer tiles from all over the world and flooring materials from every manufacturer who makes it.

Narrowing the field even further are the specialty distributors who sell only one material, such as a tile and stone supplier or a hardwood or ceramic floor center. Because of the narrow focus of these stores, they carry a broad spectrum of products in their category. Designers, builders, and remodelers are their primary customers, but homeowners can shop there, too.

The big boxes and lumberyards

Believe it or not, the large home improvement stores are designed to make your shopping experience pleasant and convenient. This comes as a shock to anyone short of time and lung capacity trying to find a particular item buried in the back aisles. But when it comes to bathroom materials, they do a pretty fair job of displaying everything they have available. Admittedly, looking at the many varieties of wallboard does not excite the senses, but these suppliers provide a place where you can see and touch the stuff that will become part of your new bathroom — wood and vinyl flooring, ceramic and stone tiles, solid surfaces, laminates, and a lot more. The larger stores, which feature kitchen and bathroom design centers, get an A-plus for their room display setups that let you walk through different bathroom vignettes designed with a selection of materials and fixtures.

If your town doesn't have a large home improvement center, then visit your local lumberyard. You may be surprised to find that they don't just sell lumber anymore. Some of the larger independent yards have expanded to include full-line hardware departments, and some even have design centers.

Many of these retailers have sort of one-stop remodeling sales programs. For a fee, they'll manage and hire subcontractors to do all the work or some of the work. You can pay them to deliver the materials to your house, or they'll rent you a truck (conveniently parked in their lot) so you can do the work yourself. If you need any specialty tools for the project, you can rent or buy them there. Need money? They're happy to sign you up with a home improvement loan to finance your project. We're waiting for the day they offer dental and health care.

Specialty shopping options

A typical decorating center or specialty retailer offers an almost endless selection of materials for your bathroom. If you can't find what you want, these places probably offer you information about other materials they can order. These companies distribute materials to people in the business of building and remodeling, so they have a broad selection of moderately priced to luxury-tagged materials. Most offer the installation of the materials they sell. Some subcontract the work out to specialty installers; others refer customers directly to installers.

Some people are overwhelmed by the choices and prefer fewer products; others thrive on the unique and unusual materials found only at a design center or showroom and enjoy the pursuit of finding something special. Find the shopping style that you feel comfortable with and limit your choices or go hog-wild finding the unique and unusual. You know how you like to shop, so follow your instincts to discover products and materials for your new bathroom.

In the paint section, you'll find more information and choices than you ever wanted and thousands of paint color samples to choose from. Every manufacturer has a palette of colors from which to choose your shade and type of paint.

The wallpaper area of a retailer usually has wide counters where you can open up and browse through the large sample books. Some are more comfortable than others and offer places to sit while you consider the options.

Ceramic tile and stone, like wallpaper, are available in many sizes, shapes, and colors, so selecting tile can be a mind-numbing experience. Retailers sometimes use sample boards of tiles as displays so you can see what the tile looks like on the wall or floor.

Many retailers sell window treatments in a wide range of designs, including basic ready-to-hang, custom-made miniblinds, narrow louvered wooden shutters, and 1-inch-wide plantation-style shutters. You also can find plain shades, honeycomb shades, fabric Roman-style shades, and even shades that fold flat on a roller. Looking for a window topper? You'll find window cornice kits to assemble and finish yourself and custom-order cornices made of wood and fabric.

In flooring, you'll find large displays of wood, laminates, tiles, stone, marble, carpeting, even cork, and all the related underlayment materials involved in installing flooring. If you're looking for one place to get an overview of flooring choices for your bathroom, look in the Yellow Pages under "Floor Material."

Knowing about what's offered at specialty retailers may not be helpful if you don't live near any. You can order many materials and fixtures online, but for heavy materials like wallboard, choose a retailer near your home.

Online suppliers and retailers

Ordering materials and fixtures online is becoming more popular every day. People are especially likely to shop online when buying a stock item that they've seen on display and know what to expect when it's delivered to their doorstep. And that delivery part is key to why many people do order online: The product is delivered to your door.

But there are downsides to ordering materials and fixtures online. What if you don't want a product after seeing it? What if it comes damaged? How do you return large items such as a toilet or bathtub? Not easily. The sites selling these materials usually explain their policies, which you should read carefully before placing an order.

Some people say that buying something online is much cheaper than buying it at a store. And that just may be the case. Use the technology on the Internet to price shop an item you want. With the name of the item, its manufacturer, and item number, use these sites to compare different materials and fixtures for their features, cost, and availability. We caution you to factor in all related costs like the delivery charge and returning it, if necessary, and then making a cost comparison.

Here are some e-commerce sites that sell materials that you'll use when remodeling your bathroom:

- ✔ Smith+Noble (www.smithandnoble.com): This site, an extension of the catalog of the same name, features an extensive line of window treatments.

- ✔ The Internet Wallpaper Store (www.wallpaperstore.com) and wallpaper wholesaler.com (www.wallpaperwholesaler.com): These sites showcase thousands of wallpaper patterns. Get a sample (approximately 12 x 24 inches) of wallcoverings for $2 or $3 a sample, plus a small shipping charge.

- ✔ Ifloor.com (www.ifloor.com): This site sells all types of flooring material, including hardwood, carpeting, vinyl tile, ceramic tile, cork, and linoleum, and offers a contractor search as well as online installation videos.

- ✔ Plumbing Mall (www.plumbingmall.com) and WhirlpoolBathStore.com (www.whirlpoolbathstore.com): These sites have a wide selection of bathroom faucets, lavatories, showers, tubs, toilets, bidets, fans, and much more.

Exploring some shopping strategies

When you're looking for ideas, materials, and fixtures to remodel your bathroom, go with a clear, well-rested head. Don't go when you're tired or hungry. You're making a major investment, so do it once and do it right. Go with a list of ideas you want to pursue and products or materials you want to look at, and shop with more than enough time to peruse everything that there is to see. Then do it again. You'll be amazed at what you like the second time that you didn't even notice during the first trip.

Go shopping with your bathroom notebook (which we describe in Chapter 2) full of dimensions and measurements and know how much material and what size fixtures you need. With this information available, you may be able to take advantage of a sale on discontinued tiles that would be just the right size for your new bathroom. (But make sure that you buy enough of them!)

Discovering the Many Faces of Wallboard

Gypsum wallboard is the mainstay of the construction industry. Most walls and ceilings are now constructed with this inexpensive and durable product. Through the years, special-purpose wallboard panels like green board and cement board have been developed to overcome wallboard's primary enemy: moisture.

Wallboard is one of the popular choices for a surface material of your new bathroom. It is also the preferred base for many other types of covering, ranging from wallpaper to paneling and wainscoting. In Table 5-1 you find a rundown of the basic types of wallboard and their characteristics.

Table 5-1		Wallboard and Its Uses	
Name	*Thickness*	*Size*	*Use*
Standard wallboard	¼ inch	4 x 8 feet	Wall, ceilings in dry areas
	⅜ inch	4 x 12 feet	Wall, ceilings in dry areas
	½ inch	4 x 12 feet	Wall, ceilings in dry areas
	⅝ inch	4 x 12 feet	Wall, ceilings in dry areas
	¾ inch	4 x 12 feet	Wall, ceilings in dry areas
Foil-backed	⅜ inch	4 x 8 feet	Wall, ceilings where vapor barrier is needed
	½ inch	4 x 12 feet	Wall, ceilings where vapor barrier is needed
	⅝ inch	4 x 12 feet	Wall, ceilings where vapor barrier is needed
Green board	½ inch	4 x 8 feet	Walls in high-moisture area
	⅝ inch	4 x 12 feet	Walls in high-moisture area

(continued)

Table 5-1 *(continued)*

Name	Thickness	Size	Use
Cement board	½ inch	32 inches x 5 feet	Walls, wet areas, tile underlayment
	½ inch	36 inches x 5 feet	Walls, wet areas, tile underlayment
	5/16 inch	48 inches x 48 inches	Floors, underlayment

Note: The ¼- and ⅜-inch drywall is primarily used for lamination. It may be used to create curved surfaces and installed over old plaster. Several layers may be glued together so the top layer hides the fasteners.

Standard wallboard

Unless you live in a house constructed before the 1950s, you're surrounded by wallboard panels, also called drywall. The panels have a gypsum plaster core covered by a paper facing. The joints between the panels are concealed with fiberglass or paper tape embedded in wallboard compound. After the wallboard is painted, the paper facing absorbs some of the paint and dries to a smooth surface.

The panels come in ¼, ⅜, ½, ⅝, and ¾-inch thicknesses. Standard panels are 4 feet wide and come in lengths of 8 or 12 feet. Most home centers and lumberyards carry 4-x-8-foot sheets in ⅜, ½, and ⅝-inch thicknesses. You'll also find some 12-foot-long sheets.

Foil-backed wallboard

Standard wallboard with an aluminum foil backing is a material that serves as a vapor barrier, which can be an effective solution to preventing condensation. Exterior walls, especially those in high-moisture areas such as a bathroom, must contain a vapor barrier to prevent condensation from forming in the wall cavity. This type of drywall should not be installed over an existing vapor barrier.

Green board

The gypsum plaster core of standard wallboard will absorb water and begin to separate from the paper face if exposed to excessive moisture. The paper covering will also mildew if exposed to dampness for extended periods of time. To help prevent this problem, moisture-resistant wallboard, called green board because — duh — it's green, was developed. It's designed to be installed in high-moisture areas, such as a bathroom, and is the preferred substrate or base for tile in high-moisture areas. But it's not waterproof, so we don't recommend it as a base for tile around tubs and in shower stalls.

Don't install tile over green board that is applied over a vapor barrier. Use cement backerboard instead.

Cement board

To overcome the shortcomings of wallboard, manufacturers developed a ½-inch-thick board that has a cement-based core rather than plaster. Cement board, also called backerboard, is water resistant and is the ideal backing for tile in wet areas such as the bathtub surround and shower stall.

Cement board is available in ½-inch and ⁵⁄₁₆-inch thickness. The ½-inch-thick board is used as a backer for tile and is available in sheets that range from 32 to 48 inches wide and 3 to 8 feet long. The thinner ⁵⁄₁₆-inch board is used for floor underlayment and is available in the same sizes. Manufacturers' specifications and sizes do vary, so check with your lumberyard to find out what sizes they stock.

Wrapping Your Room in Wallcoverings

The wallcoverings in a bathroom set the mood and style by creating a backdrop for the fixtures and furnishings. Flowers and fluff say a feminine person inhabits the space, while soccer balls and scooters running across the walls scream that it's a kids' bathroom. And that's exactly what wallcoverings do — define the room and reveal who uses it. In the same sense, a subdued pattern or subtle design on the walls create a muted backdrop to show off colorful fixtures and furnishings.

Don't overlook the wallcoverings of the room or hall leading into the bathroom. Designers recommend melding colors, patterns, and textures from one room into the next so that you don't walk from a vertical striped wallpaper in a bedroom to a horizontal pattern in the adjoining bathroom. Think about a continuing flow of patterns and colors from one room into the next as you consider wallpaper for the new bathroom.

Today you can choose from a staggering number of colors, styles, patterns, and textures of wallcoverings. Most of the wallcovering companies create collections that group patterns together that complement each other. The collections usually include companion designs of a print, a plaid, a solid, and borders, along with fabric to use as a window covering, shower curtain, or other furnishing.

Samples of wallcoverings are featured in large (24-inch-square) books with themes like Kitchen and Bath and French Country Victorian, or by categories such as textures, small and simple prints, or natural neutrals. You won't find these books in a library, but you will find plenty of them at retailers that sell wallpaper. Look for them at paint and decorating centers, as well as in the wallpaper departments of home centers and lumberyards and hardware stores.

Tricking the eye with wallcoverings

The guidelines for choosing a wallcovering pattern for a bathroom, like any other room, suggest that you consider the size and shape of the room. A small, as opposed to a large, pattern is a good choice in a small bathroom. A large overpowering design will overwhelm a powder room but may be a nice choice in a more spacious master bathroom. You may want to consider a small print or geometric design that's scaled to a small space.

Use a wallpaper pattern to trick the eye. For instance, a pattern with a light background makes the bathroom appear larger. A vertical pattern or stripe draws the eye to the ceiling, making the room appear higher. Conversely, a horizontal pattern or stripe widens a room, bringing the ceiling down in appearance.

Most experts agree that a vinyl-coated, fabric-backed, prepasted wallcovering that is durable, pliable, and easy to hang is a good choice for any bathroom. In a seldom used powder room where there's little chance of splashing water, you can use a less durable wallcovering, but in general, bathrooms are busy places where moisture is an issue, so choose a wallcovering durable enough to withstand the harsh elements.

For budgeting purposes, figure that a double roll will cover approximately 56 square feet and cost about $45. If the wallcovering is in stock at its distribution point, it takes a few days to a week to arrive after ordering. If not, you may have to wait longer, but the person at the order desk should give you a reliable estimated delivery date.

Walk into any decorating center or wallpaper store and look at the enormous selection of wallpaper books on display. You'll quickly realize that choosing a wallpaper pattern can be a daunting experience. When you find a few patterns that you like, or think you like, check out the books (just like at the library) and bring them home to see how the patterns look where you'll actually be using them.

Auditioning wallpaper

To get an idea of what a pattern may look like in your bathroom, open the book to the pattern page, secure both sides with a heavy rubber band (the kind that broccoli and asparagus are bound in) and prop the book on a chair or ladder in your bathroom. Leave it there for a few days and make a point of viewing it in daytime and evening to see how different lighting affects it. You'll surely get comments from family members (whether you want them or not).

Practice this little exercise with all the patterns you're considering to see what appeals to you after seeing it for several days.

Don't be tempted to take your scissors or X-Acto knife and cut out the pattern page from wallpaper books. Larceny in any form is never a good thing. If you really need individual samples that you can tape on your wall, look for wallcoverings in home centers and paint-and-wallpaper retailers. They spare you from the temptation of defacing wallpaper books by providing handy samples you can take home. These stores also have less-expensive wallcoverings in stock that are ready to hang.

To find out about the nuts and bolts of measuring, ordering, and hanging wallpaper, see Chapter 13.

Tapping the Power of Paneling

One of the most popular looks in bathrooms today is wrapping the walls or part of them in paneling. Whether finished naturally or painted, wood adds warmth and interest to any room, no matter how small or large. It's a good coverup for less than perfect walls, and provides an attractive wall detail to an otherwise ordinary bathroom.

Beadboard

Traditional vertical boards called beadboard are often used as wainscoting in a room to add Old World charm and appeal. You'll find beadboard made of wood or a composite material. The unfinished wooden panels, measuring ⅜ inch thick, 4 feet wide, and 8 feet long, cost about $25 each and have decorative grooves running the length of the panel that are designed to replicate the look of beaded boards. You can get the same look with a prefinished white composite panel for about $18.

Beadboard usually is installed one-third up the wall and capped with a chair rail molding or installed two-thirds of the way up and topped with a plate rail shelf, creating a handy storage and display space. A wooden baseboard completes the installation, concealing the floor joint. You can install the material, sold at lumberyards and home centers, directly over walls with construction adhesive or nail it to *furring strips,* or thin pieces of wood fastened to the wall. Find out more about installing beadboard in Chapter 13.

Frame-and-panel wainscoting

For a more formal or traditional look, consider frame-and-panel wainscoting, also called raised paneling. The material is sold as components and comes precut and milled to fit together. The panels, which you fasten to the walls with adhesive and nails, come unfinished and ready to paint or prefinished in different wood shades.

The materials to install raised paneling on the lower third of the walls of a 12-foot-x-17-foot room (approximately 58 linear feet), including a top rail and baseboard molding at the floor, cost about $1,500. The material is sold at building material outlets and lumberyards, where you can get help measuring and ordering the components for your room. At New England Classic's Web site (www.newenglandclassic.com), you can use a calculator and get a detailed design layout and bill of materials to plan your project.

Hardboard

Hardboard is a generic term the lumber industry uses to describe a panel that is made from specially engineered fibers that are pressed together under heat and pressure. Other materials may be added during manufacturing to improve certain properties such as stiffness, hardness, resistance to abrasion, and moisture. Hardboard is used as a base for several types of paneling suitable for the bathroom.

The basic hardboard panels are manufactured with two smooth sides rated S2S and a single smooth side rated S1S. You can install the S1S panel with the smooth side out for easy painting or place the rough side out (it has a fine texture surface) to provide a good base for wallpaper or some other covering. They come in two grades:

- ✔ **Standard hardboard:** This grade is suitable for interior uses such as paneling, partitions, flush doors, garage doors, and so on.

- ✔ **Tempered hardboard:** This grade is impregnated with a special oil that is polymerized by heat treatment. It is suitable in applications that need extra moisture resistance, surface hardness, rigidity, bending, and tensile strength. This product is used in the manufacture of cabinets, doors and decorative paneling. It is a good choice for custom vanity doors and side panels.

Melamine panels

Melamine panels are made from decorative papers that have been impregnated with melamine resin that are then fused to the surface of the hardboard or particleboard. The finished surface of these panels becomes very hard, scratch resistant, stain resistant, and colorfast, similar to high-pressure plastic laminate.

Melamine panels are an inexpensive wall treatment and with proper installation can be used in tub surrounds and shower areas. This panel has a rather utilitarian look but is easy to clean with a damp cloth and ordinary soap or household ammoniated liquid detergent.

Tileboard

Tileboard is an embossed melamine hardboard panel that has the look of ceramic tile. This material combines the look of ceramic tile at a fraction of the cost. It is approved for use in high-moisture areas, such as bathrooms, or anywhere an easily cleaned wall surface is required, such as kitchens and laundry rooms. Tileboard comes in 4-foot-x-8-foot sheets and is installed with adhesive.

Opening up Spaces with Glass Block

In the 1920s, glass block was all the rage, and it's making a big comeback today. Glass block has many advantages for use in and around the bathroom. First, it is totally waterproof, and second, it transmits light while still providing a high level of privacy. The more heavily patterned blocks provide more privacy but also block more light. Conversely, less pattern in the block means less privacy.

Available in many sizes and shapes, glass block can be fabricated into windows, wall partitions, and shower stalls by a skilled mason. It's available in colors and many finishes — from crystal clear to frosted glass — and many different patterns.

Most home centers stock the standard 6-inch, 8-inch, and 12-inch square blocks. Prefabricated windows and partition wall and shower wall assemblies of glass blocks can also be custom built by the manufacturer and shipped to the building site. These can be installed by carpenters, which makes a bath remodeling project run smoother because finding a mason to install the glass blocks can be a challenge in some areas of the country.

Glass block shower stall kits, available from several manufacturers, include a prefabricated shower pan, or floor, with the base for the glass block walls molded into the pan. Several styles are available, including a stylish enclosure with a curved wall.

In the past, custom shower pans to accommodate curved glass block shower walls had been a source of leaks. Today prefabricated shower pans simplify the installation of a glass block shower stall with rounded walls.

Introducing Glass's Second Cousin, Acrylic

Acrylic block combines the beauty of glass block with a tough scratch-resistant acrylic plastic, making it considerably lighter than glass block. It is available in prefabricated window and door panels that are fully glazed. These acrylic block assemblies are held together by resilient polymer clips and encased in aluminum or vinyl frames. The window and door panels are easy to install with standard tools, and because acrylic block is installed without mortar, there's no mess and fewer headaches. The blocks are available in three finishes: clear, patterned, and frosted. They come in standard 6-inch and 8-inch square sizes and 2- and 3-inch thicknesses. The block can be used for custom windows, door inserts, wall partitions, and curved shower enclosures.

Tooling Around with Ceramic Tile

Ceramic tile is made of clay. The raw materials — clays, talc, and other minerals — are quarried and refined. The tile manufacturer must be careful to get the proper mixture of these materials. The ratio of the mix of these ingredients determines the characteristics of the tile. After the formation of the tile body, ceramic tiles go through a firing process in a kiln under very high heat (2,000 degrees F) to harden the tile body (and undergo a second firing to create a surface glaze). Today some tile manufacturers use a single fire process that forms the body and glaze together.

Common uses for tile

The variety of sizes and shapes of tile is nearly matched by the many places it is used in bathrooms and throughout the house. Tile can be just about anywhere in a bathroom, from the walls down to the floor, surrounding bathtubs and showers, even on the ceiling of tub and shower enclosures.

The durable surfaces that tiles provide make them a good choice for a bathroom. Tiles designed for floors are heavier than wall tiles, and they're slip- and abrasion-resistant. The highly glazed wall tiles are not recommended for the floor because they become very slippery when wet. For cleaning purposes, avoid tile patterns with deep crevices or voids, which can make the floor harder to clean. Tiles are installed on a sound subfloor in thinset adhesive. Grout fills the joints, creating a watertight surface.

Shower stalls and tub surrounds are generally wet areas and require a tile with a high-temperature glassy glaze. The glazing on tiles prevents the tile from absorbing water and makes the tile easy to clean. Use only slip-resistant glazed tiles on shower floors.

If you're tiling a small bathroom, you'll probably want to choose a small tile that is scaled to the room. Larger tiles are more appropriate in a large, wide space. However, large tiles mean fewer grout lines, which adds up to fewer visual distractions in a small room. Consider combining square or hexagon-shaped tiles in the center of a room with a border of rectangular tiles as an edging to trim out the room.

You'll get the best selection of tiles at a tile retailer, where large display areas illustrate just how creative you can be with tiles.

Standard sizes

Tiles are available in a wide variety of sizes, ranging from small 1-inch mosaic tiles to large floor tiles:

✔ **Mosaic tile:** These small tiles can be difficult to handle and come mounted on fabric backing or paper sheets or held together with silicone adhesive. Nominal sizes of the tiles are 1 inch x 1 inch, 2 inches x 1 inch, and 2 inches x 2 inches, all ½-inch thick. Additional standard patterns and solid-colored sheets of tile in custom designs can be ordered from many tile outlets. Mosaic tile works well on floors or walls and can be used to line a shower pan because the small tile can conform to curved surfaces.

✔ **Wall tile:** Glazed wall tile is lighter weight than floor tile and comes in nominal dimensions of 4¼ x 4¼ inches, 6 x 4¼ inches, and 6 x 6 inches. They're all 5⁄16-inch thick. To trim around the edge of tiles where they meet a different surface, such as a tile wainscoting on a wall, accent tile pieces are available. These edging pieces come in strips and ropes and are designed to go around outside and inside corners and do a nice job of edging the tile. You'll find them to match the tiles you choose. In Chapter 10, you find out how to install wall tile in a bathtub surround.

✔ **Floor tile:** Some of the most popular size floor tiles are 6, 8, and 12 inches, but you'll find them sold in many more shapes and sizes. The nonslip surfaces are designed to ensure safe footing. Trim pieces for the walls are available that take the place of a base shoe molding. In Chapter 14, you can find out how to lay out and install a tile floor.

Considering the Solid Characteristics of Solid Surfaces

Today's solid surfaces are durable, long-lasting, and low-maintenance materials used for countertops, backsplashes behind sinks, shower and bathtub enclosures, and flooring. Many of these materials are available, and you'll find them in displays at home design centers and at bathroom design firms, where you'll find qualified fabricators to install them.

Synthetics

These materials, first introduced in the early 1970s are made up of polyester or acrylic, resins, and fillers. They come in a palette of colors, textures, and patterns and are sold at kitchen and bath design centers, as well as home centers and lumberyards. Synthetics withstand dirt and bacterial growth and can be repaired with a light sanding.

Giving your ceiling the top treatment

Years ago, some decorating magazine must have featured a picture of a bathroom with wallpaper on the ceiling. It was a bad idea then, and it still is today, but many people thought it a clever idea. Unfortunately, the moist conditions in even the best-ventilated bathroom will force the corners of paper to peel off. Avoid the temptation and save the wallcovering for the walls.

Another not-so-good idea for a bathroom ceiling is using a suspended ceiling made of metal grid that holds acoustical tiles. The strips of metal grid tend to rust, and with age, the tile discolors, so it's not a good ceiling material.

Paint the ceiling. Period. Choose a good-quality latex paint like Perma-White, a mildew-proof bathroom paint that prevents mildew growth on the paint film. It is self-priming, and you can tint it any color. Whether the ceiling is wallboard or plaster, paint it.

Within the confines of a tiled bathtub or shower enclosure, it's a good idea to continue the tile on the ceiling. The tile creates a durable surface that's easy to clean and care for.

Designers love to use synthetic material as wall cladding, or paneling, because of its versatility. It can be fabricated or "sliced and diced" with intricate edging details or configured with inlaids and intricate designs. This isn't a do-it-yourself material. In the hands of a fabricator, the material can line the walls of a shower stall, seal the floor as a threshold, trim out a window, or be custom cut as shelving. It costs approximately $75 a linear foot or more. Typically the material is sold in sheets that are ¼ inch, ½ inch, and ¾ inch thick, from 30 to 60 inches wide, and from 84 to 145 inches in length.

When synthetic sheets are used as wallcovering in a bathroom, they are installed with silicone sealant behind each seam on the wall, or with a narrow strip of the material called a *batten* over the joint to seal the seams. In some installations, corner pieces with routed edges are used. All joints are sealed with an adhesive caulk to prevent gaps.

Natural materials

The most popular natural materials used in bathrooms today are granite and marble, both of which are installed as walls, floors, and countertops. On a wall, marble tiles are a striking accent or durable surface enclosing a bathtub or shower. The high-tech look of a granite vanity countertop looks great when set against a granite backsplash.

We've seen marble in the bathrooms of old hotels and homes that withstands the test of time, but marble stains and scratches easily. Some marbles require a periodic sealing.

Polished natural materials are fine for walls and countertops, but can be too slippery for floors. A better choice is stone with a matte or honed surface that's safer to walk on, especially when wet.

When selecting natural materials, consult with a stone contractor about the installation, especially regarding weight, which can be an issue on second-story rooms. A good resource for information on stone is the Marble Institute of America (www.usenaturalstone.com).

Floor Surfaces and Underlayment

Beneath any great flooring materials is a great underlayment or subfloor. The purpose of the underlayment is to create a flat, sound surface for installing the flooring material. And you've never had more choices for flooring material for a bathroom. From simple vinyl floor tiles to designer ceramic tiles, the floor in a bathroom is a backdrop just waiting to happen.

Hardboard

Hardboard underlayment is a grade of hardboard that is designed to be applied over wood or plywood subfloors or old wood floors. Never apply hardboard directly to concrete. These underlayment panels, which come in 3-feet-x-4-feet and 4-feet-x-4-feet sizes, provide a smooth base for various floor coverings. This underlayment bridges small cups, narrow gaps, and cracks in the subfloor. Fill large irregularities or low portions of the floor with a surface filler and sand high spots smooth to provide a structurally sound base. Hardboard is affected by moisture, so you should condition it by placing it in the area where you're going to install it for at least 48 hours before installation so it can adjust to the level of humidity in the room.

Plywood

Plywood is used as a subfloor and as underlayment for most types of flooring, such as carpeting, tile, and vinyl products. It is also a good choice as an underlayment over existing flooring. Plywood is a sandwich of at least three layers of wood veneer; the thicker the plywood, the more layers make up the sheet. Plywood used for underlayment must have at least one smooth side. It comes in standard 4-x-8-foot sheets and in thicknesses ranging from ¼ inch to ¾ inch.

Particleboard

This board is composed of small particles of wood bound together with resin to form a uniform board. Because particleboard is less expensive than plywood, it has replaced plywood in many applications, including underlayment. Particleboard is available in standard 4-x-8-foot sheets and in thicknesses from ¼ inch to ¾ inch.

Because flooring and its underlayment are subject to high humidity and moisture, most floor manufacturers don't recommend particleboard for installation in the bathroom.

Vinyl Flooring

Vinyl flooring is durable, water resistant, and easy to clean. Available in sheets and 12-inch square tiles, vinyl flooring is a composite material made up of a sandwich consisting of the top wear layer, a mid layer, and a backing layer. Printed floors are made by taking a picture of a pattern and placing it on a foam layer that is then placed on the backing material. On inlaid floors, small vinyl granules are placed directly on the backing. On both types of floors, the wear layer is placed on top of these layers, and all the layers are fused together with heat and pressure.

For the most durable vinyl flooring and one that will resist damage, choose a top-quality floor with a vinyl inner layer or an inlaid floor.

When shopping for vinyl flooring, read the installation and maintenance information supplied by the manufacturer and compare the installation requirements, especially if you plan to install the material yourself. Some vinyl materials can be installed over existing surfaces, and some require underlayment.

Wear surfaces

There are three types of wear surfaces on vinyl tile and sheet goods: the original no-wax surface, urethane, and enhanced urethane. Each manufacturer has a unique name for its wear layer, but all of them fall into these categories. The thickness of the wear layer isn't as important as what the layer is made of. The real function of the wear layer is to maintain a scuff-free, easy-to-clean surface. The following list introduces a few options:

- ✔ **Vinyl no-wax:** The original wear layer on most vinyl products, this finish is somewhat stain resistant and resists scuffs. Sooner rather than later, it will require regular washing and occasional floor polishing, especially in heavy traffic areas. This type of wear surface is found mostly on lower-priced entry-level floors.

- ✔ **Urethane (PVC):** Urethane wear surfaces do a better job of resisting scuffs, scrapes, stains, and heel marks than vinyl no-wax surfaces. This surface retains its new look longer and requires less scrubbing and waxing.

- ✔ **Enhanced urethane:** Vinyl flooring with an enhanced urethane wear layer is the best at resisting household stains. Maintenance for the most part consists of sweeping the floor with a broom and an occasional mopping with an approved floor cleaner or vinegar and water.

Plank and tiles

Vinyl tile and planks are an easy-to-install flooring options, and because the tiles or planks go down piece by piece, they're easier to handle than a large sheet. The square tiles come in many patterns, and planks are manufactured into rectangular strips that can simulate wood boards, and other surfaces. Some tiles and planks have a self-adhesive backing that only requires peeling off the protective paper backing and pressing them down. Vinyl without the backing requires spreading an organic tile adhesive over the floor with a notched trowel and then setting the pieces in place.

Sheet vinyl

Sheet vinyl is manufactured in rolls that can be up to 12 feet wide. Because most bathrooms are under 12 feet in any one dimension, most can be covered with a single sheet. Unless your bathroom is rectangular in shape, have a professional floor installer measure the room and determine the correct amount of vinyl you need. Consider the pattern match of the flooring for any area where you'll need to make a seam. Aligning the patterns may require additional material.

Laminate Flooring

Laminate flooring is a popular choice for any room in the house. This product was developed in Europe and introduced to the United States market by Pergo. Manufacturers like Wilsonart, Mannington, Formica, Bruce, and others now offer laminate flooring systems. This hard-working surface continues to be a popular choice because it can withstand heavy traffic and is easy to clean.

Laminate flooring is a composite product made up of several layers glued together. The composition of each layer varies by manufacturer, but all laminate flooring products have basically three components: the surface wear layer, the core, and the backer.

- ✔ **Wear layer:** The top layer is typically a high-pressure laminate made of aluminum oxide applied over a photographic reproduction of the floor's pattern. Because the manufacturer can photograph just about anything, the top layer can be made to look like wood, stone, or just about any other surface.

- ✔ **Core:** The laminate core can be made from a variety of materials but is usually high-density fiberboard (HDF). Depending on the manufacturer, a tongue-and-groove is milled into the edge of the core, or a metal interlocking strip is fastened to the core. This feature assures a tight interlocking joint between the boards.

- ✔ **Backing:** The backer used for the bottom layer of laminate flooring products ranges from paper to a plastic laminate. Of course, for use in and around potential damp areas such as bathrooms, the plastic-backed laminates are the best choice.

Each manufacturer has specific recommendations as to where their products can be installed. When shopping for a floor for your bathroom, read the installation and warranty information supplied by the manufacturer. Most products can be installed in a bathroom if proper installation procedures are followed, meaning that the floor boards must be glued together and floated on a foam pad. The perimeter must be sealed with a silicone caulk to keep moisture out.

Cork

Americans have been putting cork on their floors since the turn of the century — the twentieth century, that is. Cork is a very versatile product made from the bark of the cork oak tree. Cork flooring, which you can find in parquets, tiles, or sheets, is warm, comfortable, and easy to maintain. The cork doesn't look like your bulletin board; it's available in colors and patterns and assures a soft-on-your-feet surface.

Cork is a good choice for any room, but the glue-down tiles are the only types of cork flooring we know that are recommended for use in a bathroom. After the cork is installed with adhesive, you apply two coats of polyurethane as a topcoat to the tiles and then seal the edges around the room with silicone. You can find out more about cork floors on the Web sites for Natural Cork (www.naturalcork.com), Dodge-Regupol (www.regupol.com), and Globus Cork (www.corkfloor.com).

Cork trees are stripped of their barks every ten years or so, and the tree begins to regrow the bark. Most of the cork harvest goes into wine cork production. The poor-quality cork and the waste from wine cork production are ground up to produce cork granules that are bound together under pressure with resin to produce flooring.

Part II
Take Control: Planning the Project

The 5th Wave   By Rich Tennant

"Douglas, I don't recall beer taps being a part of our bathroom remodeling plan."

In this part . . .

Control freaks, listen up. In this part, we talk about estimating how much a bathroom remodeling costs, how to budget it from start to finish, and ways to finance the project. We discuss the ins and outs of doing some or all of the work yourself and how to hire a professional when you prefer to take that route. As a foundation for planning a project, we discuss what specialty contractors do and explain the framework of how all the work they do fits together. You also find out what should be in the contract and get an idea of what to ask before you hire someone to do your remodeling work. We explain the basics of Bathroom Building 101 — all the mechanical, electrical, and plumbing systems that converge inside the walls of a bathroom. Don't worry about doing it wrong because we explain what's behind building codes and how they affect a bathroom remodeling project.

Chapter 6

Establishing a Budget, Finding the $

*B*efore you can begin to plan your bathroom makeover or addition, you have to get a realistic handle on how much the job will cost. This chapter gives you a ballpark idea of what you'll probably have to shell out to accomplish a simple bathroom makeover, a deluxe master bathroom addition, or anything in between.

Adding Up the Costs

The least expensive type of remodeling project is a simple face-lift, but depending on the materials you choose, the cost can vary by thousands of dollars. With this in mind, go over the different scenarios and the estimated costs in this chapter and zero in on the type of project you think you can afford.

The cost figures in this chapter are national in scope and are compiled from the same data that contractors use to establish their estimates. Some good references are *Repair & Remodeling Costs Data* by RSMeans Company, Inc., *National Repair & Remodeling Estimator* by Craftsman Book Company, and *Remodeling Cost Book* by BNI Building News. These estimating books are intended for members of the trades, but are good references for homeowners, as well. You can find them at bookstores or directly from the publisher.

If you can write a check for the project, then you already have a handle on the amount you have to spend. But if you have to rely on financing to supply funds for at least part of the project, first go to the section "Exploring Some Financing Options," later in this chapter, and decide what type of financing best fits your situation. Contact a lender and see how much money you actually have available before you start planning your budget.

Making cosmetic changes

In many ways, you get the biggest bang for your buck with a simple makeover. An outdated color scheme, old mildew-spotted paint, and pitted or rusty fixtures can make an otherwise usable bathroom look like the restroom at the local truck stop. A few basic changes can breathe new life into and create a fresh clean odor in the dingiest of bathrooms. Depending on the state of your loo, you may decide to choose one of these scenarios or combine several for a complete makeover. If you decide that new paint and wallpaper and a vanity and countertop swap will fill the bill, add the cost for the two projects together.

The difference in price between a basic remodeling project and a deluxe job depends on the type of materials you choose. In most cases, choosing the best materials you can afford works out in the long run to give you the best return on your investment.

Changing the paint or wallpaper

Bathroom color schemes come and go, and if yours has gone, some paint or wallpaper can be a remarkable improvement. Of course, you may be faced with finding a color and pattern to match a turquoise tub and toilet, but be assured, there are hundreds of them to choose from. Although the bathroom isn't a large room, painting or wallpapering in tight quarters takes time. Expect to pay $300 to $600 to have a typical bathroom painted and new wallpaper hung. This work is labor intensive, so if you do the work, you could cut this figure in half. The largest variable is the price of wallpaper.

Replacing the vanity and countertop

If your bathroom vanity is showing its age, a new paint and wallpaper face-lift will probably make you see just how dated it is. Replacing the vanity with a new sink and faucet goes a long way to enhance the style and appearance of the room. The installation of a new vanity and countertop, sink, and faucet is straightforward and can most likely use the existing plumbing. A small 24-inch vanity, sink, countertop, and faucet cost between $300 and $500, while a larger top-of-the-line unit with double sink and faucets can cost as much as $2,000. In this case, the materials are the largest component of the cost because the installation of a small sink or a large one is roughly the same.

Putting in tile walls and floor

Replacing old or installing new ceramic wall or floor tiles makes a dramatic change in the look of any size bathroom. Tile costs $5 to $8 a square foot installed and is one of the most expensive wall or floor coverings, but if properly installed, it is easy to maintain and will last for years. The cost of materials and labor to install tile depends on the amount or surface area covered. For example, tiling the three walls of a bathtub, approximately 60 to 70 square feet, costs $300 to $400 depending on the condition of the walls and the type of tile. Tiling a floor may cost slightly more than tiling a wall because the sub-floor may need to be beefed up to hold the tile.

Upgrading fixtures

Replacing outdated or worn fixtures can give bathrooms a new lease on life. A new toilet, sink, or bathtub can make the whole room appear new. Unless your plumbing is very old, replacing a toilet or sink is straightforward, but swapping out a tub is a major project. To get the most value out of installing new fixtures, combine it with a decorating face-lift — paint or wallpaper — and add new wall accessories.

The following guidelines can help you estimate costs:

- ✔ To upgrade the sink and toilet in a half bath with midgrade products, expect to pay between $1,500 and $3,000.

- ✔ To upgrade the sink, toilet, and tub in a full bath with midgrade products, expect to pay between $3,000 and $5,000.

- ✔ To upgrade the fixtures in a full bath with top-of-the-line products, expect to pay between $8,000 and $15,000.

Doing major reconstructive surgery

Remodeling a bathroom is expensive because of all the plumbing pipes and electrical wiring that are under the floor and behind the walls and therefore expensive to relocate. You can change the infrastructure of your house, no matter how complicated, but you'll pay the price. With few exceptions, there's very little that can't be rearranged in your bathroom, but the cost of the project can double if the existing plumbing has to be modified.

As a new design unfolds, keep in mind that there are good reasons to redraw the floor plan of your bathroom. Just remember that moving a toilet on a floor plan is a whole lot easier than actually doing it.

The most economical approach to adding space to an existing bathroom is taking space from an adjacent room, such as a closet of a bedroom or linen closet next to the bathroom. Because converting space requires removing walls and framing, that job is best left to the professionals.

Estimating the cost of this kind of project is difficult because you have to estimate more than materials. Incorporating new plumbing into the existing system is a major cost factor, and unless you are an experienced do-it-yourselfer and have completed large plumbing projects, you have to get bids for the work. Major remodeling of a large master bath can run from $15,000 to $30,000 for the materials and labor and can cost several times more if you include luxury fixtures in the design.

Deciding If It's Worth It

Remodeling magazine, owned by Hanley-Wood, LLC, publishes an annual "Cost vs. Value Report," which you can find at www.remodeling.hw.net. This annual survey compares the cost of a typical remodeling project with the value of the property after the completion of the project if the house were sold, for whatever reason, a year later. The figures used in this section are a national average, but you'll find figures adjusted for different regions of the country at the magazine's Web site.

Bathroom improvement projects are consistently at the top of the "Cost vs. Value" report. According to the 2002 report, the cost recouped for a $9,720 bathroom remodel by a professional remodeler was $8,506, or 88 percent. This project was for updating an existing bathroom that is at least 25 years old. The work included installing a standard-size tub with ceramic tile surround, toilet, solid-surface vanity counter with integral double sink, recessed medicine cabinet, ceramic tile floor, and vinyl wallpaper.

The cost recouped on a $15,058 bathroom addition was $14,180, or 94 percent. The project was adding a full 6-x-8-foot bath to a house with one or one and a half baths. The new bathroom was located within the existing footprint of the home near the bedrooms. The materials included cultured-marble vanity top, molded sink, standard tub/shower with ceramic tile surround, low-profile toilet, general and spot lighting, mirrored medicine cabinet, linen storage, vinyl wallpaper, and ceramic tile floor.

This large payback reflects the value of an additional bathroom in a house. Maybe someday bathrooms will be like closets and come with every bedroom in a house. (If you look at any new model homes, that's certainly the case.)

Can you expect to recover at least 80 percent of the money you put into your bathroom remodeling project? Yes and no. (You knew we'd say that!) Here's some advice to help you spend your money wisely:

✔ Be careful not to overimprove your house with the project. Every neighborhood has houses that are valued within a certain range. If the cost of the project raises the selling price of your home way above the other houses in the neighborhood, you can't expect an 80 percent or better return on your investment.

✔ Make sure that the overall design of the project is good and fits the house. The design and scope of an addition must fit and complement the rest of the house. Building a high-end master bathroom next to a small attic bedroom that is served only by the back stairs will not return its value.

✔ Make sure that the materials and workmanship are quality and that workmanship meets all national and local building codes. All remodeling work must meet code. Homes sold today must pass inspections, and poor-quality materials and sloppy or bad workmanship will be pointed out during the inspection. A botched remodeling project can actually lower the value of your house.

The "Cost vs. Value Report" assumes that the house is sold in a year, so unless you're in the home renovation business and plan to sell the house right away, the immediate return on your investment isn't as important as the satisfaction and convenience your new bathroom will provide to you and your family. If you use quality materials, the improvements will look great and perform for years. During that time, the value of your house and its new bathroom will appreciate.

Creating a Budget

Making a budget for the project is a bit like forecasting the weather. If everything is on schedule, the cost will probably be close to your estimate, if not right on target, at least for the material portion. But not all remodeling projects go per schedule.

When you compile your cost figures, don't use sale costs. The item may not be on sale when you actually get around to purchasing it. It's better to list the everyday price and then be under budget if you can take advantage of sales. Also include any extra charges, such as shipping or special handling, if you plan to use special-order items.

Use the Bathroom Worksheet (see Figure 6-1) to compile cost data for materials if you plan to do the remodeling yourself, or use it to compile subcontractor bids if you're going to hire out some of the work.

Bathroom Worksheet						
Items Description	Materials				Bids	Total
	Unit	Amt.	Cost	Total		
Permits						
Building						
Electric						
Plumbing						
Site Preparation						
Dumpster						
Dust protection						
Design						
Floorplan						
Walls and Ceiling						
Tub surround						
Ceramic tile						
Stone						
Solid surface						
Wallpaper						
Paint						
Flooring						
Subfloor						
Ceramic tile						
Stone						
Vinyl						
Wood or laminate						
Windows/Doors						
Windows						
Skylights						
Glass block						
Entry doors and frames						
Plumbing						
Fixture - Toilet						
Fixture - Tub						
Fixture - Tub/Shower						
Fixture - Vanity base						
Fixture - Countertop						
Fixture - Whirlpool						
Fixtures - Rough-ins						
Faucets, drains, valves						
Electrical Work						
Lighting fixtures						
GFCI outlets						
Heating/cooling						
Ventilation						
Carpentry						
Framing						
Shelving						
Built-ins						
Closet						
Medicine Cabinet						
Other Items						
Mirror						
Accessories						
TOTAL						

Figure 6-1:
Use this worksheet to keep track of the cost of materials and track contractor bids.

A general contractor that does the whole job manages the subcontractors, so the overall bid for the project is entered in the total column. In this case, use the worksheet to list the materials you want, such as fixture styles, colors, style of tile, and wallpaper. By presenting this specific information to a subcontractor or general contractor, you can expect to receive bids on exactly the same materials. You get more accurate bids, and you know the bids are for the same work and can be compared for the price differences.

Some items in the materials column on the worksheet in Figure 6-1 will show "1" for the unit and "1" for the quantity (for example, a toilet). Other items, such as tile or drywall, should have units such as square feet. The amount will be the square footage of the surface being covered, and the cost will be the cost per square foot. Or, use the total column to enter the total cost for the materials you have priced out at your supplier. Many home centers list the cost per square foot of many materials on the cost label displayed on the front of the shelf.

All estimates must account for waste, and contractors build this into their bids. If you plan to do the project yourself, allow for mistakes. An allowance of 20 percent or more for these contingencies is not out of line. Consider this extra expense as tuition as you work your way through the DIY school of hard knocks.

When you plan to do the project

Getting a handle on the total cost of a remodeling project isn't easy, even for an experienced contractor. Tackle the easiest part of the process — estimating the cost of the materials — first. Because you're going to supply the sweat, the labor isn't a factor in the budget for a do-it-yourself project.

Throughout this book, the projects describe the tools and materials needed to install fixtures and materials. Make sure to include the costs of these tools to make your estimates accurate and complete. As the list grows, enter the totals on the estimate sheet and total all individual items. This figure is the estimate for the materials needed to complete the project. Remember, it's only an estimate but should give you some guidance and help you budget the job.

When you plan to work with subcontractors

If you're going to act as the general contractor on the project and hire subcontractors to do most, if not all, of the work, use the worksheet in Figure 6-1 to track their bids. Gather up your preferences for the materials and then enter the specifications, including such things as tile size, color, and brand.

When getting bids from subcontractors for the same work, give the specifications to them so that they bid on the same project. In your discussion with different contractors, don't let them talk you into changing the specifications without good reason. If after listening to their recommendations, you think they have good suggestions, then you can consider incorporating their ideas into the specifications.

You can't compare bids unless all contractors bid on the same project. For example, if the third tile contractor you interview talks you into switching the tile style and installing them with epoxy thinset mortar instead of organic mastic, you can't compare his bid with previous bids. Is one process better than the other? Hard to tell, but the third bid will be more expensive.

Enter the contractor's bid in the Bids column of the worksheet. Identify each bid with a label like "Bid A" so you can keep track of them. When the bids are in, you can go over the worksheet and decide which contractor offers the best overall value — not necessarily the lowest bid. Then move these totals to the Total column and add them up.

When you hire a general contractor

The best method to approach a major project is to work up a plan; decide on the type of fixtures, wall, and floor treatments you want; and get several contractors to bid on the project. Discuss the options with the contractors and how each decision affects the bottom line, but be sure all the contractors end up bidding on the same project.

If the bids come in way over what you think you want to spend, call the contractors back and schedule a meeting. Go over the bid and probe for areas where you can trim the costs. The materials, especially the fixtures and faucets, represent a major portion of the budget. Changing the style or finish of the faucets can save big money. Settling for a vinyl floor instead of tile is a compromise that can make the project more affordable.

Also find out whether you can do some phases of the work, such as demolition, yourself. Many contractors are willing to work with homeowners if everything is spelled out upfront. See Chapter 7 for more information about working with contractors.

Exploring Some Financing Options

Funding a remodeling project is usually easier than other projects because you own a valuable asset, your home. The bathroom remodeling you're looking to fund adds value to this asset, so it's the type of loan lenders like to make. But keep in mind that you can choose from many ways to finance a remodeling project, and some are more expensive than others. If you're planning to undertake a major bathroom remodeling project, you probably want to at least consult with your local banker or financial advisor. They just so happen to already have several types of loans designed for exactly this expenditure. While you're talking to the professionals, don't forget to get the input of a realtor. These professionals can give you some guidance to use the right financing tools and give you some assurance that the improvements you plan to make are financially sound.

One nice aspect of home ownership and improvement is that the interest you pay on your mortgage and or home improvement loan is tax deductible. In addition, the interest rates on mortgages and home improvement loans are at a historic low point (at least they were at the time of this writing). They won't stay there forever, but in the near future, these rates are expected to remain reasonably low. Mortgage and home equity rates are downright cheap when compared to consumer credit (credit cards), which is not tax preferred and has not followed the drop in the prime rate.

Depending on the scope of the project, you may be able to fund the remodeling out of savings or other funds. But before you put all your available cash into a project, heed the advice of a financial planner and maintain a cash reserve of several months of living expense. Improving your house is one of the best investments you can make, but remember that you can't use the cash you invested in drywall and tile to pay emergency medical bills.

Home equity loan

One of the best sources of funds to remodel your bathroom is your house itself. Chances are that if you've owned your house for more than a couple of years, it has appreciated in value. Lenders have programs that allow you to withdraw this new equity in the form of a loan.

Most lenders make loans up to 100 percent of the value of your house less the current mortgage. In most cases, the interest on the loan is tax deductible, like the interest you pay on your mortgage. You receive the balance of the loan in one payment. You can renegotiate repayment terms with the lender.

Because you're using the money you're borrowing to remodel your home and increase its value, you have the option, after the remodeling project is complete, to refinance and roll the home equity loan into a new mortgage. Doing so may make a lot of sense if the interest rates are favorable. But remember, if your equity in your house falls below 80 percent, you may be required to take out mortgage insurance that will add to the cost of the new mortgage.

Home equity line of credit

A home equity line of credit allows you to tap into your home's equity. The line of credit allows you to draw out the funds as needed and pay interest only on the amount of money you use. A line of credit works well for financing a remodeling project because all the funds aren't needed at the start of the project. The interest rate is usually fixed for an initial period of time; after that, the rate is usually tied to an index like the prime rate plus a margin.

Second mortgage

A second mortgage is just what it sounds like: an additional mortgage on your property. This mortgage stands behind the first mortgage in claims against the property if you can't make the payments. Of course, home equity loans also fall into this category.

Most lenders will write a second mortgage for the full value of the property, and some will go even higher, less the balance of the first mortgage. These loans are structured with fixed or variable rates and are available with terms similar to first mortgages, but at a higher interest rate. The interest is tax deductible.

Construction loan

This short-term type of loan is designed to finance new and remodeling construction. The bank makes a loan that is paid to the homeowner as work is completed. During the construction period, you pay the interest only on the amount dispersed, and after the construction is completed, the loan is due. Most lenders make a construction loan that will roll into and replace your existing mortgage with a refinance deal, which can save you money because you go through and pay for the application process only once.

If the lender doesn't offer this combined loan, you have to arrange long-term financing to pay off the construction loan. A refinancing of some sort will be needed.

Personal loan

If you have already established a relationship with a lender and have a good credit rating, you may qualify for a personal loan. The difference between this type of loan and an equity loan is that your property isn't used as collateral.

You may use other assets, such as a valuable stamp or art collection or certificate of deposit, as collateral, or the lender may make a signature-only loan. The interest rates are higher for a personal loan than for a loan that ties in to your mortgage, and the interest is usually not tax deductible.

Credit card

The most expensive method to finance a remodeling project is with a credit card because the interest rates are much higher than other types of financing. On the other hand, credit cards can come in handy for short-term needs, such as purchasing materials, when cash is short. Pay down the balance as soon as possible or roll the credit card debt into a home equity debt consolidation loan.

Borrowing from a contractor

Many large remodeling companies offer their own financing. At first, this option may seem convenient, but in the long run, it may not turn out to be such a good idea.

If you're dependent on the contractor for funds, you have less leverage with the contractor should a dispute arise. Think twice before you borrow a large sum of money from the same firm that will do the work. Unless there is a very compelling reason, such as below-market interest rate, you're better off securing your own financing and having total control of the purse strings.

Completing Your Project in Stages

Another strategy that allows you to afford a complete bathroom makeover is to break the project up into stages, and fund each stage through your cash flow or financing. For example, break the total job into several smaller projects. Make the first phase a face-lift of new paint and or wallpaper. Later replace the vanity and countertop. In the third phase, replace the toilet and install tile on the walls and floor. In between the major phases, replace the accessories such as towel bars and soap trays. Keep in mind, however, that although this approach makes the project easier to afford, the downside is that it keeps the bathroom in a state of limbo for a long time.

Remodeling your bathroom on a budget

Remodeling can put a big dent in anyone's budget, but it doesn't have to be that way. Try these ideas to trim down the cost:

✔ Plan! Plan! Plan! Don't rush the process and allow yourself the time to fully work through all aspects of the project.

✔ Avoid cutting up your house. Try to be as creative with the space you have and avoid structural changes.

✔ Curves are in, but costly. Curved walls and other difficult-to-build features can add up quickly. Simple straightforward designs are the least expensive to build.

✔ Concentrate the plumbing in one location. Place new bathroom additions adjacent to or above existing facilities to reduce rough-in plumbing costs.

✔ Use professionals. Architects and kitchen and bath planners can actually save you money because their designs are efficient. They're familiar with working with contractors and giving advice to their clients.

✔ Stick with standard finishes and items. Bath fixtures in custom colors or high-end finishes cost several times what standard fixtures cost. Check the price of any nonstandard fixture in your plan and compare its price against the standard version. Standard may seem boring, but the savings are sure to get your attention.

Chapter 7

Doing It Yourself or Hiring a Pro

. . . .

In This Chapter

▶ Serving as your own contractor

▶ Splitting the work with the professionals

▶ Letting the professionals do it all

▶ Figuring out who does what

▶ Recognizing what's in a good contract

▶ Coping with remodeling disruption

. . . .

Remodeling can consume your life from the very beginning. It can easily become the most important thing in your life from the second the thought of remodeling creeps into your mind to the time when you actually say, "Honey, let's redo the bathroom," to the point where you think, "Whose idea was this?" to the day when you finally say, "Glory be to God, it's finished." Everyone is affected by remodeling, even in a house with multiple bathrooms. That's why in most cases the faster the bathroom remodel, the better. To achieve that goal means putting in the time before the tear-down so that the redesign and rebuilding process can take place on time and on budget. This can mean hiring professionals for all or some or none of the job. Your participation can range from managing the work of others to doing all or some of the work yourself.

To help you decide whether you want to hire professionals or do the work yourself, begin by thinking about your time, talents, and budget. You may know exactly what you want in a new bathroom and want to do some, but not all, of the work, so hiring contractors is the way to go. Or you may be clueless and need input and advice and someone to oversee the project, such as a general contractor, a designer, or design center professional. You may fall somewhere in between and want to manage the project and hire the contractors needed, or perhaps do some of the work yourself while getting reassurance and advice from a bathroom designer. Or you may want to do it all from start to finish. It's one small room with many options, so make it the best it can be.

Figuring Out What You Can Do Yourself

Before you don your hard hat, call your local building inspector to find out what type of jobs you can and cannot do during your bathroom remodeling project. Some jurisdictions allow homeowners to do all the work, some require you to pass a proficiency test first, and others require pros to do all the plumbing and electrical work. Checking in with your building department and being honest with yourself about your skill level are the best policies.

Pick up a copy of local building codes that pertain to bathrooms and become familiar with the specifications. If you decide to do the work yourself, you're responsible for making sure that all materials and workmanship meet those codes.

Know what type of wiring, electrical boxes, and plumbing pipe that your local code requires before purchasing and installing anything. Just because something is sold at your local hardware store or home center doesn't mean that it meets your local building codes. If in doubt, take a sample to the building department and ask questions.

After you know the requirements of the local code, you can decide just what makes sense for you to do. All codes basically allow you to do the grunt work, and much of bathroom remodeling work is just that. *Grunt work is* our affectionate term for unskilled labor that even unskilled laborers don't want to do. This work includes jobs such as removing wallpaper, scraping tiles off the wall, removing layers of flooring, unhooking and removing old fixtures and faucets, and repairing a water-damaged window. *Note:* Any and all repetitive jobs like these — you know, the kind that require more brawn than brains — are ideal for homeowners.

The only reason to do the work yourself is to save on labor charges. Hey, that isn't so bad, is it? Some of you may even enjoy the extra cash in your pocket. It at least makes grunt work bearable. Understand, however, that you don't have to do all the work yourself, and to help you save on labor, the rest of this chapter explores the different roles contractors and subcontractors play in a remodeling project. From there, you can decide just how much or how little you want to be involved. But, whatever you do, don't skip this section when you're hiring out the project, because understanding the players can save you big bucks when you do.

Acting as Your Own Contractor

A skilled and savvy homeowner can do just about anything, including remodeling a bathroom. The ideal situation for this scenario is when the homeowners have more than one bathroom, so they don't feel pressured to complete the job quickly and possibly short-circuit the work. When you have the time and want to tackle the job, go for it.

Acting as a contractor is a full-time job. For putting up with all the hassles of supervising subcontractors and trying to keep the customer happy, contractors usually earn about 20 percent of the total cost of the remodeling project. That can run into some real dough for a large project.

When you're willing to take on this role, you deserve that 20 percent savings. The most important point to remember is that you have to earn this money by taking on the role of general contractor, and you need to know that doing so doesn't always mean an automatic savings. Exact duties of the general contractor are outlined in the section "Kicking Back While the Pros Do the Work," later in this chapter. Remember to always hire pros. If you hire inept subcontractors and don't manage them well, that 20 percent saving may seem like petty cash when the wrath of your household descends on you.

On the other hand, if you have managerial skills and a flexible work schedule and enjoy a confrontation or two, you can be good at the job. You have control of the project and get a bathroom that is exactly what you want. Another nice thought is that general contractors usually don't do the actual work; instead, they watch others do it. So if you think you can do it, you can cut your budget and still not get splinters.

Sharing the Workload with the Pros

Another alternative is to do some of the work yourself. You may be a whiz-bang painter or want to hone your skills at installing floor tile. You can do part of the work, but be forewarned that you better be on schedule and not delay the work progress, especially when the work involves sequential steps that tie into the inspection process. If you're going to do part of the job, do it right the first time and do it on time.

Of course, in the best of all worlds, you have a talented relative who just loves to help out. Uncle Harry may be a plumber, or your sister-in-law's favorite pastime is laying tile. For the cost of a couple of beers and a bratwurst, you may be able to tap into these sources of help or at least get some valuable advice. But be advised that financial dealings with friends and relatives can get a bit sticky if they don't work out as planned. Just imagine yourself in small claims court facing down Uncle Harry.

If you want to be a part of the crew but lack the know-how, be a gofer. Instead of paying a skilled tradesperson to make a coffee or materials run, you do it.

Kicking Back While the Pros Do the Work

If you decide to hire professionals for your remodeling project, they'll take care of it all — from the designer who plans the layout of the room and all its fixtures, to the plumber who runs the pipes and sets the fixtures, to the electrician who installs the wires, outlets, switches, and lights. In addition, many specialty contractors lend their talents, including workers who install ceramic tile, cabinets, countertops, windows, doors, wallboard, and flooring; the painters; and the wallpaper hangers. Considering that bathrooms have a relatively small square footage, a disproportionately large number of specialty workers and skill sets are involved.

Meeting the players and knowing what to expect when you hire them

The bathroom remodeling professionals who perform services and provide skills are many and varied, and you may encounter and employ some or all of them for your project. Understanding what they do and where their input falls in the work process gives you an overview of who does what and when they do it.

Design professionals

The National Kitchen & Bath Association (NKBA) is a nonprofit trade association that educates kitchen and bath professionals and has been a leader in the industries for 40 years. The association trains kitchen specialists as certified kitchen designers (CKD) and bath specialists as certified bathroom designers (CBD). These individuals enroll in extensive study courses and pass design and safety certification exams given by the NKBA.

These specialists work at independent design firms and at home centers such as Home Depot and The Great Indoors. They work at kitchen and bath centers and design showrooms, too. You can locate a certified bath designer online at the association's Web site, www.nkba.org. The "Find an NKBA Professional" page directs you to type in your zip code and check whether you want an independent designer or one who works at a retailer design center or both.

Many of the retail design centers offer free design services when you purchase the materials there. They usually charge a $50 to $100 detail fee for an installer to come to the house and inspect the bathroom to determine the scope of the project and extent of the work required, plus a $100 charge to measure the room for accurate dimensions. Most of what you pay to a retail design center for a bathroom remodeling goes for materials and installation.

Design showrooms, which are usually provided by large bathroom and kitchen remodeling firms, offer free or reduced-cost design services if you hire them to do the work. Although some showrooms will design a bathroom for free, others charge an hourly rate ranging from $50 to $100. Others have designers who work on a retainer basis, and some of the fee is deducted if they do the work. Some bath showrooms charge you for the design of a new bathroom, but won't release the design to you unless you pay them an additional fee. The extra fee is intended to discourage you from hiring someone else to do the job.

Independent bathroom designers charge a fee for their services that can range from a flat fee to a percentage of the total cost of the project. These designers have the freedom to use any products and materials available on the market and aren't limited to the brands and product lines that a showroom or home center carries. These designers usually get discounts on materials and fixtures, so some of their fee can be offset by these savings.

Many design firms apply the cost of the design to the total cost of the job, a good deal for both of you.

A bath designer who works as an independent or for a design firm may be able to spend more time offering you suggestions about alternative design plans. Most people are stymied by all the choices of fixtures and cabinetry, and the help of a professional can save you time and money in the long run.

Maybe the greatest difference between an independent design firm and a retail design center is how they manage the project.

- ✔ **Independent design firms:** Independents can take on the role of the general contractor and coordinate all the specialty contractors. They'll assign a project manager who is there every day and responsible for all materials that go into the new bathroom, including shipment, inspection, and installation of those products. A design firm takes on the day-to-day supervision and inspection of work and has a staff of subcontractors it regularly uses, workers it relies on for their quality and workmanship. A firm like this isn't likely to want a client who wants to do some of the work, because it has no control over the quality of your work. The design firm may suggest that you can prepare the bathroom and remove the wallpaper and cabinets, but it isn't likely to want you to do anything else.

- ✔ **Retail design centers:** A home center designer will check on the materials and installation and assign a representative to check on the progress of the work, but that rep won't be there every day. A retail design service is your best bet whenever you want to do some of the work yourself.

Although making a cold call and simply walking into a design center or independent designer's office to discuss your project is okay, your best bet is calling ahead to schedule an appointment and time to peruse the showroom.

Take along some snapshots of your bathroom (don't be embarrassed — they've seen worse) and the rough dimensions of the room. When you're considering enlarging the room by taking space from an adjacent room, take along a picture of that room as well. Such documentation isn't absolutely necessary at the first meeting, but it gives the designer more to work with. Bringing along pictures, magazine clippings, books, and anything else that gives the designer a hint about the direction of the look and components you'd like in your new bathroom also is a good idea.

Know your budget and tell the designer at the initial meeting how much money you can spend to remodel the bathroom. When your budget isn't carved in stone (lucky you!), give the designer a range of what you'd like to spend. Talking about money upfront helps focus the design and choice of materials and, in the end, saves everyone much time and anguish. Even with a limited budget, a good designer can offer design solutions with plenty of materials and fixtures to choose from.

General contractors

The cast of characters in a bathroom remodel is orchestrated by someone in charge who has an overview of the project and knows how to time and coordinate the work process. Enter the general contractor. The general contractor is a combination of director and producer and, in some cases, does part of the work. If you're working with a bath design firm or showroom or a remodeling company, someone is assigned as project manager and takes on this important role. This person's job begins with ordering materials and ends when the project is done to your satisfaction.

The general contractor or project manager coordinates the work of subcontractors and specialty tradespeople, helping to ensure that the work progresses in a timely fashion. For example, plumbers and electricians need to do the rough-in work for water lines, fixtures, and wiring before the walls are finished. But somewhere in between those jobs, inspections are required. A good general contractor or project manager coordinates the schedule of all this work so there are no delays and so workers don't end up standing around waiting for material to arrive.

Subcontractors and specialists

Knowing exactly who does what in a remodeling project gives you an idea of what to expect. Here's an A to Z rundown of subcontractors and specialists involved in a bathroom-remodeling project. Not all of them may be involved in your bathroom remodeling, but we're sure you'll meet some of them.

Carpenters

Carpenters build the framing for walls, doors, and windows, including any repair work around bathtubs or showers before tile or a surround is installed. They also return after the walls are up to install cabinets, countertops, medicine cabinets, and any built-in units, such as a window seat or storage cabinet.

Drywall contractors

These installers hang wallboard over the framing built by carpenters. They're the ones who screw the heavy 4-x-8-foot or 4-x-12-foot sheets of wallboard to the framing and then hide the joints between the sheets with a mesh or paper tape that is covered with drywall compound. They make the cutouts for the electrical outlets, switches, lighting fixtures, and vents.

When the compound is dry, these workers sand it smooth so that the sheets of wallboard appear not to have any joints or seams. To make the walls smooth, they usually apply three rounds of compound and sand after each application. They hang the wallboard, do the taping, and apply the first coat of compound on day one, but each subsequent application takes a day to dry before workers can resume sanding and apply another application of compound, so this process involves several return trips. Be prepared for clouds of drywall dust after each sanding.

Electricians

These licensed professionals or their apprentices are responsible for all the sources of power needed in a bathroom. They run cable for the lighting switches and fixtures and install outlets for personal appliances and exhaust vents. They also install any other electric devices, such as heaters, towel warmers, ceiling fans, and their controls. Their work must pass inspection by a local building inspector before the walls are finished and again after they install and hook up the devices and appliances.

Flooring installers

These contractors specialize in laying new floor material, as well as removing the existing floor and what's beneath it. Some floor installers specialize in vinyl sheet flooring, tile and stone, or laminates. Their job begins by preparing the floor so that it's smooth, level and structurally sound. They remove the baseboard around the room and the threshold at the door and replace any damaged subfloor, which is often found around toilets and tubs that have leaked. If uneven surfaces require leveling, they apply a leveling compound before the underlayment. After laying the new material, they install a door threshold and then they (or carpenters) install baseboard around the walls.

Masons

Tile masons install ceramic, stone, glass block, and marble wall and floor tiles. Masons who install tile often spend more time laying out the tiles than actually installing it, which is especially the case if the job involves an intricate design of tiles or angled or odd-shaped surfaces. Masons who want to do a good job make sure they're working on a level, sound surface, whether it's the walls, ceilings, floors, or countertops.

Specialists who install solid surface materials like Corian, Silestone, and Zodiaq are trained by the material manufacturers, so they're qualified to work with the material. This experience assures you, the customer, that the material is properly installed. If there's a problem with the materials or the labor, the manufacturers will probably make it right.

Painters

Whether you want plain vanilla walls or a fanciful faux finish, a painting contractor somewhere is ready to splash some color on your walls. If new wallboard and/or wallpaper is involved in the remodeling project, the painters will first prime the walls with a special paint designed to seal the porous wall surface. On new wallboard it's particularly important to apply primer so the new walls can absorb the primer and create a nonporous surface for either paint or wallpaper. It's almost impossible to remove wallpaper from unprimed walls without severely damaging the wallboard's paper face. The painter will choose a specialty primer designed for the finish surface.

A decorative painter, someone who specializes in faux finishes, stenciling, *trompe l'oeil,* and other creative finishes, gives new meaning to a fresh coat of paint. A general painting contractor will paint the walls with two coats of paint, but a decorative painter offers unique designs, textures, and finishes that are limited only by your (or the painter's) imagination.

Plumbers

These licensed professionals or their apprentices who work with them are responsible for the delivery of fresh water and the removal of wastewater from the bathroom. They run and reroute water pipes and lines; install fixtures and valves at sinks, tubs, and showers; and hook up toilets and bidets. Their work is done in several stages: first behind the wall and then after the walls are finished. First, they rough in the location for new valves and fixtures, and then they extend the existing drain lines and water supply pipes. Their work must pass inspection by a local building inspector before the walls are installed. After the rough-in inspection, the walls are installed, and the plumbers return to hook up the fixtures.

Wallpaper hangers

A good vinyl wallcovering in a bathroom provides a durable surface that usually outlives its design. You'll probably get tired of the pattern before it wears out. Wallpaper hangers choose the appropriate adhesive and primer based on the condition of the walls and the type of wallpaper you choose. These workers also have the tools and skills to remove old wallpaper.

Don't let anyone talk you into papering over old wallpaper. The new wallpaper will be glued to the old wallpaper, so the whole job will be hanging on the old paste, which is certain to fail eventually. Painting over wallpaper is even worse: It makes the wallpaper almost impossible to strip later because the paint seals the paper and prevents water from penetrating the surface to soften the paste.

Special services

The two face-lift services in the following list reuse, not replace, your existing furnishings as a budget-wise option to replacing them. Removing an old bathtub can be downright impossible without chopping it into pieces, which can be dangerous and damaging to surrounding surfaces. If a cabinet or bathtub is sound and in the right location, consider these choices as a way to extend their useful life at a fraction of the cost of replacing them. You'll find companies that provide these services advertised in the Yellow Pages and on the Internet.

- **Cabinet refinishing:** You can give a trendy new look to a white and gold French Provincial vanity cabinet by refinishing it like a piece of furniture and replacing the hardware. Do it yourself or hire a furniture refinisher, who can work on it in place by priming, sanding, and applying a new finish.

- **Cabinet resurfacing:** A cabinet resurfacing, also called refacing service, involves removing the cabinet doors and applying a new laminate surface to the cabinet frame and sides and replacing the old doors with new styles. When the finish is complete, add new hardware to complete the transformation.

- **Sink and tub refinishing:** A sink or tub can be refinished through a process of reglazing the surface. The tub is scraped and etched to roughen up the old finish, and all imperfections in the old finish are filled and sanded. The new polyurethane finish is sprayed on the surface and polished. You get what you pay for with resurfacers. Look for one that will do extensive prep work and apply a bonding coat and at least three coats of glaze. This isn't a good solution for a sink or tub that's you use daily, because it's not as durable as the original, but if you treat it with care, it's one way to go.

- **Lining an old sink or tub:** To create a tub liner, an installer measures the old tub, which is then matched with the tub manufacturer's specifications, and a matching acrylic model is made. The liner is trimmed to fit, slipped over the old tub, and fastened with adhesive and tape. You can also have matching wall panels made and installed at the same time.

Finding your professionals

Some people brag about their fancy car, and others praise the expertise of their wine merchant. Most of our friends brag about having the best and the brightest contractor, and they won't tell you his name because they want to keep him to themselves.

These selfish souls make it tough on the rest of us who are always on the lookout for a good contractor or tradesperson to do some work on our houses. It isn't as easy as letting your fingers do the walking, but there are ways and means of finding and hiring good workers.

Word-of-mouth referrals

Ask your friends, neighbors, relatives, and work associates for names of good contractors they have hired. Usually a word-of-mouth referral is the best you can get.

Ideally, you can find a contractor who has remodeled a bathroom similar to your own so that you can make a comparison of the transformation as well as the quality of workmanship. That approach works if you live in a subdivision of similar homes and can nose your way into a house similar to your own that has a remodeled bathroom.

Questions to ask when you interview a remodeler

When you interview contractors for a bathroom project, use these qualifying questions suggested by the National Association of the Remodeling Industry (NARI) to find out more about their business:

- **How long have you been in business?** A company with an established business history in your community is a good choice.

- **How is the business organized and how does it operate?** You need to know whether the company has employees who will do the work or whether the company uses subcontractors, or a combination of both. Make sure to know the name and contact information for the project manager who is responsible for the successful completion of the work.

- **What percentage of your business is repeat or referral business?** This number is a good indication of customer satisfaction. According to NARI, most remodeling businesses attribute over 50 percent of their annual volume to customer referrals.

- **Does your company carry workers' compensation and liability insurance?** Ask for copies of the insurance certificates to verify coverage and call the agency to make sure the policy is current. Even if the certificate has an expiration date, you can't tell whether either party has canceled the insurance. In addition, some states require licensing and registration. If your state has construction licensing laws, ask for the contractor's registration and license

and then confirm the license number and expiration date with your local building department.

- **What is the approach to a project of this scope and what is the time frame?** Answers to these questions give you an idea of how the contractor works and what to expect. Ask about work schedules, completion date, and workers' starting and quitting times. Ask what the procedure is for schedule delays or changes and how you'll be contacted. Find out how many other jobs the contractor is working on at the same time yours will be underway so you know where yours falls in the schedule.

- **How many projects like mine have you completed in the past year and can I have references for them?** If the contractor does a lot of bathroom remodeling jobs, you should be confident he has the experience to handle yours. Ask for the names, addresses, and phone numbers of customers so you can visit some of them to see whether their projects are similar in scope and to get a look at the quality and workmanship of the company.

- **Is a permit required?** Most cities and towns require building permits, and failure to obtain one and the necessary inspections can be illegal. You should know when a permit is required and whether the contractor will obtain one before beginning the work.

In your neighborhood, look for contractor trucks and their signs in front of houses where they're working. Notice the times they arrive and leave and try to catch them to introduce yourself and describe your project.

Home shows and local sources

You can often meet and talk to contractors at home shows, where they exhibit samples of their work. These shows provide a nice opportunity to talk in general about your project before setting an appointment. In many cities, you can now find remodeling tours where contractors show off their work.

Also look for contractors' business cards or fliers at home centers and suppliers where they buy materials. Talking with Realtors, designers, and home inspectors is another source of names of contractors.

Online referral services

You can use an online referral service on the Internet to find a local contractor, too. Web sites such as ServiceMagic.com (www.servicemagic.com) and ImproveNet.com (www.improvenet.com) offer matchmaking services for homeowners looking for a contractor. At the Real Estate or Home Improvement channels of portals like Yahoo! or MSN, you'll find banner ads for "Find a Contractor," which is a link to an online referral service. Contractors join online services and pay for referrals or leads to potential customers in their work area. A homeowner fills out a request for service that describes the project, and that request is forwarded to contractors, who then review the request and decide whether they want to bid on the job. If they do, they contact the homeowner directly.

Retailer-installed sales

Some retailers offer installed sales of everything from appliances to windows. The retailer acts as the general contractor and assigns a project manager, who orders material, sends out an installer, and takes responsibility for the job being done to your satisfaction.

Realtors, designers, architects, and home inspectors are other sources to ask for the names of contractors.

Recognizing a Good Contract

A contract may be one page that describes a basic service or installation if you're hiring a subcontractor, or it may be a lengthy document that outlines in detail a major renovation that a general contractor will perform. NARI recommends that you consult with your attorney or personal advisor whenever you have questions or concerns about a remodeling contract.

A contract is the key document between a homeowner and contractor that connects the job together and verifies that the parties who signed the document share the same vision and scope for the project. The devil is in the details in this case. That fact underscores the importance of taking the time to review a contract before signing it and raising any questions or concerns before — not after — the work begins.

Here are the key details to look for in a bathroom remodeling contract:

✔ Contractor's name, address, telephone number, and license information.

✔ Homeowner's name, address, telephone number, and the location in the house where the work is scheduled.

✔ A detailed account of what the contractor will and will not do, including protecting the area surrounding the bathroom, daily cleanup of the bathroom and surrounding area, and final cleanup when the work is completed.

✔ A detailed list of all the materials used in the project, with specifications of the brand name and model number of all products, including the size, color, style, and any other descriptive information.

✔ A specification that all the work performed will meet or exceed the building code.

✔ Starting and completion dates, work hours, and days that workers can be expected on the job.

✔ Financial terms that are clearly spelled out, including the total price, payment schedule, and any cancellation penalty or early completion incentive. A typical payment schedule is divided into thirds: 30 percent as a down payment, 30 percent midway in the project, 30 percent at the completion of the job, and 10 percent when work on the *punch list* (the list of things that *still* need to be done or fixed after the project is "finished") is completed to the satisfaction of the homeowner.

✔ A stipulation that your signature is required for approval before work begins.

✔ The notice of right of recession, which specifies that a homeowner can cancel a contract within three business days of signing it.

✔ Procedures for change orders during the course of the project. A change order that includes the cost of the modification should be written and signed by all parties before the new work begins and any time delays occur that will affect the overall timetable for the work progress. Use a change order in the following situations:

  • If you change your mind about a design or product

  • If the contractor recommends changing some aspect of the design

- • If a change is required because of an unexpected situation, such as a broken pipe or termite damage

- • If a code violation affects the project

✔ A binding arbitration clause that enables both parties to resolve a dispute quickly and effectively without costly litigation if a disagreement occurs.

✔ A warranty covering materials and workmanship for a minimum of a year. This warranty should be identified as either full or limited, with an explanation of these terms. A full warranty means a faulty product must be repaired or replaced or the homeowner's money returned. A limited warranty indicates that replacements and refunds of damaged products are limited in that regard. The warranty must identify the name and address of the party who will honor the warranty and must also specify the time period for the warranty.

✔ Assurances that you won't be liable for any third-party claims for non-payment of materials or subcontractors. A contractor's Affidavit of Final Release or Waiver of Mechanic's Lien Rights from the general contractor, the subcontractors, and suppliers should be provided as a claim for money owed.

Making It Legal: Remembering Building Codes

The building codes that are decided by the city or county where you live are designed for new homes and renovations to existing ones. So remodeling a bathroom will put you in touch with your local building department. The codes are created as a way to protect you from poor workmanship, which can be dangerous, and to provide a standard and uniform way that work, especially electrical and plumbing work, is completed. A building permit is issued by your local building department, which follows up with a series of inspections during various stages of the construction process and at its completion.

In every bathroom, two key utilities — water and electricity — can present potential safety issues, so they're on the radar screen of your local building code inspector. Make a visit to your local building department and ask about the codes. This agency usually charges a fee for a building permit, which has an expiration date and must be posted in a window of your house. Before the permit expires, the building inspector must inspect the work. If the work isn't finished by the permit's expiration date, the permit usually can be renewed — for a fee.

Many plumbing codes let the homeowner do most of the work inside the house, but if the job requires a connection to the city lines, a licensed plumber is needed. (Just imagine how much damage a dimwit homeowner could do polluting the city water system!) Both the plumbing and electrical codes explain who can do the work, what materials may be used (and those that may not), and how the job should be done. This means that codes can specify how many electrical outlets there should be, where they should be installed, the thickness of the wallboard, and the size of drains and pipes.

When a bathroom remodeling project involves an addition to and expansion of the footprint of the building, you need to be aware of zoning law restrictions that stipulate the percentage of land that can be covered by buildings, and how and what percentage of open property is distributed among the side, back, and front yards. Take a look at your property survey and find out just how close your house is to adjoining property lines.

If you want to build where the zoning law prohibits, you must apply for a variance to the zoning law, which requires submitting property plans and blueprints of the bathroom addition, making an appearance at the appeals board, and posting a notice so your neighbors have an opportunity to respond to your plans — and possibly object. Then comes a hearing where you or your attorney present your request for a variance. Sure, it's a long and arduous process, but don't consider skipping it.

Warning signs of questionable practices

Anyone who enjoyed watching the movie *Tin Men* may remember some of the deceitful business practices of the main characters. You need to be on the outlook for some of these practices, too. If you notice any of the following during or after an interview with a contractor, don't hire that person:

✔ You can't verify the name, address, telephone number, or credentials of the contractor.

✔ The contractor tried to pressure you into signing a contract, said your home will be used for advertising purposes so you'll receive a special low rate, or the price quoted is available only if you sign the contract that day.

✔ No references are furnished.

✔ The information you received is out of date or no longer valid.

✔ You're unable to verify the license or insurance information.

✔ You're asked to pay for the entire job in advance or to pay in cash to an individual instead of by check to the company itself.

✔ The company isn't listed in the telephone book, with the Better Business Bureau, or with a local trade association, such as NARI.

✔ The contractor doesn't tell you of your right to cancel the contract within three days.

The contractor, not the homeowner, should apply for a building permit because the name on the permit is the person who is responsible for meeting the building code.

Discovering Some Coping and Scheduling Strategies

Some simple tips on when and when not to schedule a bathroom remodeling can make your life much easier. For example, do not remodel your bathroom in time for a major event such as a graduation or birthday party. You'll create undue stress that can't be avoided and make the project much worse than it has to be. It's better to schedule the project when you're not facing an imminent deadline and keep everyone happy.

Summertime is often a good season for a bathroom remodeling project because you probably have fewer deadlines with the kids out of school. Many folks arrange to remodel when the kids go to summer camp so fewer people are in the household.

If you're tempted to go on vacation and return when the work is done, think again. Being home to make on-the-spot decisions is key to getting the new bathroom you want. But if you can arrange to escape for the time the drywallers are sanding, you'll be glad you did.

Resign yourself to the fact that life will not be normal when a bathroom is being torn apart and rebuilt. Water is turned off, electricity gets shut down, and a pile of material and fixtures fills up the garage or porch. Deal with it.

Your pet may have an anxiety attack when a daily contingent of unknown contractors armed with tools arrives on your doorstep. Show extra kindness and patience to your four-legged friend.

Drink wine. At the end of the day, as you inspect the progress (or the lack of it), consider the restorative value of merlot, or maybe a nice chardonnay. Save the champagne for completion day.

Chapter 8

Behind the Scenes
of Your Bathroom

· ·

· ·

*U*ntil you have a nasty water backup in your bathroom, how often do you ponder where water goes when the shower drains or when you push the flush lever? Or where the water comes from in the first place when you turn on the faucet? Modern plumbing is so reliable that most people tend to take it for granted — that is, until it malfunctions. Most of the time you deal only with the fixtures that are located at the top of the proverbial plumbing tree.

And what about the outlets in the bathroom that turn on hair dryers and curling irons? What keeps the air fresh and dry? For you to make intelligent decisions about your bathroom remodeling project, you need to know a bit more about the key systems of your house: the plumbing, electrical, and ventilation systems. In this chapter, you take a look behind the walls, beneath the floor, and above the ceiling to see how these systems work together to supply water, electricity, and fresh air to the bathroom, and you'll be amazed at what you find.

Going with the Flow

A house gets its supply of water from a municipal water utility or from its own water utility, a well. If the water is supplied by a municipal utility, it's carried through the community in *water mains* that are buried under streets or other public easements. The *curb stop* is the main valve between the public water main and the pipe leading into your house. This valve, which controls the water flow out of the water main, is usually located close to the street or curb, if there is one. It may be located far below the surface and require a special handle to operate. This valve is operated by the water department and is closed only if there is a problem with the pipe leading from the main to your house — or to shut off the water if you don't pay your bill. During a major remodeling project, the water meter may need to be replaced or moved. If that's the case, have the water department come and close the curb stop.

In most municipalities, you're responsible for maintaining the pipe that runs from the curb stop into your house, which is called the *house water service pipe.* This pipe leads from the water meter to the *main house shut-off valve,* which is the main shut-off valve controlling water flow into your house.

If you use a well, the water is drawn from the ground by a well pump. Either system — municipal water utility or your own well — eventually connects to the water distribution piping of your house, which is similar in all houses.

The water supply pipes from the main shut-off valve branch off to supply cold water to the rest of the house and to the hot water heater. Hot water supply pipes from the water heater distribute hot water throughout the house.

Everything you've ever wanted to know about your house's water systems

People often tend to rely on gravity to do its thing (for a variety of reasons), and so does the plumbing system of a house. The whole system relies on the fact that water seeks its own level, or to put it in plain English, water runs downhill.

That's a pretty simple idea, but when you connect a bunch of pipes together and pour some water in at the top, that's not always what happens. The water may start down, but if it meets resistance, it may get diverted. If designed correctly, modern plumbing prevents this from happening by assuring that all the horizontal drain pipes slope downward and connect to vertical pipes that are sized to handle the water flow. To keep the water flowing, air must enter the drain system, which it does through properly placed vent pipes (see Figure 8-1).

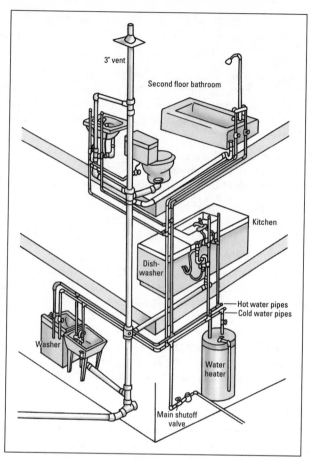

3" vent

Second floor bathroom

Kitchen

Dish-
washer

Hot water pipes
Cold water pipes

Washer

Water
heater

Main shutoff
valve

Figure 8-1:
The
drainage,
waste, vent,
and water
delivery
system of a
typical
house.

The DWV system

Ever wonder why your house has one or more small chimneylike pipes sticking
out of the roof? They're part of a system of vents to assure that air can get
into the drainage pipes so the water flows downhill smoothly. Meet the vents
and the drain pipes that form the drainage, waste, and vent (DWV) system.

At first it may seem like a no-brainer to get water to run down the pipes, but
it's not that simple. Just fill a soft drink bottle full of water and turn it upside
down. Out comes the water in a nice even flow, right? Wrong. No water comes
out until a big gulp of air gets in, which allows the water to come out in gurgling
gushes. For the water to get out of the bottle, air has to get in.

All those pipes under the sink and behind the walls actually have a name. Here's a list and a brief explanation to help you understand any "plumberese" you may encounter during your project.

- **Fixture drain and trap:** This system of pipes connects fixtures such as sinks to the main drainage pipes. Most building codes require bathroom fixture drains to be at least 1¼ inches in diameter or larger. The trap holds water in the U-shaped portion of the pipe, preventing sewer gasses from passing.

- **Waste pipe:** This pipe, which is usually 2 inches in diameter, collects waste from several fixtures, possibly the sink and shower, and marshals it to the larger diameter drain pipe called the *soil stack*.

- **Soil stack:** This is the large-diameter vertical pipe — at least 3 inches — that the waste pipes and the discharge of toilets empty into. Because the soil stack is the only pipe that can take the discharge from a toilet, the toilet must be located close to the soil stack.

- **Vent:** To assure that water flows quickly through these pipes, a vent is required to let air into the drainage system. The vent helps prevent the gurgling sound you sometimes hear after you empty a sink full of water and prevents the water from siphoning out of the trap under each sink.

As you can see, the DWV pipes control the wastewater inside your house, but unless it has someplace to go, you're going to have a major problem. Fortunately, you have a sewer system to handle that job.

The sewer system

After the wastewater finishes flowing through the DWV system in your house, it reaches the sewer system. This is actually a very large DWV system that collects waste from the entire neighborhood. The neighborhood sewers eventually connect to the sewage plant. If you have a septic system, your sewer line connects to the septic tank, which acts as your private sewage plant. Here's a rundown of the major parts of the sewer system.

- **Building sewer:** The soil stack attaches to the building sewer, which exits the house and connects to the municipal sewer system.

- **Public sewer:** Large-diameter pipes connect the municipal sewer system together. These pipes carry the discharge from all the houses in your neighborhood to the sewage treatment plant.

- **Septic field:** In communities that are not serviced by a public sewer system, each house has a private sewer system called a septic system. The building sewer of a house connects to the septic system instead of the sewage plant.

Now that you know the names of the major parts of the DWV of your house and the sewer system, you can impress your friends with this new knowledge at your next party. But we would hold the discussion of the soil stack until after dessert.

DWV connections

Drain and waste pipes and fittings are designed to carry the water and waste out of the house to the sewer or septic system. Water flows through the system, and if it and the waste don't encounter resistance, they end up in the sewage plant.

Drainage pipes are installed so they pitch downward at ¼ inch per foot. Maintaining this pitch is important. If the pipes are pitched too steeply, the water runs off too fast and leaves the waste behind. If not pitched enough, the water and waste sit in the pipes.

The fittings that join the pipes together have sweeping bends and smooth joints between the fitting and pipe to promote easy passage of the sewage (see Figure 8-2). If you're going to install the DWV system, work carefully and follow the plumbing codes carefully. It's not enough to have a system that doesn't leak; it must keep in the waste that could cause a serious health risk if it leaked. The only way to assure this is to provide proper venting and use the recommended diameter drainage pipes and vents and install them correctly.

Figure 8-2: Drainage fittings have a gentle sweeping bend for a smooth flow of liquid and waste.

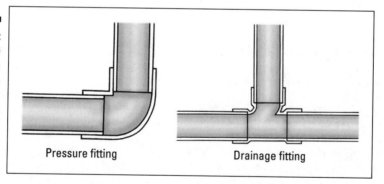

Pressure fitting   Drainage fitting

The power of pressure in a water system

If water flows downhill, how can you get it to the second floor? In the not-so-good old days, that was usually accomplished by carrying the water to wherever it was needed. Today, pressure pushes water through pipes. The pressure is generated by a pump, which may be in your basement if you have a well, or at the municipal water department if you're on city water. In either case, the pump pushes the water through pipes inside the wall of the house and makes it available at the faucet.

Making Pipe Connections that Matter Most

Sometimes you can't avoid moving fixtures if you're remodeling, and if you're building a bathroom from scratch, you're most likely using new fixtures. In either case, moving or installing fixtures means that you have to tap into a DWV system, and doing so can be expensive. Some of the expense is based on the fact that the DWV pipes themselves are large, but most of the cost comes from complying with the plumbing codes that may require additional piping, such as new vents, that sometimes penetrate the roof.

Extending or moving the water supply pipes to a relocated or new fixture is much easier than modifying the DWV system. They're smaller in diameter, and the building code is pretty straightforward when dealing with this system.

As you remodel, you must be aware that there are limits to what your pipes can handle. If you add fixtures to an existing bathroom or build an additional bathroom, the existing water-supply pipes may not have the capacity to carry the extra load, which causes the all-too-familiar problem of the shower water temperature drastically changing when someone flushes the toilet. Increasing the diameter of the hot and cold water pipes supplying the bathroom will usually solve this condition. A pressure-compensating shower valve also allows you to flush without worry.

Meeting drain requirements when you add or move a fixture

Different fixtures have different drainage system requirements. If you're planning to add a new fixture or move an existing one, first figure out how many fixture units (the amount of water the fixture normally drains into the system) you'll be adding to the drain load and what size trap you'll need. A correctly sized trap allows fast drainage of water and keeps sewer gases from entering the bathroom by retaining water in the U-shaped part of the trap.

Use Table 8-1 as a guide to determine the drainage system requirements when you're planning your project. It has the fixture units that each fixture is assigned by the plumbing code and the minimum trap size required to service that fixture. For example, a clothes washer requires a 2-inch trap and drain pipe and puts a 3-unit load on the drain. Enlarging a bathroom to include a bathtub and a clothes washer will add five fixture units to the drain load.

Table 8-1	Fixture Units and Trap Size	
Fixture	*Units*	*Minimum Trap Size*
Sink	1	1¼ inches
Bathtub	2	1½ inches
Shower	2	1½ inches
Clothes washer	3	2 inches
Toilet	4 (3 units for a 1.6 gallon toilet)	3 to 4 inches

Can the drain handle it?

Your drains may not be up to the challenge of your bathroom remodeling project. Table 8-2 helps you figure out whether your current drains can handle the extra load of new fixtures you plan to install. For example, a 2-inch drain can carry six fixture loads. If an existing sink is all that is connected to the drain, it is probably acceptable to use that drain pipe to service the existing and new sink fixtures. However, if other fixtures are dumping into the drain pipe and each has a two-unit fixture load, you have to increase the size of the existing drain or plan to install an additional drain.

Table 8-2 Pipe Fixture Capacity and Maximum Distance from Vent			
Pipe Size	*Maximum Fixture Units*	*Maximum Distance from Stack or Vent*	*Minimum Vent Size*
1¼ inches	1	2½ feet	1¼ inches
1½ inches	3	3½ feet	1½ inches
2 inches	6	5 feet	1½ inches
3 inches	20	6 feet	2 inches
4 inches	160	10 feet	3 inches

To vent or not to vent

The vent is designed to allow air to enter and exit the DWV system so the water can flow freely. The plumbing code requires all fixtures to be vented and governs the size of the vent and the distance a fixture can be from the vent.

Moving an existing fixture may require replacing the existing plumbing with the correctly sized drain pipe and new vent. For example, if you move the toilet to the other side of the bathroom, you may not be able just to extend the drain pipe. To assure that the toilet will empty properly through a 3-inch horizontal pipe, the toilet can't be more than 6 feet from the stack or it must have an additional vent. Refer to Table 8-2 to find out which pipe diameters require what kind of venting.

The plumbing code allows *wet vents*, meaning that the pipe can act as its own vent because the pipe is not totally full of water and air can get into the pipe to aid the flow of water and waste, but wet vents are limited in length. The larger the pipe, the longer the wet vent can be. For example, a sink with a 1½-inch drain can be located no more than 3½ feet from the soil stack or it requires an additional vent. If the sink is served by a 2-inch pipe, it can be located up to 5 feet from the stack without additional venting (see Figure 8-3).

Figure 8-3:
The size of the drain pipe and the distance of the fixture from a vent or stack determine if additional venting is required.

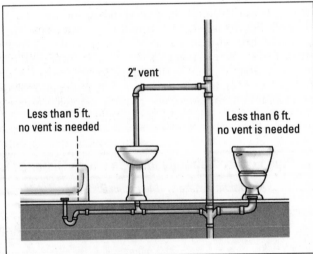

2" vent

Less than 5 ft. no vent is needed

Less than 6 ft. no vent is needed

Use the tables in this section for planning purposes only. The plumbing code is not exactly user-friendly, and not every issue is covered here, especially in dealing with the DWV system. If you do the design, take the plan to your local building department and sit down with the plumbing or building inspector and go over it point by point. The inspector will suggest changes to the plan as needed. Making changes on paper is easier than flunking a plumbing inspection and having to tear out the plumbing and start over.

Factors affecting water delivery

The amount of water that a pipe can deliver in any given time depends on two factors: the diameter of the pipe and the water pressure. If you increase either one, the pipe will be able to deliver more water within the same amount of time. In most cases, the public utility supplies water to your house at a steady pressure through a ¾-inch to 1-inch pipe. The flow through this pipe into your house is usually adequate for all your needs. The pipes inside your house that distribute this water to the various fixtures can vary in size from ⅜ inch to ¾ inch in diameter. The smaller diameter pipes are adequate to supply water to a single fixture, but the flow of water through the pipe may not be adequate to supply additional fixtures. Increasing the diameter of the pipe is the only parameter that can be easily altered to increase the water flow rate.

Branch pipe sizes

The water supply pipes that distribute hot and cold water throughout your house are called *branch pipes*. The plumbing code takes the size and length of these branch pipes into consideration. The longer the pipe run, or distance the water must travel through the pipe, the more resistance the pipe itself provides to the water flow (see Table 8-3). The code lists the maximum amount of fixture units, or capacity, each pipe size can deliver. For example, if a house has a 35-foot-long ½-inch pipe supplying water to a bathroom, you can hook up a toilet, sink, and bathtub to the pipe and meet the code requirements.

Table 8-3	Fixture Units by Pipe Size and Length				
Water Main Size 30-45 PSI	**Distribution Pipe Size**	**Fixture Units at Different Pipe Lengths**			
		40 feet	60 feet	80 feet	100 feet
¾ inch	½ inch	6	5	4	3
¾ inch	¾ inch	16	16	14	12

Table 8-4 shows you how many fixture units various pipe sizes can serve. The water pressure plays a factor here, so a conservative 30 to 45 pounds per square inch (PSI) is used in the table. If your pressure is higher, you can have a bit more expansion capacity. For example, if your present bathroom is 35 feet from the water meter and is supplied with a ½-inch pipe, you can add a shower (2 units) to the bathroom, for a total of 6 units, but not a shower and clothes washer (3 units), for a total of 9 units. To add both of these fixtures, you must increase the diameter of the supply pipe to ¾ inch or run an additional ½-inch supply pipe.

Table 8-4	Fixture Units and Minimum Pipe Sizes		
Fixture Name	*Units*	*Pipe Size*	*Supply Tube Size*
Toilet	3	½ inch	⅜ inch
Sink	1	½ inch	⅜ inch
Shower	2	½ inch	½ inch
Bathtub	2	½ inch	½ inch
Clothes washer	3	½ inch	½ inch

Plugging in the Power

In most municipalities, you don't need electrical permits for replacing switches, outlets, or lighting fixtures. More extensive work, such as adding additional lighting or installing a heater, most likely does require taking out an electrical permit and having the work inspected by the electrical inspector. If you're in doubt whether you need a permit, check with your city's building department before starting the job.

In most areas, you or an electrician or electrical contractor can do the work because most codes allow homeowners to do electrical work inside their own houses. This rule is changing, however, so check with your local building department first.

If your remodeling does need a permit, you'll have to go through two inspections:

✔ First at the rough-in stage to check that the wires and electrical boxes are correctly installed

✔ A final inspection after the devices are installed and the walls are finished

Don't cover any wiring circuits or boxes with wallboard before the rough-in inspection because the inspector may require you to remove it so he can see the wiring.

Electrical service upgrade

Newer homes get power from the utility pole with a three-wire system that delivers both 120- and 220-volt service to the main service panel. The higher 220 voltage is used to power large appliances, such as electric ranges, water heaters, and air conditioners. Most three-wire systems provide at least 100- or 150-amp (the total capacity of the panel) service. Today a 200-amp service is becoming the norm.

Most municipalities don't require you to upgrade an older service unless you're doing major remodeling. If you're planing a bathroom remodeling project that involves more that a face-lift, you're required to get a building permit, and you may have to upgrade your electrical system to meet the current code requirements This is not a do-it-yourself project and must be done by a licensed electrical contractor, along with the local electric utility. Even if you aren't required to upgrade your service, all new electrical work must meet the building code.

Most electrical codes have specific requirements for the placements of outlets, switches, and ground-fault circuit interruption (GFCI) protection and cover a long list of other issues. Seek professional help in designing the electrical plan for your bathroom. A professional can help you make the right choices for features such as vent fans, the proper placement of GFCI receptacles around the sink, and the required placement of switches and outlets.

A modern bathroom can consume an amazing amount of electrical power and require many individual circuits. Plan for multiple users and install two GFCI receptacles at the sink or dressing table, each on its own circuit, to allow for running two hair dryers or a hair dryer and a curling iron. Plan additional circuit(s) for ventilation, space heaters, heated towel bars, and a GFCI circuit for a whirlpool tub.

Running a wire from a box to a ceiling fixture

Remodeling a bathroom means adding conveniences such as new lighting and better ventilation and maybe a whirlpool tub. These upgrades require a source of electrical power. Usually you can tap into the existing lighting circuit to handle the additional lighting fixtures.

If you're adding a whirlpool bath, the electrical code won't allow you to tap into an existing lighting circuit. Whirlpool motors require a 20-amp GFCI circuit. Have a licensed electrician run a new circuit from the service panel to the bathroom to supply the power needed.

Don't put lights downstream of a GFCI because if you trip the GFCI, the lights will go out, creating an unsafe and inconvenient situation.

Short of installing a new whirlpool bath, most electrical changes are easy for do-it-yourselfers. You can extend the lighting circuit yourself and add new switches to make control of the lights and vent fan more convenient. This job is pretty straightforward if you're gutting the bathroom and exposing the studs. If not, fishing wires through the walls without doing too much damage is a challenge.

Use the following technique to run a wire from an existing electrical box in the wall to a ceiling fixture. You can also use this method to add switches to lights or fish wires to any location you need them.

Be sure that the power to the bathroom is turned off at the main service panel before you begin any work.

After you've decided where you want to place your new fixture, follow these steps:

1. **Use a sharp utility knife to cut away a small section of wallboard or plaster from the wall at ceiling height directly above the existing electrical box (see Figure 8-4).**

   This opening exposes the top plate of the wall framing.

Figure 8-4:
Cut a notch in the top plate to allow passage of the new wire from the wall cavity into the ceiling cavity.

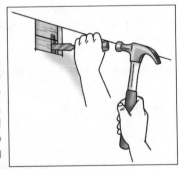

2. **Chip a ½-inch-deep notch in the top plate with a 3.4-inch chisel.**

   The notch exposes the ceiling cavity.

3. **Remove the cover plate from the existing electrical box by removing the mounting screws from the outlets and pulling them out of the box.**

4. **Use a screwdriver to open one of the knockouts in the top of the box.**

5. **Push the end of an electrical fish tape into the new opening at the top of the box.**

6. **Push the tape into the wall cavity and have a helper look for the tape end at the opening you made at the top of the wall.**

   Bend a coat hanger into a hook to make it easier to grab the end of the tape.

7. **Twist the new wire around the loop in the end of the fish tape and pull the new wire into the wall and down into the existing box.**

   Allow at least a foot of wire to hang from the box and then remove it from the fish tape.

8. **Insert the fish tape into the new electrical box in the ceiling and push it into the ceiling cavity (see Figure 8-5) until its end reaches the notched area.**

   Have your helper listening and looking for the tape end at the wall.

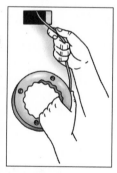

Figure 8-5:
Push the
fish tape
back toward
the opening
in the top of
the wall.

9. **Use the coat hanger hook to grab the tape and pull it out of the ceiling cavity (see Figure 8-6).**

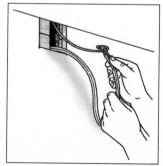

Figure 8-6:
Use the
fish tape
to pull the
new wire
through
the ceiling
cavity into
the new
electrical
box.

10. **Twist the end of the new wire around the end of the fish tape.**

11. **Pull the other end of the tape out and have your helper push the wire into the ceiling as you pull on the tape.**

12. **Pull the tape and the wire out of the new box and cut the wire off, with about 12 inches of wire extending from the box.**

13. **Nail a metal plate over the new wire.**

    The electrical code requires that the wire be protected with a metal plate (see Figure 8-7). Two plates are required if you notch the double top plate.

Figure 8-7:
Install metal plates over new wire to protect it from damage.

14. **Repair the opening in the wall with a patch of drywall and apply drywall compound.**

    Allow the compound to dry.

15. **Apply drywall tape over the joint between the patch and the wall.**

16. **When dry, apply a second coat of compound, let it dry, and then sand it smooth to match the surface of the wall.**

GFCIs: Gotta have 'em

All electrical codes require that ground-fault circuit interrupters (GFCIs) be used in bathrooms because the device reduces the danger of a deadly shock from a faulty cord or appliance. A GFCI measures outgoing and returning current and shuts off the power if it detects a possible dangerous current imbalance. It has a test button that, when pushed in, switches off the power to the outlet and any receptacles connected to it. There are three applications for GFCI receptacles:

✓ **Circuit-breaker-type GFCI:** Installs in the service panel and protects the entire circuit fed by the breaker

✓ **Termination type:** Protects only the outlet where it is installed

✓ **Feed-through type:** Protects the outlet where it's installed and all outlets that are wired to the GFCI outlet on the same circuit

If you're tearing out an old bathroom and replacing it with a new and improved one, all the new electrical receptacles need to be GFCI-protected. But you can easily replace a standard receptacle with a GFCI in an hour's time with only an inexpensive voltage tester, a screwdriver, and long-nose pliers. Have a marker and masking tape handy to identify the wires.

Follow these easy steps to replace an existing electrical receptacle with a GFCI:

1. **Turn off the power to the receptacle and use a voltage tester to make sure the circuit is dead.**

2. **Unscrew the cover plate of the receptacle and remove it.**

3. **Remove the receptacle from the electrical box by unscrewing the mounting screws and then pull it out of the box.**

   Note where the white and black wires are attached to the old receptacle and remove the wires.

   The feed-through type of GFCI receptacle may have short lengths of wires coming out of the receptacle body or screw terminals. One pair of black and white wires or screw terminals should be marked LINE, and the other pair of black and white wires or screw terminals should be marked LOAD (see Figure 8-8).

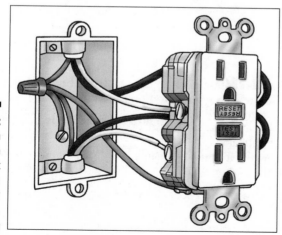

Figure 8-8: A GFCI can provide ground-fault protection to the other outlets.

4. Match up the wires on the feed-through GFCI receptacle as follows:

1. Attach the black wire or terminal marked LINE to the black wires that were attached to the copper-colored terminal on the old receptacle with the connectors called wire nuts that are supplied with the receptacle.

2. Attach the white wire or terminal marked LINE to the white wires that were attached to the silver-colored terminal on the old receptacle with the connectors.

3. Connect the green ground wire to the green terminal on the receptacle or to the green or bare copper wire or to the grounded electrical box.

The GFCI can be wired so that it doesn't provide GFCI to outlets that don't require it. To install this type, reinstall the black, white, and green wires you removed from the old unit to the same colored screw terminals on the new GFCI (see Figure 8-9).

Figure 8-9:
A GFCI can be wired so it doesn't provide ground-fault protection to the other outlets.

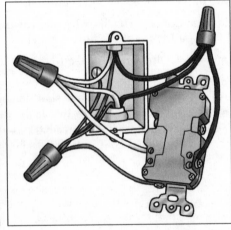

5. Push the new receptacle back into the electrical box and screw it in place. Screw on the cover plate and turn on the power.

6. To test the receptacle, plug a lamp into the receptacle and push in the reset button.

If the button pops out and the lamp stays on, the outlet is wired backward or defective.

7. Disconnect the power and recheck the wiring.

Banishing Those Nasty Odors with Ventilation

Unless you have a pot of cabbage boiling on your stove all day, your bathroom is the largest source of moisture in your home. High humidity, especially in confined areas such as the bathroom, is the primary breeding ground for mold and mildew. All building codes require some form of ventilation in the bathroom.

If a fan, light, or combination fan/light is installed in a wet area — right above the tub/shower as opposed to out in the middle of the room, it should be approved for use in wet areas and be GFCI protected.

A bathroom window has been the traditional ventilation solution, but because air conditioning is the standard in most homes, windows tend to stay closed year-round. Also many powder rooms and half baths aren't located next to an exterior wall, so they don't have access to a window. If your new bath doesn't have a window, you must install a power vent. If your existing bath has a window, you still should install a vent.

The fact that warm air can hold more moisture than cold air is one of the principles that keeps the weather systems working. That's a good thing outside but not inside. The hot water in the bathroom warms the air, and it absorbs water vapor. As long as the air stays at the same temperature, the water vapor stays suspended in the air. But if the air should cool, it can't hold the same amount of water vapor, and some of the vapor condenses back into water. You see this happen when warm, moist air is cooled by the cold window pane during the winter.

Bathroom ventilation systems are designed to remove the moist air inside the room before it has a chance to cool enough to cause condensation on the walls and ceiling, which is like a welcome mat for mold and mildew.

To ventilate a room properly, the Home Ventilation Institute (HVI) recommends that the ventilation system be capable of removing air equal to eight times the volume of the room in one hour. Depending on the size of your bathroom, this can be a lot of hot, moist air.

Picking the right size fan

A quick general rule that you can use to estimate the ventilation requirements of a typical bathroom is to multiply the area of the ceiling by 1.1. Your numerical answer gives you the cubic foot per minute (CFM) number. For example, if you have a 6-x-9-foot bath, the area is 54 square feet. Multiply 54 by 1.1, and you get 59.4. Vent fans are sold with CFM ratings in multiples of ten, so round up, and look for an exhaust fan that has a CFM rating of at least 60.

Based on this method, let the information in Figure 8-10 do the math for you. Find the length of your bathroom on the horizontal axis and the width on the vertical axis of the table and read the CFM requirement where the column and row intersect. To use the preceding bathroom as an example, go to the 6-foot width on the vertical column and over to the 9-foot length on the horizontal. Where these two columns intersect you find 59. This is the approximate CFM rating for the exhaust fan.

Bathroom Vent Size (CFM)

Width	15	83	116	149	182	215	248	281	314	347
	14	77	108	139	169	200	231	262	293	323
	13	72	100	129	157	186	215	243	272	300
	12	66	92	119	145	172	198	224	251	277
	11	61	61	109	133	157	182	206	230	254
	10	55	77	99	121	143	165	187	209	231
	9	50	69	89	109	129	149	168	188	208
	8	44	62	79	97	114	132	150	167	185
	7	39	54	69	85	100	116	131	146	162
	6	33	46	59	73	86	99	112	125	139
	5	28	39	50	61	72	83	94	105	116
		5	7	9	11	13	15	17	19	21
		Length								

Figure 8-10: Use this table to estimate the size of the ventilation fan required for the typical bathroom.

Another method HVI recommends as a way to get the right size exhaust fan is to add the individual requirements of each fixture. Table 8-5 shows the CFM requirements for a toilet, shower, bathtub, and jetted tub. HVI recommends that if you're sizing the ventilation for a master bathroom with a toilet, shower, and whirlpool tub, you get a fan with at least 200 CFM capacity. HVI suggests that in this case, installing three separate but smaller exhaust fans near the fixtures will produce the best results.

Table 8-5 Venting Requirements for Fixtures

Fixture Type	*Cubic Foot per Minute (CFM) Output*
Toilet	50 CFM
Shower	50 CFM
Bathtub	50 CFM
Jetted tub	100 CFM

When sizing the vent, make sure that it has the capacity to do its job, but don't install a fan that's oversized. The exhaust fan not only removes the moist air — which is a good thing — but also removes the air that you pay good money to heat or cool.

Instead of spending your money on unneeded CFM, spend it on upgrading to a fan that is quiet. One reason that people don't run a fan is they can't stand the rattle and roll of a noisy fan.

Letting technology take control

Yes, you should always turn off the bathroom light and fan when you leave the room to save energy, but most likely, the exhaust fan hasn't finished its work just because you're finished showering. If you have an exhaust fan with a humidity sensor, you can leave the fan running, and it will turn itself off automatically when the humidity reaches a normal level. This is a great feature, especially in the summer months when the air is humid and the exhaust must run for a longer time to lower the humidity.

Many light and fan manufacturers offer combination light/exhaust fan units that automatically turn on when someone enters the bathroom — an especially welcome feature when you get up in the middle of the night — and start the exhaust fan when they sense a rise in humidity. The light in these units also turns off automatically when you leave the room, but the fan continues to run to remove excessive moisture. Another option is to install a timer switch that turns the fan off after a set amount of time.

The brass accessories complement the fixtures in this lush master bathroom that features a marble countertop on an heirloom vanity.

The decorative window is the focus in this Victorian home with a vintage claw-footed tub set on raised flooring that conceals the plumbing pipes.

Colorful cabinetry with granite countertops and a companion armoire balance this high-style bathroom with function and flair.

The clean, contemporary lines of this subdued bathroom create a soothing warmth and appeal. The streamline vessel sink and cabinet complete the look.

Sixteen-inch black-and-white vinyl tiles create the classic look of slate in this traditional his 'n hers bathroom. A shower stall shares the wall with a platform bathtub.

A trio of skylights bring daylight into this windowless bathroom with reflective surfaces that enhance its open and airy feeling.

A round wall of glass block creates a one-of-a-kind walk-in shower enclosure that lets in plenty of daylight while providing privacy.

The acrylic block windows and marble floor and tub surround combine to create a restful retreat for a master bathroom with a separate shower. Recessed overhead lighting enhances the mood.

An ordinary double vanity steps up to extraordinary when topped with a solid surface counter and contrasting bowls. Chrome faucets complement the matching mirrors and cabinet hardware.

The strong vertical lines of the wall paneling are duplicated on the vanity doors. The stylish straight lines are echoed in the wall sconces and paned porthole window.

This basic, but beautiful bathroom features white fixtures and wainscoting on the walls, chrome accessories and a sliding door in the lighted bathtub enclosure.

This small, but mighty bathroom features a ceramic tile shower room with built-in seat and glass door.

This welcoming powder room uses a colorful print on the walls to contrast the rich white fixtures. The brass mirror and faucet make a powerful first impression.

A rich floral print on the walls, window valance, dressing table and seat cushion unify this large master bath with its bedroom suite.

The interplay of different shaped tiles and patterns in soft natural shades creates a focus for this handsome bathroom with built-in tub and shower room separated by a clear tempered glass enclosure.

Part III
Fabulous Fixtures, Vanities, and Faucets

The 5th Wave   By Rich Tennant

"What if we put the solid granite Jacuzzi on the first floor?"

In this part . . .

This part is bulging with the stuff a great bathroom is made of — toilets, bathtubs, whirlpools, sinks, faucets, cabinets, and countertops of all descriptions. You find out how to choose them, where to find them, and what's involved in installing them. Whether you're doing a basic bath remodel or an all-out luxury spa, you face beaucoup decisions. The product choices are staggering, and we tell you how to make selections that will make you happy for years to come. We talk about practical choices for a limited budget and products for a dream bath to pamper and spoil you. The key is narrowing your selection and focusing on fixtures that are well designed and well made in styles and finishes that please you.

Chapter 9

Go Flush! Selecting and Installing a Toilet

*I*f you've always taken toilets for granted, you're in for a big surprise when you find yourself in the toilet-buying market. Don't be overwhelmed by the fact that there are hundreds to choose from. Consider this chapter Toilets 101, and you'll find out everything you need to know about choosing and installing the toilet that's right for your home.

When it comes to a toilet, function follows form, so begin by pinpointing who will be the primary users of the toilet and how often it will be used. A good choice for an infrequently used powder room is a distant cousin from one that's used in a family's one and only hall bathroom. If you have large family members, you may want to consider elongated toilets, which are larger and more comfortable. Also available are elevated toilets, which are convenient for anyone who is physically challenged or has difficulty sitting down or rising. A standard toilet has a 15-inch rim height, but many of today's toilet manufacturers are now offering 17-inch rim heights, which are comfortable for most adults and meet the requirements of the Americans with Disabilities Act (ADA). Choose a toilet to fit the person who will use it.

You can buy a toilet for under $100 or over $1,000, and both of them will get the job done. But obviously the durability, design, quality, and style are what account for the price difference. Figure an average price of $300 for a good-quality toilet that may outlive the people who installed it. Actually, the life expectancy of a toilet is 40-plus years. Set your budget first because it may limit the color selection, quality, quietness, flushing mechanism, water-conserving quality, and ease of cleaning.

Taking a Tour of the Toilets

Most toilets are made of vitreous china, which means they're impervious to water. It's a durable material that is easy to clean, making it the obvious choice for a bathroom. There are two basic designs of toilets:

✔ **One-piece:** This style is seamlessly molded together, has a more streamlined look, and, consequently, is easy to clean.

✔ **Two-piece:** The more typical two-piece toilet has a separate water tank that hangs on the wall and rests on the toilet base or bowl. It is less expensive than a one-piece unit and is slightly more difficult to install.

Start paying attention every time you go to a different bathroom to get an idea of the different toilet styles available. For now, check out Figure 9-1 to see the differences between one-piece and two-piece toilets.

When you buy a two-piece toilet, you have to buy the toilet seat separately because the seat is not sold as part of the toilet. Strange, but true.

Figure 9-1:
Notice the
differences
between a
two-piece
toilet and a
one-piece
toilet.

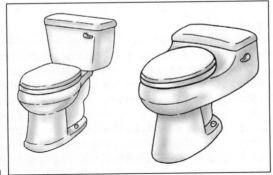

Considering flushing mechanisms

That whoosh you hear when you press the flush lever of any toilet is caused by the rush of the water through the toilet to remove the waste. The water rush can be caused by good old gravity, water, or air pressure. Depending on where your toilet is located, one flushing method is better than the other. Here are the types of flushing mechanisms:

✔ **Powered by gravity (the quiet flush):** Gravity toilets are a lesson in basic physics: Press the lever to release water in the tank into the bowl and the weight of the water, which is located above the toilet's drain, flushes the water and waste down the drain.

✔ **Pressure assisted (the big whoosh):** Pressure-assisted toilets (see Figure 9-2) use water pressure or compressed air to force water through the bowl and flush the water and waste down the drain. This type of toilet gets the job done, but because it is sometimes noisy, everyone in the house may know just what you're doing. The noise level also makes these toilets a bad choice near a bedroom or family room, but that may not always be the case: Manufacturers are working on reducing the noise.

Figure 9-2:
A pressure-assisted toilet.

Getting a good fit

The typical height of a toilet is 14 to 15 inches, a convenient and comfortable height for most people. For tall or large people, elevated toilets are available that are up to 18 inches high, which are more comfortable for them. These elevated toilets are also convenient for anyone who is physically challenged and has difficulty sitting down or rising. There are ADA-compliant toilets that meet the standards of the Americans with Disabilities Act for wheelchair accessibility, as well. And if parenthood is in your future, you may be interested in knowing that you can get a small toilet that's scaled down for a little kid and designed for potty training.

Considering features and comfort

Never use a toilet without thinking about why it's comfortable or why it's not. When you begin doing your personal survey of toilets, you'll be amazed at the differences and nuances you'll discover. Here are some things to notice in your quest for the perfect toilet for your remodeled bathroom:

✔ **Comfortable size:** Is the toilet too small for a large person's use? Consider an elongated toilet, which is usually about 2 inches deeper than a standard toilet and has an oversize seat, making it more comfortable and convenient to use.

✔ **Elevated height:** For anyone who struggles while lowering and raising themselves, consider an elevated toilet, which is approximately 2 to 4 inches higher than a standard toilet.

✔ **Cleanability:** Some people consider the ease of cleaning a toilet the most important feature. For them, a one-piece toilet with a smooth-sided bowl is the best choice. Another option is a toilet seat that pulls off without tools so it's easy to clean.

✔ **Quiet flush:** If your bathroom is next to living quarters, consider a toilet that offers a quiet flushing system. It's a lot like a dishwasher: You want it to work, but you don't want to hear it working.

✔ **Power flushing:** Many toilet manufacturers have their own patented flushing systems designed to exceed performance standards. Most of these designs use water pressure to compress air in a chamber. When the toilets are flushed, the air pushes the water out of the chamber at high velocity, flushing the toilet with less water.

✔ **Automatic seat closing:** Some toilets are designed with a slow-moving hinge that gradually lowers both the seat and lid. Does this sound like the perfect solution for the lone woman in an all-male household?

✔ **Insulated water tank:** To prevent a build-up of moisture on the outside of the tank (and, consequently, a breeding ground for mold and mildew), many toilets have an insulated water tank. The insulation prevents condensation by keeping the cold water inside. This feature is popular in homes in humid climates.

✔ **Two-lever flush lever:** To conserve water, many toilets offer a double-action flushing lever. You push the small lever to release less water for liquids or use the large lever to flush away solid waste.

Getting the lowdown on low-flow toilets

In the early 1990s, a national law was passed to conserve water. It mandated that all new toilets sold in the United States require a maximum of 1.6 gallons of water per flush. The thinking was that by reducing the water from 3.5 gallons used by the old-style tanks, a lot of water would be saved. However, these early low-flow toilets were flawed in design and required two or sometimes three flushes to empty the bowl. This, of course, gave credence to complaints of many homeowners, builders, and remodelers that low-flows nullified any water savings.

That's all an unpleasant part of our history, and hopefully if you had one of those early low-flows, you've replaced it. If you haven't, do it now with one of today's new improved-design low-flow toilets.

Reinventing your bathroom with new fixtures

Decisions, decisions, decisions — that's what you'll face when you begin looking at toilets. Fortunately, the major manufacturers of plumbing fixtures have done some of the work for you by offering eye-catching suites or collections of fixture styles. You'll find toilets and bidets, sinks, tubs, and faucets in a variety of styles that include contemporary, traditional, country, Victorian, and retro, just to name some of them.

If you're remodeling a particularly small bathroom, you'll find compact-size toilets designed specifically to fit in small spaces. Some manufacturers offer a special corner toilet when that's the only space available.

You can choose from a rainbow of colors for toilets and fixtures, as well as the more versatile white and off-white. If you're choosing a colored fixture, make sure that you see it life size, not just on a sample board. This isn't wallpaper that you can remove if you get tired of it. A toilet is a more-permanent part of your house that you'll live with for a long time.

Shopping for la toilette

Depending on where you live, you can shop for bathroom fixtures in several places. Many of the large chains of home centers have design centers within their stores, where a wide selection of toilets and related fixtures is installed in showroom settings. Kitchen and bathroom design centers feature large displays of bathrooms and a selection of fixtures and cabinetry. The more sources you can visit, the better. That way, you'll be able to preview different types, styles, and colors of toilets, along with their related fixtures.

You can also purchase toilets and other bathroom fixtures from several sources on the Internet (see Chapter 19). But if you decide to buy online, do so only after you've done the footwork and know the toilet style, model, and color you want. Before placing an order online, investigate the cost of shipping and handling, as well as the return policy.

Realtors tell us that brightly colored bathroom fixtures can be a real turnoff to prospective buyers. If you're designing your ultimate bathroom, go with hot pink if that's what you want, but if you're not going to live there forever, be more subdued in your choice of toilet colors. Basic white may be boring to you, but it can be beautiful to others.

Roughing Dimension: Measuring Your Options

The first stage of a new plumbing job is installing pipes behind the walls or beneath the floor, which is called *roughing in*. In a remodeling project, the pipes are already there but may have to be altered. In either situation, the location of these pipes must match up with the fixtures that are installed later. To make sure that pipes and fixtures are properly aligned, manufacturers provide rough-in dimensions for each fixture. For a toilet, the important rough-in dimension is the distance from the wall to the center of the drain pipe in the floor and the height on the wall behind the toilet for the water supply line. If the drain isn't located the proper distance from the wall, the toilet could be located far from the wall and look silly. Even worse, if the drain is located too close to the wall, the base of the toilet can't be aligned over the drain. (See the section "Installing a New Toilet," later in this chapter.)

If you're replacing a really, really old toilet, measure the distance between the bolts that hold it to the floor and the wall. Prior to the mid-1930s, tanks were hung on the wall, and the bowl was attached to a sewer pipe with a mounting flange located either 10 inches or 14 inches from the wall. Today, toilets use a 12-inch roughing-in dimension, so if you're replacing one of these good ole boys, you may have to hire a plumber to modify the drain pipe or install an offset toilet flange, which may give you the extra 2 inches you need to install a 12-inch toilet on a 10-inch rough-in. Figure 9-3 illustrates a rough-in position for a toilet. Toilets are available on special order to fit the old dimensions, but the choice of styles is very limited.

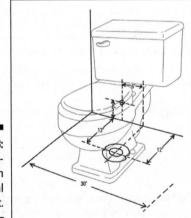

Figure 9-3:
The rough-in position for a typical toilet.

Most fixture manufacturers provide a roughing-in illustration with the product. To get a heads up about what's involved before you buy and install a fixture, go to the manufacturer's Web site and find the product specifications. These usually include installation instructions and roughing-in information. Before buying and installing any fixture, read the instructions so that you have time to think it through and plan the job before actually doing it. Ain't the Internet great?

Dethroning the Throne

Unfortunately, there's nothing regal about disconnecting an old toilet to prepare for a new one.

The steps to removing a toilet are the reverse of installing one, so you get a practice run by disconnecting the old one. Clear the floor and lay an old blanket or newspapers nearby so that you can rest the parts of the toilet there as you disassemble it.

Don't worry about touching the water! The water in the tank is clean, and the water in the bowl is flushed out before you begin. You'll need a bucket, large sponge, rags, rubber gloves, a wrench, and a scraper.

Follow these steps to remove an old toilet:

1. **Pour ¼ cup of toilet bowl cleaner or household bleach into the toilet and flush it a few times.**

2. **Turn off the water to the toilet and disconnect the supply line to it at the bottom of the toilet tank.**

3. **Flush the toilet again, lift off the top of the tank, and set it aside so it's out of the way.**

   The toilet bowl will have a small amount of water at the bottom.

4. **Wearing rubber gloves to protect against bacteria, use a large sponge to soak up the water and squeeze it into a bucket. Continue until all the water is gone and the bowl is dry.**

    You can use a wet-dry shop vacuum to remove the water left in the bottom of a toilet.

5. **Remove the gloves and wash your hands thoroughly.**

6. **Look on the underside of the toilet base where the tank rests to find the tank mounting nuts and bolts. Use a wrench to loosen and unscrew them.**

    If the nuts and bolts are corroded and won't budge with a wrench, give them a shot of WD-40 or Liquid Wrench, a spray lubricating oil. If that doesn't loosen them, try a hacksaw, using the blade between the toilet base and the nut to cut through the bolts. Place masking tape on the toilet surrounding the bolts to protect the base.

7. **Find the nuts and bolts on either side of the base of the toilet that hold the toilet to the floor. If they're covered with plastic caps, remove the caps and use a wrench to loosen and unscrew the nuts.**

   If the bolts are too corroded to unscrew, remove them with a hacksaw (see Figure 9-4). Keep a rag handy to wipe up any water that may seep out.

Figure 9-4:
Use a
hacksaw
to cut
through
badly
corroded
closet hold-
down bolts.

8. **Standing over the toilet bowl, gently rock it from side to side to break the seal of the wax ring; then lift it straight up and keep it level.**

   Water will likely be left in the trap, and you'll slosh it all over your feet and the floor if you tilt the toilet. Rest the toilet on an old blanket or newspapers.

9. **Stuff an old rag in the hole in the floor, which is called the closet flange.**

   This hole is a direct path to the soil pipe leading to the sewer or septic system, so the rag prevents sewer gases from entering your home.

10. **Find the old wax ring, which sticks the base of the toilet to the floor, and remove it.**

11. **Use a scraper or putty knife to thoroughly clean the floor of all the residue.**

12. **Wipe down the flange and surrounding area with a mixture of household bleach and water, or use a disinfectant cleaning solution.**

Preparing the Floor for a New Toilet

After you remove the toilet, inspect the underlayment for damage. The underlayment is a material that provides a flat, level surface for the finished flooring and toilet to rest on. See Chapter 14 for more information about underlayments.

Inspect the underlayment for telltale signs of moisture. Dark or discolored underlayment around a toilet indicates water damage. You can replace only the damaged sections, leaving in place what's in good condition (see Figure 9-5). To make the repairs, cut away the damaged underlayment with a circular saw, setting the saw blade depth to match the thickness of the underlayment. Cut through the underlayment with the saw and remove the bad section around the toilet. Then cut a piece of underlayment that is the same thickness as the old and replace the damaged pieces.

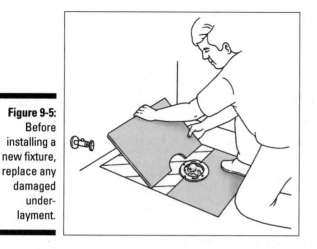

Figure 9-5:
Before installing a new fixture, replace any damaged under-layment.

If you're installing a new floor over an existing one, plan to get an extension flange that will raise the toilet up to be aligned with the new flooring height. See Chapter 14 about removing and installing flooring materials.

Installing a New Toilet

You install a two-piece toilet in three phases: First you secure the toilet base to the floor, then you fasten the tank to the base, and finally, you connect the water supply to fill the toilet with water.

A one-piece toilet is installed in the same way as a two-piece unit except that it's more cumbersome and heavier to handle. Because it's all in one piece, however, the installation goes faster as you don't need to install separately. Use the basic instructions later in this section to install both types of toilets.

To install a two-piece toilet, you need the following:

- ✔ Adjustable wrench
- ✔ Carpenter's level
- ✔ Plumber's putty
- ✔ Putty knife
- ✔ Scrap of carpeting or heavy blanket
- ✔ Screwdriver
- ✔ Toilet and its mounting nuts and bolts
- ✔ Wax ring or bowl gasket

Carefully read the installation instructions packaged with the toilet and identify the parts, then follow these steps to install a new toilet:

1. **Remove the rag in the flange hole in the floor.**

2. **Prepare the floor for a wax ring.**

   If you haven't already, scrape up any old wax and debris from the flange and surrounding area.

3. **Locate the closet bolts and attach them to the toilet flange.**

   Turn the T-shaped head of each bolt so that it slips into the slot in the flange. Push the bolt into the slot and slide it into position so it's parallel to the wall behind the toilet. Turn the bolt so the head can't be pulled out of the flange. Slide the plastic retainer washers down the threads to hold the bolts in place.

4. **Turn the toilet upside down and rest it on a padded surface.**

5. **Locate the toilet horn, the short spout in the center of the base of the toilet, and place the wax ring and its sleeve onto the toilet horn and press it down firmly (see Figure 9-6).**

   This wax ring fits around the toilet horn and compresses against the drain flange as you press it to the floor and then bolt it into place. The plastic spout must face up. You have a one-time shot with a wax ring because after the ring is compressed, it won't spring back. The key to a proper seal is to lower the toilet onto the flange without disturbing it.

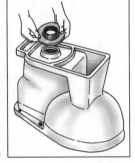

Figure 9-6: Installing a new wax ring seal.

6. **Carefully lower the toilet base on the flange by lining up the closet bolts over the holes in the toilet base (see Figure 9-7).**

   It's helpful to have another person on hand as you lower the toilet onto the floor to line up the bolts with the holes in the base. Keep the base level as you lower it to the floor.

   Put plastic drinking straws over the bolts to lengthen them and act as guides as you lower the toilet onto the bolts.

Figure 9-7:
Lower
the toilet
bowl onto
the bolts
installed in
the slots on
the side of
the toilet
flange.

Wax seal
Floor bolts
Toilet flange

7. **Gently but firmly press the base down on the wax ring.**

8. **Put a carpenter's level across the toilet base to assure that the bowl is level both side by side and front to back (see Figure 9-8), and then place the washers and nuts on the bolts, using an adjustable wrench to tighten them.**

   Alternate side to side as you tighten the nuts, checking that the bowl is still level side to side and front to back.

   Be careful not to overtighten the bolts. You don't want to tighten them so hard they crack the base of the toilet.

Figure 9-8:
Use a
carpenter's
level to
assure that
the bowl
is level.

9. **Cover the bolts with the trim caps.**

   If the bolts are too long for the trim caps to cover them, use a hacksaw to shorten them. Snap the plastic trim caps in place to cover the bolts.

10. **Install the flush mechanism (if necessary).**

    The fill and flush mechanism in a toilet tank regulates the flow of water into the tank when you push the lever. It opens a valve so that clean water in the tank flows into the toilet bowl, flushing out its contents. Most toilets come with the mechanism installed, but if yours does not, follow the instructions included with the toilet to install it.

11. **Turn the tank upside down and attach the rubber seal, called the spud washer, to the pipe that protrudes from the bottom of the tank.**

12. **Carefully turn the tank right side up and center the spud washer over the water intake opening, which is at the back edge of the bowl in the toilet base.**

13. **Lower the tank to the back of the bowl, align the tank bolts and rubber washers with the holes in the tank, and insert the tank mounting bolts through the holes in the bowl.**

14. **On the toilet bowl underside, thread on the washers and nuts, tightening by hand at first and then with a wrench (see Figure 9-9).**

    Do this carefully and don't overtighten. Be sure to turn the nut, not the bolt. Some toilet tanks have preinstalled mounting bolts, and others require that you preinstall the bolts. Follow the directions that come with the toilet.

Figure 9-9:
Use a screwdriver to keep the tank bolts from turning while you tighten the nuts from below the tank.

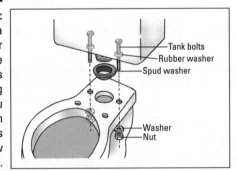

Tank bolts
Rubber washer
Spud washer
Washer
Nut

15. **Connect the riser (supply) tube and shut-off valve by fastening the coupling nut to the tank fitting and the compression fitting to the shut-off valve, first by hand and then with a wrench.**

    The most reliable risers are made of chromed brass, but they can be difficult to install. The braided steel flex supply risers with metal connectors are very reliable and easier to install.

16. **Turn on the water supply at the stop valve (see Chapter 8) to fill the tank and toilet with water, checking for any leaks and watching the toilet as it begins to fill with water.**

    The water flow should begin to slow and stop at the fill line marked inside the tank.

17. **Follow the manufacturer's directions about adjusting the water level.**

    Some valves have a float arm that can be adjusted, and others have a set screw to adjust.

Using a bowl gasket assembly

Instead of using a wax ring to anchor your toilet and seal it to the floor, you can use a bowl gasket kit, which comes with a gasket, sleeve, three sizes of O-rings, a cardboard spacer, two bolts, retainer washers, brass washers, and acorn nuts to fit almost any toilet situation.

Insert the bowl gasket assembly, wrapping the cardboard spacer around the gasket and then slowly and evenly pushing the gasket assembly downward until it is 1 inch above the floor surface. The O-ring rolls into the drain pipe and moves up the bowl gasket assembly to create a tight seal. The cardboard spacers collapse and won't interfere with the seal.

---

18. **Install the toilet seat by pushing the seat bolts through the holes in the toilet base and then tightening the nuts on the bolts from below.**

    Some seats require using a screwdriver to tighten while you hold the bolt with pliers.

Bathing in a Bidet: Personal Hygiene

A *bidet,* a sit-down wash basin with faucets used for partial bathing, is installed in some luxury bathrooms and master suites. As a small wash basin for personal hygiene, a bidet provides convenient, gentle cleansing for those with conditions such as hemorrhoids, rashes, or incontinence. The user sits astride the bowl, facing the faucet, to control the spray or fills the bowl with water. You can also use a bidet as a foot bath.

Most toilet manufacturers offer bidets in styles and colors that complement their toilets (see Figure 9-10).

The most typical bidet features a single or two-handle faucet and vertical and horizontal sprays. Although many bidets are open, others incorporate a cover in their design.

Installing a bidet requires rough-in plumbing lines for hot and cold water and a drain, just like a vanity sink. Placement of a bidet is traditionally next to a toilet, so determine the location when designing the bathroom floor plan.

To install a bidet, first determine the location for the bidet and make sure that the wall and floor are square and plumb to ensure a proper installation. Have a plumber run lines for hot and cold water and a drain to meet the rough-in specifications for the bidet.

Carefully read the installation instructions packaged with the bidet and identify the parts.

Figure 9-10:
Taking a
look at a
typical
bidet.

To install a bidet, you need the following:

✔ Adjustable wrench

✔ Bidet and its mounting nuts and bolts

✔ Carpenter's level

✔ Hot and cold riser tubes

✔ Screwdriver

✔ Silicone sealant

Follow these steps to install a bidet:

1. **Attach the faucet and drain fittings to the body of the bidet.**

2. **Move the bidet to its location and check the alignment with the drain and water supply pipes.**

3. **Draw a contour of the bidet on the floor and mark the location of the hold-down bolts on the floor.**

4. **Remove the bidet and drill pilot holes for the hold-down bolts.**

   You may have to use a carbide-tipped drill to bore through floor tile.

5. **Use the contour drawn on the floor and reposition the bidet.**

6. **Insert the hold-down bolts and tighten them.**

   Use a carpenter's level to assure that the bidet is level.

7. **Place the caps over the heads of the bolts.**

8. **Apply silicone sealant around the base of the bidet.**

9. **Connect the hot and cold riser (supply) tubes, shut -off valve, and drain.**

10. **Connect the water supply and drain and turn on the water to check for leaks.**

If the bidet water supply doesn't have a shut-off valve, add one with hot and cold flexible tubes with preattached fittings that connect the coupling nut to the bidet fitting and the compression fitting to the shut-off valve.

Chapter 10

Rub a Dub Dub! All About Tubs

● ●

In This Chapter

▶ Choosing a bathtub

▶ Getting rid of an unwanted tub

▶ Installing a new tub

▶ Replacing and building tub walls

▶ Adding a door to your tub

▶ Working with faucets

● ●

*N*ow this is where remodeling a bathroom gets really personal. Are you a tub person or a shower person or both? Shrinks probably have theories about what people's personal bathing preferences disclose about their personality, but we want to leave that one alone. We do know that most people have definite preferences, and if you're a tub person who delights in soaking in bubbles or steaming in hot bath water, you have a whole lot of options. Even if your space is limited or odd shaped, you can probably find a bathtub or whirlpool to fit your space and satisfy your desire for bathing luxury. (If you're a shower person, head to Chapter 11.)

But what if you have an old bathtub that can't be removed? Sure, with a sledgehammer anything is possible, but we discuss when it makes sense to leave an old tub in place, give it a coverup, and improve the room around it.

In your quest for the perfect bathtub, visit the Web sites for Kohler (www. kohler.com) and American Standard (www.americanstandard-us.com), where you'll get a good overview of the variety of tubs available. You'll see the colors, finishes, prices, sizes, configurations, installation notes and specifications, and complementary products.

Selecting a Bathtub

Want to soak and simmer in hot, steamy water? How about easing your aches and pains with a soothing massage? Or maybe you're an in-and-out kinda bather who wants nothing more than hot water and plenty of it? Do some noodling about what you like and don't like about your current bathtub and make a list of your likes and dislikes. After you can nail down your bathing priorities, you're in for a whole lot of choices, which, by the way, we present in the following sections. If you're looking for inspiration, see the color insert of bathroom photographs, which shows options ranging from posh platform tubs to charming replica claw-foot tubs.

Sudsing It Up in Tubs for All Seasons

The typical bathtub is 5 feet long, 14 inches deep, and 32 inches wide, but there are variations on this theme. Longer, deeper tubs are available to accommodate different shapes and sizes of bathers. Many 6- and 7-foot tubs are sized for two bathers. Square or corner tubs range from 4-feet square and larger. Most tubs are configured with either a left- or right-hand outlet for the drains to accommodate different installations.

Try before you buy. You sat in your recliner before you bought it, didn't you? Why not a bathtub? If you're embarrassed, climb in when no one is looking and see how it fits. If you're buying a two-person bathtub, definitely try it on for size.

Bathtub manufacturers offer a rainbow of colorful shades, many of them coordinated with matching sinks and toilets. Of course, the whites and neutral shades will be the least expensive and easiest to get. For resale purposes, real estate agents say that the more subtle neutral shades are the best choice. But if your heart is set on taking a bubble bath in a navy blue bathtub, go for it.

Bathtubs are made from a variety of materials:

- **Cast iron:** A cast-iron tub is the most expensive option. It's the heaviest of the materials and offers deep rich colors and a glossy surface that can't be matched. It's the best you can buy.

- **Steel:** Formed steel covered with enamel is a popular material for tubs. It is lighter than cast iron but not as durable.

- **Acrylic:** The acrylic tubs are molded and shaped in any number of configurations and feature an easy-care durable surface.

- **Fiberglass:** These tubs are lightweight, so they're easy to handle, and are an economical alternative to acrylic.

Bidding Good Riddance to an Old Tub

Anyone who has ever remodeled a bathroom will tell you that the most diffi-cult part of the project was removing the old tub. You have to remove all the plumbing fixtures, disconnect the plumbing lines — that's the easy part — and then dislodge, cajole, and finally lift out the monster. The finale involves manhandling the tub in one piece or many pieces out of the bathroom, through the house, and to the trash. It's an act of skill and brute force that everyone should experience because the sense of relief is sheer bliss.

Built-in, platform, and footed tubs offer unique challenges. An old built-in may have layers of wallboard, tile, or surround material that is holding the tub in place, so removing the walls is the first job. See the section "Taking out the tub," later in this chapter, for those instructions. That old charmer of a platform and footed tub is heavier than an elephant and just about as easy to move down a staircase. Sometimes the only way to get it out is to bust it up with a sledgehammer and remove it piecemeal.

Before you take up the old sledgehammer, check the Yellow Pages to see whether a local architectural salvage outfit will be willing to remove the tub for you. You can also advertise it in your local newspaper's classified ads as an item that you're giving away. There's a good chance that a salvage dealer or contractor will be willing to remove it for you or even pay for the tub itself.

When the old tub is removed, the bathroom will appear to have grown in size, and you'll probably discover (if you haven't already) the key to unlocking the inner workings of your bathroom plumbing.

Gaining access to the plumbing: The inspection panel

First, a word about working on the plumbing lines of the bathtub. If you're lucky, your bathtub plumbing lines are accessible through an access panel, a removable inspection panel that's often located in a hall or the closet of an adjoining room. The panel is a piece of plywood that is framed in and fas-tened by screws that probably have been painted over. If you have one of these inspection panels, working on the tub, faucet, and valve is much easier, and it won't disturb the walls around the tub.

If there's no access panel, build one so that working on the pipes will be convenient — now and in the future. Follow these easy steps:

1. **On the plumbing wall, mark off a 30-inch rectangle of wallboard so that you have full access to the pipes and fittings of the tub.**

   Use a carpenter's level to mark off the rectangular outline so that the horizontal and vertical lines are square.

2. **Use a drywall saw to cut the wallboard, following the outline to make the opening.**

3. **Make the actual panel by cutting a piece of ¼-inch plywood slightly larger than the opening and sanding the edges.**

4. **Use wood cleats or screws at the corners of the panel to secure it.**

5. **Paint your new access panel to match the wall.**

Disconnecting the plumbing lines

No matter what style tub you have, they're all connected to the plumbing lines in the same way. Turn off your water supply and then follow these steps to disconnect:

1. **Standing in the tub, unscrew the faucet handles from the valve body and remove the spout.**

   You may need a screwdriver or a hex wrench if there's a hex nut under the spout.

2. **Remove the screws holding the overflow plate in position and remove the plate.**

   You may have to pull the drain linkage mechanism out of the overflow along with the cover.

3. **To loosen the tub drain, push the handles of a pair of slip joint pliers into the tub drain, called the *spud*.**

4. **Put a large screwdriver between the handles of the slip joint pliers and turn the pliers counterclockwise to unscrew the drain from the pipe under the tub, called the *shoe*.**

Taking out the tub

Now is the time to bring in your neighbors and friends with bulging biceps. Don't attempt to do this next job alone. Get two strong helpers to assist with the pulling, lifting, and carrying. If the tub surround has tiles, use a cold chisel to chip away the lowest course of tile around the perimeter of the tub (see Figure 10-1). Remember to wear safety glasses. If there's a fiberglass enclosure, cut the enclosure 6 inches above the tub.

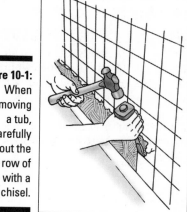

Figure 10-1:
When removing a tub, carefully chip out the first row of tile with a cold chisel.

To remove a built-in tub, follow these steps:

1. **Use a screwdriver or pry bar to remove the screws or nails that hold the tub flange to the wall studs.**

2. **When the tub is free of the walls, use a pry bar to loosen the front of the tub from the floor. Place the end of the bar between the floor and the tub and pry up to raise the tub off the floor.**

3. **Insert several scraps of plywood or cardboard skid under the front edge of the tub.**

   The wood protects the floor and makes it easier to pull the tub out of its enclosure.

4. **Slide the tub onto the plywood and pull the tub away from the wall (see Figure 10-2).**

Figure 10-2:
Using a wood or cardboard skid when removing the tub.

The challenge is safely lifting and moving the tub down a steep staircase. Be careful because making the turns can get dicey.

If the tub won't budge, you may have to cut it in pieces. A reciprocating saw with a metal cutting blade cuts through a steel or fiberglass tub. Use a sledge-hammer to break up a cast-iron tub, but cover it with an old dropcloth first. To protect yourself, wear long sleeves, long pants, and heavy leather work gloves. And don't forget to wear safety glasses to protect your eyes.

After disconnecting the plumbing lines of a platform or claw-foot tub, try to lift the tub off the floor. If it's too heavy, cover the tub with an old dropcloth and use a sledgehammer to break it into pieces.

Putting in a New Tub

Installing a new tub isn't an easy do-it-yourself project because it involves working with a large, heavy object in a small, confined space. If you have any hesitation or misgivings about doing it, hire a plumber who has the experience to install it and the license to hook up the fixtures.

If you want to do it yourself, inspect your tub before you start the installation. Measure its dimensions and check them against the size of the opening. Make sure that the drain outlet is at the correct end of the tub. Look for any signs of damage and protect the tub surface with a dropcloth.

Before you get started on the installation, inspect the floor joists and look for signs of any joists weakened by rot or any that were cut to remove pipes. Totally remove a rotten joist and replace it. Reinforce any bad joists by fastening a new joist to the existing one with machine bolts. Then install a new subfloor over the joists if necessary (see Chapter 14).

Gather the following tools and materials to install an acrylic or platform tub.

- 1-inch galvanized roofing nails
- 2-x-4s
- Carpenter's level
- Construction adhesive
- Dropcloth
- Electric drill and bits
- Measuring tape
- Mortar mix
- Pipe wrench

✔ Plumber's putty

✔ Safety glasses

✔ Screwdriver

✔ Silicone caulk

✔ Trowel

✔ Wood shims

✔ Woodworking tools

Installing an acrylic tub

An acrylic tub is set in a bed of cement (check the manufacturer's recommendations), and the sides are screwed or nailed through flanges on the side of the tub into wall studs. The tub is supported on a 1-x-4-inch ledger nailed to the wall studs. In models with integral supports under the tub, you can shim under the supports to compensate for a slightly out-of-level floor. Then the overflow assembly is connected to the tub drain and main drain line. Faucets are connected to the water supply lines, and plumbing pipes and drain lines are hooked up.

Follow these steps to install an acrylic tub.

Installing a ledger board

The first step in installing the tub is to set in place a ledger board that supports the edges of the tub that contact the walls of the tub enclosure.

1. **Push the tub into the enclosure.**

2. **Mark the top of the flange on the wall studs with a pencil.**

   Use the specifications from the manufacturer or measure the distance from the top of the flange to the underside of the tub; it's usually 1 inch.

3. **Make another mark 1 inch below the first mark you placed on the studs.**

   This is the location of the top edge of the ledger.

4. **Use wood screws to fasten the ledger board horizontally across the back wall of the alcove (see Figure 10-3).**

5. **Fasten shorter ledger boards to the ends of the enclosure level with the board you install on the back wall.**

   This creates a continuous ledge on the tub enclosure wall for the tub to rest on.

Figure 10-3:
Installing
a ledger
around the
perimeter
of the tub
enclosure.

Hooking up the plumbing

It is easier to install the drain and overflow pipes on the tub before it is permanently installed in the enclosure. Turn the tub over or rest it on its side and then follow these steps:

1. **Follow the manufacturer's directions and assemble the shoe fitting, which is placed under the tub and the waste pipe.**

2. **Assemble the overflow fitting with the overflow pipe.**

   Insert the ends of the overflow pipe and waste pipe in the T-fitting (see Figure 10-4).

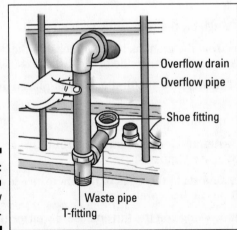

Figure 10-4:
Installing an
overflow
drain.

Overflow drain
Overflow pipe
Shoe fitting
Waste pipe
T-fitting

3. Put this assembly in place to check that shoe and overflow align with the openings in the tub.

4. Place a bead of plumber's putty around the drain flange and wrap Teflon pipe tape around the threads on its body.

5. Place the rubber washer on the shoe and position the shoe under the tub in alignment with the drain flange.

6. Screw the drain flange into the shoe.

7. Tighten the drain flange by placing the handles of a pair of pliers into the drain flange.

8. Insert the blade of a large screwdriver between the handles of the pliers and use this as a lever to tighten the drain flange.

9. Place the rubber washer on the overflow drain and install the overflow cover with the screws provided.

You may want to leave the drain linkage and pop-up assembly out of the tub until it's set in place.

Securing the tub

Follow these steps to apply mortar to the subfloor of the tub:

1. Mix a batch of mortar according to the directions.

2. With a notched trowel, spread a 2-inch-thick layer of mortar on the subfloor where the tub will be set.

3. Lift the tub in place and position it so it's tight against the walls.

Hold a carpenter's level on the tub and check that it's level. If not, adjust it with wood shims placed under the tub.

Finishing up

After the tub is level, it is secured to the enclosure to keep it that way. Secure the flange to the studs by driving 1-inch galvanized roofing nails through the holes in the flange (see Figure 10-5). If the tub is fiberglass, drill holes at each stud. If it's a steel or cast-iron tub and there are no holes or they don't align with the studs, drive the nails above the top of the flange so the head of the nail engages the flange.

Installing a platform tub

When a tub becomes the centerpiece of a bathroom retreat, it's often enclosed in a framed platform that's given a surface of tile, wood, or other finishing material. The project involves construction skills and tools to build the platform and plumbing know-how and tools to install the unit and its faucets. If you are so gifted, follow the tub manufacturer's directions for the wiring and plumbing requirements and use these guidelines for building a platform. If you prefer to sit this one out, hire a contractor. In either case, the following sections tell you what's involved.

Figure 10-5:
Securing the tub flange to the wall studs with roofing nails.

Doing the prep work

Follow the tub manufacturer suggestions and design a platform that is at least a foot wider and longer than the tub and high enough to support it. Build the framework for the platform from 2-x-4s and ¾-inch exterior grade plywood, using nails and deck screws to fasten them together. Keep in mind that the height of the platform should allow for the plywood decking plus the thickness of backerboard, thinset mortar, and tile and allow a ¼-inch expansion gap between the tub and the finish material. If you're installing a whirlpool, make an opening in the framework for an access panel for the pump and drain.

Constructing the platform for a tub isn't difficult, but it requires accurate measurements and cutting. This is a very straightforward project for a carpenter, so you may be well served by hiring out this phase of the project.

1. **Check the height of the platform that your particular tub requires and calculate the height of the platform wall studs.**

    For example, if the tub requires a 36-inch-high platform, the studs should be cut to 31¾ inches. This length allows for the thickness of the top and bottom 2-x-4 plate, the ¾-inch plywood, backerboard, mortar, and tile.

2. **Nail the studs to the top and bottom plates to form the walls for the platform.**

3. Secure the wall framework to the floor with nails, and use deck screws to cover the framework with plywood to make the deck.

4. Use a jigsaw to cut an opening in the deck for the tub, either using a template provided by the manufacturer or after carefully measuring the dimensions for the rough opening (see Figure 10-6).

Figure 10-6:
Laying out the outline of the tub so that it's centered on the deck.

5. Following the faucet manufacturer's instructions for measuring and marking the rough-in locations for supply pipes.

6. Drill the holes in the deck and then rough in the water supply and drainpipes.

Dropping in the tub

After the platform is built and the plumbing roughed in, the tub is placed in the platform. It is easier to install the whirlpool tub after you have installed the tile on the top surface of the platform, but there may not be enough room to move the large tub around the bathroom as the partitions are built. If that is the case, then install the tub before the tile. Both options are discussed here.

Follow these steps to secure the tub in the platform.

1. If the tub must be installed before the tile, apply a layer of mortar to the floor below the tub for support (following the manufacturer's directions).

1B. If the tub can be installed *after* the tile is installed on the plywood deck, apply a layer of mortar to the floor below the tub for support (follow the manufacturer's directions). The tub will rest directly on the tile and does not require wood blocks. (Proceed to Step 4.)

2. **To support the tub while the mortar sets and position it at the correct height above the bare plywood deck of the partition, place blocks of wood under the tub.**

   The wood blocks should be the thickness of the thinset mortar, backerboard, thinset mortar, and the tile, which is about 1 inch combined.

3. **Place the blocks around the edge of the cutout where the tub will be installed.**

4. **Carefully lift the tub by its rim and set it in the cutout hole, with at least one other helper guiding it slowly into the hole in the deck (see Figure 10-7).**

Figure 10-7:
Lifting the tub very carefully into position in the opening.

5 **When the mortar has set, install the drain assembly and connect the wiring to the motor and controls.**

6. **Complete the installation by finishing the surface of the deck and platform.**

   Install backerboard to the sides and top of the platform with backerboard screws (see Figure 10-8). Apply thinset mortar and install the tile or other surface material.

7. **Install the faucet on the deck of the platform. Run the riser tubes from the faucet to the rough-in water supply pipes.**

8. **Apply caulk to fill the joints between the tub and deck and between the base of the platform and the finished floor (see Figure 10-9).**

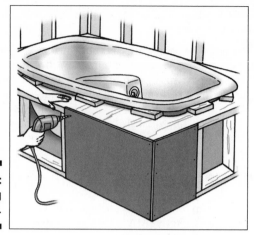

Figure 10-8:
Finishing
the platform.

Figure 10-9:
Applying
caulk to fill
the joints
between the
tub and
deck and at
the base of
the platform.

When Removing a Bathtub is Mission Impossible: Two Alternatives

When you can't remove an unattractive tub, you have two options: refinishing the surface or having a liner made to go over it. These aren't do-it-yourself options. A new tub liner, which costs about $1,000, will last longer than having a tub refinished, which can cost anywhere from $200 to $500. You can read more about these services in Chapter 7.

Of course, to complete your tub's transformation, replace the old bathtub fixtures with new ones. See the section "Flippin' over Faucets," later in this chapter, to find out more.

Reglazing

If the overall tub surface is worn or damaged, one option is having it refinished through a process of reglazing. First, the technician thoroughly scrapes the surface of the bathtub and then applies an etching solution to dull the old finish. Then the technician sands it thoroughly. A new polyurethane finish is sprayed on the surface and polished. Because of the heavy-duty sanding, this can be a messy job that sends sanding dust throughout your house.

Adding a tub liner

The second choice in covering up an old tub's surface is having a tub liner created that will exactly fit over and cover the surface of the old tub. An installer measures the old tub. Then a matching acrylic model is made, using the tub manufacturer's specifications for the contours and the exact location of plumbing cutouts. The liner is trimmed to fit, slipped over the old tub, and fastened with adhesive. You can also have matching wall panels made and installed at the same time.

Your Bathtub's Walls Inside and Out

If you're going to use an acrylic or fiberglass tub surround kit to cover up tiles, the preparation work is relatively easy. Leave the tiles in place and clean them with a random-orbit sander with 80-grit sandpaper. If a few of the tiles are loose, pry them off, and reapply them with an adhesive for ceramic tile. Then, wearing a respirator, sand the surface of all the tiles to remove any dirt and soap scum so the surround adhesive has a clean surface to adhere to. You can install the surround directly over the tiles.

Are you planning to tile the walls around your tub? From ripping out the old wall coverings to sealing the grout around the new tiles, the information in the following sections can show you how to make your tile dreams come true.

The walls come tumbling down

If the walls around the tub are spongy when you touch them or if they have mildew or structural damage, you have to replace the walls behind them before you do anything else. You have to remove the walls, dry out the area, fix the source of any leaks or dampness, and build a sound wall framework with a rot-resistant underlayment material.

To get ready to rip out damaged walls, remove all the soap, shampoo, and personal items in the bathtub area. Protect the surface of the tub by lining the tub with heavy cardboard or covering it with an old blanket. Assemble the following tools and materials, and let 'er rip!

- Cold chisel
- Hammer
- Hex wrench
- Phillips screwdriver
- Pliers
- Pry bar
- Putty knife
- Respirator
- Slotted screwdriver

Removing the faucet and spout

Turn off the water and grab your screwdriver. The hardest part of this process is figuring out where the manufacturer is hiding the screws that hold the handles in place.

1. **Look for a fastening screw in the center of the faucet to remove the handle.**

   Sometimes it is concealed by a plastic trim piece that you can pop off with the flat blade of a screwdriver.

2. **Loosen the screw with the screwdriver and remove the handle.**

3. **Look for screws that hold the trim piece and loosen them and pop the trim piece off the wall.**

4. **Use the handles of a pair of pliers to unscrew the spout by rotating it counterclockwise.**

   Some spouts require an Allen wrench to remove screws holding them in place.

Removing wall panels

If the walls are covered with plastic panels, most likely they're glued to the wall, and the cover seams and top have a trim piece of plastic that is screwed or glued in place. Here's how to get rid of the old wall panels:

1. **Use a screwdriver to remove any screws.**

2. **Beginning at the top of the panels, slide a putty knife behind the panels, trying to ease the panel away from the wall.**

   You may need to gently tap the end of the handle of the putty knife with a hammer to force it behind the panels.

3. **Work your way across the panel with the putty knife.**

   It may come off in one large piece, or it may come off in pieces, depending on the type of adhesive that was used to install it.

Removing tiles

If any of the tiles are loose, usually closest to the tub where the walls behind them may be water damaged, you need to pry them off. Just insert the rounded end of a small pry bar behind a tile and, with a hammer, gently tap the bar to force the tile to pop off the wall.

Another tactic is using a wide putty knife rather than the pry bar. Wedge it behind the tile and then tap the end of its handle with a hammer. Some tiles will pop off intact, but others will come off in chips and pieces, so wear eye protection and a dust mask for protection. To remove a tile soap dish, use a cold chisel and hammer to knock it off the wall.

Appraising the walls

After you remove the panels or tiles, look at the walls. If they're pocked with holes and gashes, you can resurface them with wallboard compound and then paint them.

If the wallboard is wet from water damage and mildew, replace it with cement backerboard before tiling. The backerboard panels are reinforced with fiberglass or are fiber-cement products and act as a rigid waterproof underlayment for tile.

Installing cement backerboard on tub walls

The ideal underlayment for ceramic tile is cement backerboard, which comes in ¼- and ½-inch-thick panels measuring 3 x 5 feet and 4 x 8 feet. The dense gray material is very heavy, so use the smaller size for replacing tub walls.

The panels are nasty to handle because of their sharp edges, so wear heavy leather gloves. Protect the surface of the tub with a heavy dropcloth.

Be prepared for a noxious odor when you cut cement backerboard. No kidding. We don't know what causes the unpleasant scent, but your dog will sit up and snarl. Wear a respirator when cutting this or any other cement-based product.

Installing cement backerboard is not on our top ten lists of fun projects because the material is difficult to handle. But working with the panels is a short-term stint compared with the long-lasting and durable surface they provide. Before you get started, have the following tools and materials handy:

- Carbide-tipped hole saw (or a jigsaw with a carbide blade)
- Carbide-tipped scoring knife
- Carpenter's level (4-foot length)
- Caulk gun
- Cement backerboard
- Electric drill/driver
- Fiberglass tape
- Galvanized backboard screws
- Silicone caulk
- Thinset mortar
- Trowel
- Wedges or shims

There's really room for only one person to stand in the tub while installing the panels, but it's useful to have a helper who measures and cuts and then hoists the panels into the tub area for installation.

Measuring the walls and panels

Follow these directions to measure and cut the panels.

1. **Measure the length and width of the middle tub wall.**

   Plan the layout of the backerboard panels to use as many full-size panels as possible. You should install the cement backerboard only as high as the top of the tile or wall panels.

2. **Score the face of the panels with a carbide-tipped scoring knife, and then hit the panel behind the score line to snap the panel (see Figure 10-10).**

3. **Cut through the fiberglass mesh on the back of the panel to separate the pieces.**

Figure 10-10:
Snapping the backer-board along the score line.

Cutting openings for plumbing

The shower valve controls and shower head must reach through the new wall. Lay out these openings carefully.

To cut openings in backerboard, follow these steps:

1. **Make a cardboard pattern of the location of the valve, spout, and possibly the shower head.**

2. **Transfer these locations to the cement backerboard, using the cardboard as a template.**

3. **Use a carbide-tipped hole saw or a jigsaw with a carbide blade to cut the openings.**

Positioning the panels on framing

Follow these steps to make sure you get your panels where you want them:

1. **Before attaching the backerboard, use the straight edge of a level to make sure that stud faces are all on the same plane.**

2. **If they're uneven, plane down any high spots.**

3. **Install blocking for future grab bars while the walls are open.**

4. **Carefully lift the backerboard panel into the tub area and set it on several shims placed about a foot apart to maintain a ¼-inch gap between the board and tub (see Figure 10-11).**

5. **Secure the panels to the wall framing with galvanized backerboard screws.**

The fasteners should be flush with the surface.

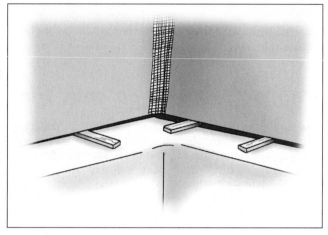

Figure 10-11:
Using wood wedges as shims to maintain a ¼-inch gap between the panels and the tub.

6. **Continue measuring and cutting panels, aligning and fitting them together with a ⅛-inch gap between panels for expansion and contraction.**

Finishing the seams

To finish the seams of the panels, follow these steps:

1. **Measure and cut to length fiberglass tape to seal the seams of the panels.**

2. **Reinforce the seams by applying thinset mortar with a trowel (see Figure 10-12).**

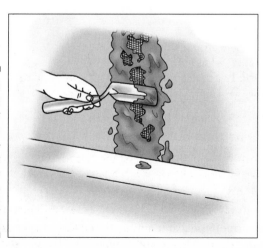

Figure 10-12:
Smoothing the mortar over the tape — quickly remove any mortar drips that fall on the tub.

Caulking the gaps

Apply a silicone caulk around the perimeter where the backerboard meets the surface of the tub.

Surrounding a tub with ceramic tile

The traditional appeal of ceramic tile makes it a good choice for covering the three walls surrounding a bathtub, and it comes in virtually any color and countless styles and designs. You can install ceramic tile directly over wallboard, plaster, or existing tile, but the best underlayment is cement backerboard. Figure on spending two days on the job: the first day to install the tile on the walls and the second day to apply the grout between them. For more about ceramic tile, see Chapter 5.

The following is a list of the tools and materials you need to have on hand to get the job done. You can rent (and sometimes borrow) most of the tools at the tile retailer or home center where you buy the tiles.

- 4-foot carpenter's level
- Ceramic tile
- Craft stick
- Grout and rubber float
- Hammer and finish nails
- Marker
- Notched trowel
- Plastic spacers
- Plumb
- Sponge
- Squeegee
- Tile adhesive
- Tile cutter
- Tile nippers
- Toothbrush
- Towels
- Tub/tile caulk

Before you get started, turn off the water supply to the tub fixtures and remove them, following the instructions in the section "Removing the old valve," later in this chapter. With the water off and fixtures removed, you're ready to tile.

Marking layout lines on the walls

The key to a professional-looking tile installation is aligning the tiles perfectly. Spend time to mark the wall with accurate horizontal and vertical layout lines (see Figure 10-13).

Figure 10-13:
Marking
layout lines.

1. **Place your carpenter's level on the back edge of the tub to determine whether the tub is perfectly level.**

   If it's not, you need to measure the first horizontal layout line from the low end of the tub. By starting the horizontal layout line at the low end of the tub, you'll be able to cut the tiles down to size as you reach the end of the tub instead of having to cut thin pieces of tile to make up for the gap between the tile and tub.

2. **Starting at the low end the tub, measure from the tub up the wall the height of a tile plus the width of a grout line plus ¼ inch for a gap between the tile and tub and make a mark on the wall.**

   For example, if you're using a standard 4¼-inch tile, this layout line should be located 4⅝ inches above the tub's edge (the size of the tile plus ¼ inch for the gap and ⅛ inch space for the grout). Adjust this measurement to fit the size of tile you plan to use.

3. **Place the top edge of the level at the mark you just made and draw a level horizontal line across the back wall.**

   Depending on the length of your level, you may have to make the line in several segments.

4. **If you're tiling only partway up the wall, mark another horizontal line to indicate where the tiles stop.**

   It's helpful to divide the wall up into smaller 3- or 4-foot sections with additional layout lines. Don't worry — the sections and lines will be covered with adhesive and the tiles.

5. **Make a plumb vertical layout line near the center of the wall to act as a reference point.**

6. **Mark the locations of any ceramic accessories, such as soap dishes or towel racks.**

Cutting tiles down to size

Use a tile cutter when it's necessary. The tool has a metal frame with an adjustable fence that holds a tile while it creates a straight even cut (see Figure 10-14). Rent or borrow a tile cutter where you buy tiles. Before you leave the store with it, ask to try it out so that you know how to operate it correctly.

Figure 10-14: Working with a tile cutter.

1. **Score the glazed surface of the tile with the cutter.**

2. **Press down on both sides of the tile to snap the tile in two pieces.**

3. **Use a carbide-tipped hole saw or drill a pilot hole and use a rod saw to make openings for the pipes leading to the faucets.**

   If the opening falls between tiles along a tile edge, you can use a tile nipper to nibble away the tile to make the opening. Don't worry if the opening isn't perfectly even, as the escutcheons will hide the cuts.

Applying tile adhesive

When you apply tile adhesive, it's important to work small sections at a time so that the adhesive doesn't skin over. Start from the center vertical line and work outward in one direction.

1. **Spread the adhesive with the smooth edge of the trowel, creating a level base for the tiles, as shown in Figure 10-15.**

   Try not to thoroughly cover the layout lines.

2. **Use the notched edge of the trowel to spread uniform ridges over the area.**

Figure 10-15: Combing tile adhesive with a trowel.

Setting the tiles in place

As you set the tiles in place, use a slight twisting motion to ensure that there is full contact between the back of the tile and the adhesive. Most ceramic wall tile has tiny spacing lugs along the four edges that automatically space the tile, creating ⅟₁₆-inch grout joints. If the tiles you use don't have spacers, or if you would like to have wider grout joints, use X-shaped plastic spacers that align the tiles and then remove them before grouting.

Insert one leg of the X-shaped spacer into whatever joint needs help. This leaves the rest of the spacer sticking out of the tile surface and easy to get a grip on for removal later.

1. **Place the first tile with one edge aligned with the center vertical layout line and in alignment with the horizontal layout line.**

2. **Working outward toward each end, set the adjoining tiles, maintaining alignment with the horizontal and vertical layout lines.**

3. **Use a tile cutter to cut the tiles at each end of the wall to fit.**

4. **Use a craft stick to scrape out any tile adhesive that gets in the grout joints or between the tile and the tub.**

5. **Let the adhesive set, usually overnight.**

Applying the grout

Follow the mixing and application directions on the grout; then follow these easy steps to apply the grout:

1. **Use a rubber float to spread the grout over the entire tiled area.** Rock the float back and forth, using the lower edge as you push up and across the tile and the upper edge as you pull down and across the tile. Make several passes, using firm pressure to make sure that the joints are packed full (see Figure 10-16).

Figure 10-16: Getting the grout into all the joints around the tiles.

2. **Using the handle of an old toothbrush, strike the tile joints to force the grout deep into the seams.**

3. **When the grout is firm, use a large damp grout sponge with rounded corners and water to wash away excess grout.**

   Rinse the sponge often (and change the water often) to get the most grout off the tile faces. If a slight haze remains on the tiles after the grout has dried, use clean towels to buff it away.

Sealing the tub and tile joint with caulk

Apply a good-quality tub/tile caulk with a caulk gun to seal and waterproof the joint at the bottom of the tile where it meets the bathtub and the corners where tile walls meet. This grout joint will crack over time. Use clear caulk that will let the color of the underlying grout show through.

Adding a Tub Door

Tired of dealing with a shower curtain that never quite contains the shower spray and develops an unpleasant mildew stain on its bottom corner? Instead of replacing the curtain, add a tub door. The installation is a no-brainer. It involves measuring and cutting the top and bottom horizontal tracks to the appropriate width of your tub, fastening the tracks to the sides of the tub wall, and mounting the door panels in the tracks.

Getting started

Remove all your personal toiletries, soaps, and rubber ducky from the tub and thoroughly clean the tub walls and surfaces around it.

Take a look at the parts of the door assembly and identify the frame and track and hardware. Set the door panels aside and lay out the parts as you read the installation instructions supplied by the manufacturer. Most of them are installed in the same way.

Gather up the following tools, and you'll be ready to go:

- Carpenter's level
- Caulking gun
- Center punch
- Electric drill and bit
- Fine file
- Hacksaw
- Hammer
- Masking tape
- Masonry bit for ceramic tile
- Measuring tape
- Phillips screwdriver
- Pliers
- Safety glasses
- Silicone caulk
- Slotted screwdriver

Door to door from start to finish

The few hours it takes to install a tub door will provide years of useful service and good looks in the bathroom. The following sections tell you how to get the job done.

Measuring and cutting the bottom track

The bottom track supplied by the manufacturer is longer than needed for most applications to allow the door to be installed in a variety of enclosures. This track usually must be cut slightly shorter than the width of the opening to accommodate the side jambs. As always, read the manufacturer's installation directions carefully before you do anything; then follow these steps:

1. **Use a measuring tape to find the distance from wall to wall along the top edge of the tub.**

2. **Follow the manufacturer's directions and subtract the thickness of the side jamb from the total width of the opening.**

3. **Cut the bottom track to this length and smooth any rough edges at the cut end with a file.**

   Use a hacksaw and a miter box to assure a square cut. A block of scrap wood in the track helps keep the track square while you cut it.

Locating the bottom track

The bottom track is installed on the top edge of the tub.

1. **Place the bottom track on the flattest part of the tub ledge, following the manufacturer's instructions to determine which side of the track faces out.**

   Make sure that the space between the wall and the ends of the track is the same on both ends.

2. **Temporarily fasten the track to the ledge with masking tape.**

3. **Make a pencil mark on the tub along the front edge of the track.**

Locating the wall jambs

The wall jambs are fastened to the tub surround and support the top track that the doors hang from. Ideally, you will screw the wall jambs directly to the studs. You can also use sturdy metal anchors to secure the jambs.

1. **Place a wall jamb against the wall and push it down over the end of the bottom track so it's fully engaged with the track.**

2. **Hold a carpenter's level next to the wall jamb and adjust it to be plumb.**

3. **Make a mark in the hole locations.**

4. **Remove the wall jamb and drill the holes with a $\frac{3}{16}$-inch bit for the mounting screws or wall anchors.**

   If you're drilling into ceramic tile, use a masonry drill bit.

5. **Repeat the drilling in the opposite wall for the other wall jamb.**

Caulking the bottom track

Lift the bottom track and apply a bead of silicone caulk into the groove on the underside of the track. Then reposition the bottom track into its proper place.

Installing the wall jambs

Work on one wall jamb at a time.

1. **Place one wall jamb into or over the bottom track (depending on the design). Then align the holes in the wall jamb with the holes in the wall (see Figure 10-17).**

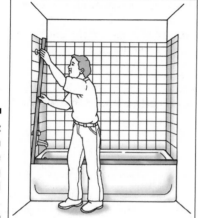

Figure 10-17:
Don't get in a jam while installing the wall jambs.

2. **Secure the jamb with the screws supplied by the manufacturer or the anchor.**

   The door kit should include rubber bumpers. Install them over the screws at the top and bottom of the jamb.

3. **Repeat the installation on the other jamb.**

Installing the top track

The top track must be cut to length like the bottom track. Follow the manufacturer's directions; they state how much allowance must be made for clearance. The distance from wall to wall may be different at the top than it is on the bottom, so be sure to measure carefully.

1. **Use a measuring tape to find the distance from wall to wall.**

2. **Cut the top track slightly smaller than the distance measured according to manufacturer's directions.**

3. **Smooth any rough edges at the cut end with a file.**

Installing the hardware on the door panels

Place the rollers on the top frame flange of both door panels and secure them with lock washers and machine screws.

Positioning the door panels

Positioning the door panels is easiest from outside the shower.

1. **Install the inside panel first by lifting it up inside the top track and hanging the rollers on the inside rail of the top track.**

2. **Align the inside panel with the wall jamb.**

3. **Install the outside panel by lifting it up inside the top track and hanging the rollers on the outside rail of the top track.**

Each manufacturer has a unique method of securing the sliding panels in the track. Follow the installation directions provided.

Finishing up with caulk

Apply a bead of caulk where the jambs and wall meet and where the bottom track and wall jamb are joined.

Flippin' over Faucets

If you think that choosing the name for your firstborn child was difficult, just wait until you see the choices you're confronted with when choosing a faucet for your bathtub. There are three basic types of faucets for wall-mounted installation:

✔ A single-handle tub faucet has one valve that controls the water flow and temperature. The flow of water goes to the tub spout or a shower head via a diverter.

✔ A two-handle tub faucet has one hot and one cold water control, which both flow into a mixing chamber and then through the spout. If there is a shower, a diverter directs the flow of the mixed water.

✔ A three-handle tub and shower faucet has one handle for hot water, another for cold water, and a third handle for the diverter that directs water to the tub spout or the shower head.

If you're considering a deck-mounted faucet, there are basically two types of spouts:

✔ **A bath-mount installation** mounts directly to the rim of the fixture. Acrylic or fiberglass composite baths can be drilled to accept this faucet. Some faucets are designed by the tub manufacturer to go with the tub.

✔ **A deck-mount installation** features a longer spout that reaches over the bath rim, making its placement more flexible. Because a cast-iron bath is difficult to drill, a deck-mount faucet is the best choice.

Wall-mount faucets and adapter kits are also available to convert some deck-mount units to wall mount for baths and whirlpools.

You can also choose between single controls, dual controls, lever handles, push-up levers, and pull-down levers, just to name a few. The finishes include chrome, nickel, bronze, and brass that is brushed, satin, or polished. You can choose from colorful, practical, or luxurious finishes that resist corrosion and tarnishing, and many offer a lifetime warranty. The styles of faucets range from sleek contemporary to traditional brass. Many manufacturers make it easy to choose by putting together a collection or suite of faucets and their fixtures.

Whether you're installing a new tub faucet or replacing one, the same process is involved. The job is doable by a gifted do-it-yourselfer. The challenge is not in the plumbing work; the challenge is getting access to the valve behind the faucet without destroying the wall that covers it up.

The ideal time for replacing a tub faucet and valve is when you're rebuilding the walls surrounding the bathtub, because the plumbing is exposed at that time.

If you're replacing a single-handle tub and shower valve with a large-diameter trim cover, the job is easier. When you remove this cover, also called an *escutcheon,* you'll expose the valve body, and you usually have enough room to work on the valve through this opening.

Even if you have access to the old valve behind the wall, consider the type of pipes that are supplying water to the valve before you decide to do this yourself. If the valve is installed with plastic or copper pipes, they're relatively easy to work with; if not, heed the warning. If the old valve is hooked up to galvanized pipes without pipe unions, you must cut the pipes to remove the valve. Working on old galvanized pipes requires special tools and skills. To install the new valve, you then must thread the ends of the old pipe and use a dielectric fitting when connecting galvanized pipes to copper to prevent galvanic action. Leave this project to the plumber.

If you decide to tackle this job, you can rent the necessary tools.

Removing the old valve

If there are no shut-off valves for the tub/shower, turning off the water supply to the whole house is necessary. If there is a shut-off valve for the tub/shower, turn it off. Then lay down a heavy dropcloth, blanket, or heavy cardboard from a shipping box to protect the bottom of the tub while you work on the faucet and valve. You may need to reach the valve via an access panel, so protect the floor around it in the same way.

Removing the old valve requires the following tools:

- Groove-joint pliers
- Hacksaw or reciprocating saw
- Hammer
- Pipe wrenches (2)
- Screwdriver

For the first part of this project, you work on the bathtub side of the plumbing wall that contains the faucet and valve. Then you complete the job by working at the other side of the wall. Before you get started, open the valve and let the water drain out to empty the pipes.

Taking off the handles, spout, and shower head

Faucet designers don't like to show the screws that hold the handles in place, so many are hidden behind covers. If the screws aren't obvious in the center of the handle, they're under the cover. Most spouts just unscrew, but some may be held in place by a setscrew. Shower heads unscrew from the pipe leading out of the wall.

1. **Standing in the bathtub, use a screwdriver to remove the screws holding the handles to the valve stems.**

   You may have to look under the cover to find the screws.

2. **Pull the handles off the valve stems.**

   They may be difficult to remove if the handle shows signs of corrosion. Squirt some WD-40 into the screw hold and wait a bit for the handles to loosen before removing them.

   Some older faucets have a diverter handle to direct water to the shower. Remove it in the same way as the other handles.

3. **Remove the spout by placing the handle of a large screwdriver into the opening in the end of the spout and turning counterclockwise to unscrew the spout.**

   Some spouts, especially plastic ones, may have setscrews holding them in place. If so, loosen the setscrew with a hex wrench and twist off the spout.

4. **Remove the shower head by gripping its body with a groove-joint pliers and turning it in a counterclockwise direction to unscrew it from the pipe coming out of the wall.**

Freeing the valve body from the pipes

Working on the other side of the wall, free the old valve from the existing pipes. This is easy if unions are connecting the valve to the hot and cold water supply lines. But if the valve doesn't have unions, then the pipes must be cut to free the valve.

1. **Loosen the pipe union with two pipe wrenches.**

   Place one wrench on the pipe and the other on the union. Then push and pull the wrenches in opposing directions.

2. **If you have copper or plastic pipes or galvanized pipes without a union connection, use a reciprocating saw to cut the pipes a foot below the valve (see Figure 10-18).**

   Cut carefully so you have a clean, square end to solder the new valve to. You can also use a hacksaw to do this job.

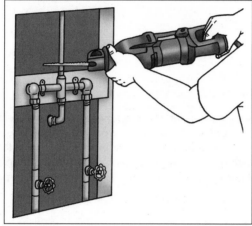

Figure 10-18: A reciprocating saw with a metal cutting blade is handy when cutting pipes.

3. **Remove the valve body from the wall by using a hammer to remove the nails holding the pipe straps in place.**

4. **Pull the valve body out of the wall.**

   Save the pipe that leads to the shower head so you can reuse it.

Installing a replacement valve

The type of valve you removed determines the style of replacement valve unless you're going to change the wall. If the old valve has two handles, the distance between the handles of the new valve must match the old valve, or you must change the openings in the wall. Also, pressure-balancing shower valves are usually one-handled. Many require changing the wall if the old valve was two-handled.

Some valve faucet combinations require threaded fittings, and some have the supply pipes soldered directly into the valve. Most faucet valve sets also serve a shower.

Most valves come with specific installation instructions, which are important to follow exactly. Think of installing the new valve as reversing the process you use to remove it. Here's a list of the tools you'll need to install the replacement valve:

✔ Fittings

✔ Marking pen

✔ Pipe dope (pipe joint sealer)

✔ Pipe reamer, file, or sandpaper

✔ Pipe wrench

✔ Propane torch

✔ Screwdriver

✔ Solder and flux

✔ Valve

A transition fitting allows you to connect copper pipe to galvanized pipe. So if you have a propane torch and a tubing cutter, working with copper pipe isn't difficult. Also, several transition fittings are available in copper, plastic, and galvanized steel designed for attaching different piping systems to a new valve. Check your local building code to make sure that you use approved materials.

Dry-fitting for practice

Before you begin to install the valve, familiarize yourself with the valve parts and check that the valve fits the existing openings in your wall.

1. **Remove the hardware from the packaging.**

2. **Dry-fit it with the valve in the opening in the wall.**

   Hold the valve stem body in place and check to see that it will fit. If the space is too tight to work in, you may have to enlarge the opening in the wall.

Attaching the transition fittings to the old piping

Visit your local home center or hardware store to purchase a transitional fitting that adapts the end of the existing pipe to copper. The counter person should be able to suggest the proper type of fitting for your pipes. If you have galvanized pipe, use a dielectric fitting that prevents electrolysis between the steel and copper.

Install the transition fittings on the ends of the old hot and cold water pipes.

Old galvanized pipes are difficult to work with and require special tools to cut threads on the end of the pipe. Unless you've worked with this material before, you're better off calling in a plumber to install the valve. You have completed a large portion of the project, so the plumber's bill won't be too steep.

Connecting the piping to the valve

The ends of the existing pipes must be connected to the valve body by short pieces of new piping.

1. **Begin at the transition fitting and cut and fit new sections of copper pipe for the hot and cold supply pipe to the new valve.**

2. **Disassemble the new sections of pipes and clean the ends of the pipes with sandpaper or emery cloth and the inside of the fittings with a wire brush or sandpaper.**

3. **Apply flux to the ends of the pipe and inside the fittings to clean them and ensure that the solder will flow into the joint.**

4. **Reassemble the pipes.**

5. **Apply heat to the fittings — not the pipe. When the fitting gets hot, the solder will begin to melt and flow into the fitting.**

   Allow the fittings to cool.

Installing the tub spout

Read the installation instructions to find the size, type, and length for the pipe leading from the valve to the tub spout. Depending on the valve, you could be required to use either copper or a combination of copper and a short section of galvanized pipe.

If you're using galvanized pipe, apply pipe dope to the threads and install the pipe with a pipe wrench. Otherwise, cut and install new copper piping and solder it in place.

Finding the shower riser pipe and installing it

The supply pipe attached to the top of the valve is the shower riser. In some cases, you may have to use the old pipe if you can't get it out of the wall.

1. **Measure the distance from the top of the new valve to the opening in the wall where the shower came out.**

   If there is little room, use the old riser, if possible. You can use a pipe union to join the old pipe to a short section of new pipe. If the old pipe is galvanized steel, the end must be threaded, which is why galvanized pipes are best handled by a plumber.

2. **Cut a new section of pipe and solder an elbow to the top of the pipe.**

3. Push the pipe into the wall, aligning the elbow with the opening in the shower wall, and solder the lower end to the valve.

   To make sure that the elbow is properly aligned with the wall opening, insert the nipple for the shower head through the wall and thread it into the elbow. Then check that the pipe coming out of the wall is straight before you solder the shower riser pipe to the valve.

4. Nail a piece of wood between the wall studs to support the elbow at the top of the riser pipe and screw the elbow to the brace.

Installing the handles and trim and testing for leaks

The final step is to install the trim and handles and turn on the water.

1. Follow the installation instructions to assemble the escutcheons and handles.

2. Test-fit the valve by turning the water back on at the main shut-off valve.

3. When the water flows out of the tub spout, turn off the water.

4. Inspect the joints between the valve and the new piping, looking for leaks.

5. Turn on the water and start the shower.

6. Check for a leak in the pipes leading to the spout and the shower head.

Chapter 11

Showered with Possibilities

Are you a showerhead? You know what we mean. Nothing gives you greater pleasure than standing in a shower with an invigorating spray of water that lets you shut out the world. There's no other place where you have such profound thoughts and insights than when mesmerized by the steady stream of refreshing water. If that's you, get ready for some major life choices when selecting a shower for your bathroom. Sure, you'll find the basic enclosure in all shapes and sizes, but you'll also discover shower rooms and systems with body sprays and jets designed to pamper and massage, faucets and fixtures that range from simple showerheads to panels with body sprays and jets, and shower environments with lighting and audiovisual equipment. All these elements let you adjust water intensity and coverage, from relaxing to invigorating, to create a shower that's custom made for you.

Creating a shower oasis is not as difficult as you may think. In this chapter, we show you how to choose the shower that meets your space requirements and offers the options you want, and we show you how to install it, too.

Standing Room Only: Selecting a Shower Unit

Today's showers range from basic shower enclosures to custom-designed systems that stand alone as the centerpiece of a bathroom. You can see examples of some of these not-so-ordinary showers in the color insert. The custom units are best installed by a bathroom design firm and their fabricators, because they're familiar with installing those systems. But if you want to install a shower unit yourself, consider a fiberglass or acrylic enclosure or a glass block system, both designed for do-it-yourself installations that we explain later in this chapter.

The two things that determine the size and shape of a shower unit are the floor space where it will be installed and the features you want it to perform. In a large master bathroom suite, you may have plenty of room for a separate shower and bathtub, but in a small guest bathroom, a corner unit, called a neo-angle unit, may be the only thing that will fit. Refer to the basics of laying out a floor plan in Chapter 2 and use your bathroom dimensions as your guide.

Most manufacturers have the size and specifications for their shower units on their Web sites, so the Internet is a good starting point. But to test-drive a shower unit, go to a bathroom design showroom or home center where you can walk in, move around in, and actually see how you fit in the space. Another option is to check out the showers when you spend the night with friends or relatives. If they have a shower you like, step inside to see if it feels right and then measure its size to see whether it will fit in your new bathroom. The more opportunities you have to test-fit a shower, the more likely you'll choose a style and size you'll enjoy for years to come. Try them on for size, but no singing in the shower.

Shower surrounds and enclosures

The most typical units are made of fiberglass and acrylic and come in one, three, or four pieces made up of wall surrounds, some of which include a receptor or floor pan that you stand on. The multipiece designs let one person bring the unit into a house in sections, so it's handy for a do-it-yourselfer to maneuver through the rooms. These units are installed in place, and then the joints are sealed with caulk. Some shower units have wall components with a tongue-and-groove interlocking system that eliminates the need for caulk.

The advantage of a one-piece unit is there are no joints — translated: no caulking required — so there are no openings where mold can grow. However, getting a large one-piecer inside a house requires a wide access or an open wall or window, so it isn't the unit of choice to transport into a tight space or up a narrow stairway.

You can use one of these enclosures as a stand-alone shower in a wall recess or as a free-standing unit. When a tub and shower are both included in a bathroom design, the shower and bathtub often are back to back to take advantage of running the plumbing lines next to each other.

Glass block systems

For years, glass block has been used in bathroom windows to provide privacy because it distorts light shining through it. Today, glass block and acrylic block provide a stylish and symmetrical appearance as shower walls, creating a new high-tech look and appeal. The transparent quality of glass block makes it a good choice for transforming a dark bathroom into one with lightness and visual interest. You can use glass block as part of a custom shower wall treatment framed in wood or choose a block system designed for do-it-yourselfers to create walk-in, rounded wall, and classic style showers.

Acrylic block looks just like the original glass block, but it's much lighter. In some cases, this may be an important factor to consider if you're planning a bath-remodeling project for the second floor. In any case, both glass and acrylic block are available in kits and prefabricated modules to fit just about any project.

Installing a Shower Enclosure

A shower enclosure makes good use of a small space, because it takes up limited floor space in even the smallest bathroom. For the installation to be a success, spend some time upfront planning the project and assessing any groundwork that's needed.

Laying the groundwork

Before you begin installing a shower enclosure, you need to address a couple of points. First, the shower requires a wood framing to support the walls of the enclosure (see Figure 11-1). If the shower is placed in a corner only, fewer walls must be constructed. In either case, the manufacturer will supply a layout plan for the enclosure. Follow it carefully. The wall studs are usually placed closer together than on a standard wall.

Figure 11-1:
Non-bearing partition walls support the shower stall wall panels.

One advantage to installing this type of shower enclosure is that the wall panels are mounted directly to the wall studs, so drywall or backerboard isn't necessary. Before the shower stall is installed, you can plan ahead and install wood backing for grab bars. Consult the manufacturer's installation instructions to find out the type of backing that is needed to support a grab bar. In most cases, solid backing of 2-x-6 lumber nailed between the wall studs is required.

Second, you'll want to hire a plumber to install the rough-in plumbing. The shower enclosure requires a 2-inch drain centered in the enclosure. The rough-in dimensions give the exact measurements for its location. Unless you're experienced with plumbing, this part of the project is best left to a professional plumber. Have the plumber also install the drain fittings in the shower receptor that meet the local plumbing code requirements.

Installing a shower enclosure

To install a shower enclosure, you need these materials:

- 2-x-4s or 2-x-6s
- 2-inch masking tape
- Carpenter's square
- Dropcloth
- Electric drill
- Hammer
- Hole saw or jigsaw with fine-tooth blade (32 teeth per inch)
- Large-head nails

✔ Level

✔ Measuring tape

✔ Pliers

✔ Putty knife

✔ Safety glasses

✔ Screwdrivers

✔ Silicone sealant (for shower door installation)

✔ Utility knife

✔ Woodworking tools

Follow these instructions to install a shower enclosure.

1. **Open the packaging and identify all the parts and components of the enclosure.**

2. **Place the shower receptor in the enclosure and check that it's level and doesn't rock back and forth.**

   You may have to install shims under the receptor. Put the necessary shims in place and retest the level of the shower. When the surface is solid, remove the shims one at a time, apply construction adhesive to them, and replace them.

3. **Use galvanized roofing nails to secure the receptor to the wall framing (see Figure 11-2).**

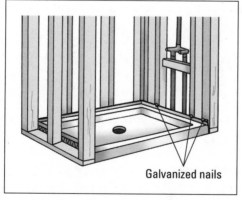

Figure 11-2: The shower receptor is secured to the framing with galvanized nails.

Galvanized nails

Follow the manufacturer's recommendation and drive the nails through the predrilled flange holes or place the nail against the top of the flange so that the head of the nail catches the flange.

4. **Position the panels in the enclosure.**

   Some kits have wall panels that interlock with one another to form water-tight seals. In this case, follow the manufacturer's directions and position the panels in the enclosure in the proper sequence so they can interlock.

5. **Check that the panels fit snugly against the wall framing.**

   The panel at the shower valve end of the enclosure can't be placed against the studs yet because of the rough-in plumbing.

6. **Mark the location of the shower valve and shower riser pipe by making a cardboard template of the location of the valve and shower head pipe.**

7. **Place the template on the shower enclosure panel and drill a pilot hole at the center of the cutout to guide the hole saw.**

   Use a hole saw or jigsaw with a fine-tooth saw blade to make the holes for the valve controls and the shower head pipe.

8. **Install the shower wall panel on which the valve is located.**

   Check that all panels are properly aligned and square and the shower valve and shower head pipe are properly aligned.

9. **Fasten the panels to the wall framing with galvanized roofing nails (see Figure 11-3).**

   Whenever there is a gap between the wall stud and the shower wall panel, insert a wood shim before driving the nail.

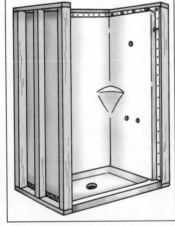

Figure 11-3:
Fasten the wall to the wall studs with galvanized nails; shim where necessary.

10. **Apply silicone caulk to all joints in the enclosure.**

    Follow the manufacturer's instructions and use a top-quality caulk.

Installing a Glass Block System

If you liked working with building blocks or LEGOs as a kid, you'll enjoy building a glass block shower, because all the pieces fit together to create a dramatic new shower room. Gather the material and tools together so you can make progress through the building process.

To install a glass block shower kit, you need the following:

- Bucket
- Carpenter's level
- Drill
- Drill bits
- Glass block shower enclosure kit
- Margin trowel
- Masking tape
- Mineral spirits
- Mortar or plaster mix
- Paintbrush
- Rubber gloves
- Safety glasses and respirator (for mixing mortar)
- Silicone sealant
- Slotted screwdriver
- Tape measure
- Tin snips

The directions in the following sections are for installing a walk-in shower block enclosure kit. The receptor and drain are best installed by a professional. If the plumbing is already in place, you can install the pan, but hire a plumber to connect the shower pan to the drain.

Preparing the subfloor

The shower receptor base requires a bed of mortar or plaster mix placed under it for proper support.

1. **Apply mortar on the subfloor 2 inches thick in a 12-inch-x-12-inch grid pattern the full length and width of the shower base.**

   Be sure that the grid extends under the vertical support board of the curb.

2. **Use a carpenter's square to level the shower base around the perimeter.**

   Avoid standing in or loading the base until the mortar has set.

Installing the shower base

Follow these directions for installing the receptor or the floor of the shower.

1. **Sand a 4-inch-wide area along the top of the acrylic shower pan's curb with 80-grit abrasive paper.**

2. **Drill two $\frac{3}{16}$-inch-diameter pilot holes in the curb for attaching each of the metal panel anchors.**

3. **Mix three parts of the primer with one part water.**

4. **Brush the diluted primer onto the area you just sanded.**

5. **After the primer becomes tacky (3 to 5 minutes), predrill the curb that the block rests on and fasten the metal panel anchors to the shower pan with 2-inch screws and washers.**

   Note that the first anchor is 10 inches from the wall.

Building the glass enclosure

When you're ready to build the glass walls, follow these steps:

1. **While the primer is still sticky, apply a $\frac{1}{4}$-inch bed of glass block mortar to the curb with a small trowel.**

2. **Place the $\frac{3}{8}$-inch-thick foam expansion strip between the first block and the shower wall.**

3. **Place a 4-x-8-inch block against the shower wall and use the trowel handle to tap it down into the mortar.**

4. **Next to the block against the wall, begin laying 6-x-8-inch blocks, placing the panel anchors between the vertical mortar joints (see Figure 11-4).**

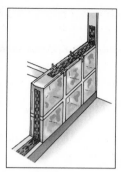

Figure 11-4:
The metal panel anchors hold the glass block to the wall and shower pan.

The combination of 4-x-8 and 6-x-8 blocks gives the proper spacing so the end of the wall aligns with the end of the curb molded in the shower pan. Repeat every other row of block, using reinforcing mesh. Check that each block is plumb with the level.

5. **Place spacers between the blocks to ensure consistent, evenly spaced mortar joints (see Figure 11-5).**

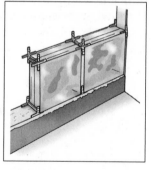

Figure 11-5:
Spacers help maintain even mortar joints between the blocks.

6. **Install reinforcing in the last vertical joint of the straight section just before starting the curved section.**

7. **Form the curved section of the shower by laying four consecutive curved glass blocks using spacers.**

8. **Put an end block that has a rounded corner (to give the wall a finished look) at the ends of the walls.**

9. **Install a second row of blocks.**

   As you install the blocks on a mortar bed, use the level to ensure the wall is straight and level.

10. **Tie the glass block to the shower wall with metal panel anchors placed on every other row of blocks.**

    Apply mortar to the block and then place the anchors on the glass block and secure the anchor to the wall stud with several screws. If there is no wall stud behind the anchor, use wall anchors.

11. **Install metal horizontal reinforcing strips on tops of the blocks to hold them together.**

    Cut the inner edge of the metal reinforcing strips so they can be bent to follow the curve of the wall.

12. **After you finish the fifth or sixth row of blocks of the curved wall, begin the short straight wall.**

13. **Repeat Steps 1 through 6 and 9 through 11, but no curved blocks are used in this wall.**

14. **After laying the final course, and before the mortar stiffens up, check the walls one last time to make sure they're vertical.**

15. **After the mortar has fully cured, fill the joint between the wall and the glass block with clear silicone sealant.**

16. **Put on a rubber glove and wipe the silicone with your finger dipped in mineral spirits to smooth it for a finished professional look.**

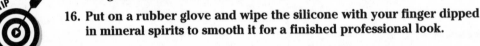

Adding accessibility to your shower

Shower units that comply with the Americans with Disabilities Act (ADA) are designed for people with limited physical abilities or those confined to a wheelchair. The key to their design is a low threshold so that you can enter them without an obstacle or so that a wheelchair can be rolled into them. These showers are usually one-piece units with integral grab bars and a built-in or fold-up seat. A person in a wheelchair should be able to roll up next to the shower unit, adjust the controls to the right water temperature from the outside, and then use grab bars to transfer to the seat inside the shower unit. The faucet control should be a single-lever handle and include a hand shower that can be operated by someone seated or standing.

You're not going to find too many examples of ADA-compliant shower units at retailers, but you can find them featured on manufacturers' Web sites, such as Kohler.com (www.kohler.com). Use Kohler's search boxes to refine the search by specifying "ADA compliant," and you'll narrow the selection. The sites also have the cost of the units, installation requirements, specifications, rough-in dimensions, and the actual installation manuals — all valuable planning material.

Hanging a shower curtain rod on tile

The biggest challenge to installing anything (shower door track, towel bar, or curtain rod) in a bathroom with ceramic tile is making a hole in the tile without cracking it. The job is easy, however, if you have a masonry bit and a roll of masking tape.

Place the bracket for whatever you're installing in position and mark its general area on the tile.

Then place a couple of strips of masking tape over the area. Place the bracket in the exact position and mark the location of the mounting screws on the tape with a felt pen. Then drill through the tape. The masking tape will keep the drill from moving off the mark until the bit starts penetrating the tile.

Installing a Shower Door

The clean lines of a shower door give a streamlined look in a bathroom. The panels come in a range of clear to opaque glass with patterns and styles that match just about any decor. The components include the door, a bottom track, wall and strike jambs, hinge and jamb, seals, and a single or double panel. There's also an array of end caps, anchors, and screw covers to be assembled.

Shower doors are sold as separate items, usually not a part of an enclosure kit. They protect the room and floor from water spray — a more permanent barrier than a shower curtain. Carefully read the installation instructions for the type of door you choose and identify all the parts and components. You can find basic door installation instructions in Chapter 10.

Fixtures and Faucets for a Shower

With the right fixtures, you can take the fine art of showering to new heights. New bathroom technology allows you more control of the temperature and volume of the shower spray from a single shower head. You can install an elaborate system of sprays, jets, faucets, and valves that converts a simple shower to a home spa.

When selecting these components, first consider what you like and don't like about your existing shower. Have you noticed an especially comforting shower head in a hotel? If so, think about what feature you enjoyed so that you can include it in your new shower. Use this criteria as a baseline when looking at fixtures and faucets that will make the shower as basic or luxurious as you want.

To design your own shower spa, go to the Moen Web site (www.moen.com) and use its "Design your own vertical spa" feature. You choose the style of shower and then decide which components you'd like, such as a small body spray or a hand shower on a slide bar, and where you'd like them placed. You can come away with a printout of the customized shower you created.

Replacing a shower valve

Whether you're installing a shower valve or replacing an old unit, the process is the same. The biggest difference is that you have better access to the valve during new construction because the walls are open. In either case, the job is straightforward as long as you're working with copper or plastic pipes.

If you have an older house with galvanized steel pipes, you're better off calling in the pros who have the specialized tools to cut and thread this type of pipe.

Most of the newer shower valves install the same way. This project illustrates the basic steps to rough in a shower valve, which is unique in that it has additional water jets in the valve assembly and an oversize opening that makes replacing an old shower valve easier. The jets not only tickle your middle with water, but for remodeling purposes, they're covered by a larger-than-normal escutcheon plate. The escutcheon conceals the control handle and jets, and allows you to cut a large opening in the wall.

The particular shower valve you choose may not be exactly like this unit, but the installation is basically the same. Manufacturers include installation instructions with their units along with the rough-in dimensions.

To replace a shower valve, you need these materials:

- Emery cloth
- Flux (to coat copper joints when soldering)
- Hand saw, jigsaw, or spiral-cut saw
- Pliers
- Propane torch
- Putty knife
- Screwdriver
- Shower valve
- Solder or plastic pipe cement

Follow these steps to install a new shower valve. When you're replacing an old shower valve, rather than installing a new one, do Step 1 and then jump to Step 9.

1. **Turn off the water.**

2. **Remove the escutcheon from the existing valve.**

   Take off the control handle first. Then remove the screws holding the plate against the wall. If the escutcheon was installed with caulk, score it with a utility knife. Try to avoid scratching tile you plan to leave in place.

3. **Use the template provided by the manufacturer or the escutcheon plate from the new valve to locate the position of the new hole in the wall.**

   If there is no template trace around the escutcheon, use a pencil to make a new line about ½ inch inside the escutcheon profile line (see Figure 11-6).

Figure 11-6:
Use the escutcheon as a template to position and cut the hole to access the pipes.

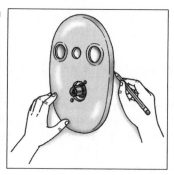

4. **Use a hand saw, jigsaw, or spiral-cut saw (see Figure 11-7) to cut the opening in the wall for the new valve by following the outline of the cover plate.**

   Carefully check inside a wall for the location of the existing pipes before you cut into it. To get a good view, shine a flashlight on the hole as you hold a small mirror in the hole. Look for electrical lines and water and vent pipes that may be in the way.

Figure 11-7:
You can use a spiral-cut saw to cut the opening for the valve.

5. If the old pipes are copper, unsolder the valve body from the water pipes.

6. Heat the valve close to the pipe, gripping the valve body with pliers.

7. As the solder melts, twist the valve body and pull it off the pipe. Do the same for the remaining pipes.

   Wear leather gloves because the copper will be hot.

   Plastic pipes can't be removed from the valve body and must be cut. Use a hacksaw to cut them as close to the valve body as possible.

8. The new valve requires support. If no blocking is behind the old valve, cut a 2-x-4 and insert it between the wall studs behind the valve.

   Check the roughing-in dimensions for your particular valve and adjust the position of the support so that the valve protrudes the proper distance from the wall.

9. To connect the valve to the water supply pipes, first clean the ends and inside of the pipes with flux.

   Clean the end of the pipe with emery cloth and then use a wire brush to clean inside the fitting. Apply the flux to the outside of the pipe and the inside of the fitting. Flux prevents oxidation, helping the solder form a good bond.

10. Insert supply pipes into the valve body.

11. Consult the instructions for the lengths of the supply piping that leads to the water jet assembly.

12. Cut, clean, and flux these fittings, and then cut the shower riser to length and insert it into the assembly.

13. Check alignment and then solder the unit together (see Figure 11-8).

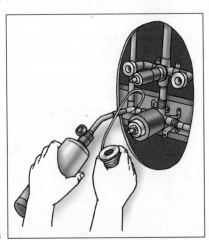

Figure 11-8:
Solder the water supply pipes to the valve body.

14. **Test the unit for leaks.**

    If this is a new installation, screw a ½-inch galvanized plug into the shower head pipe so you can test the unit for leaks without the shower sprinkling water all over the place.

15. **If the tub or shower is already in place, install the shower head.**

16. **Turn on the water and check for leaks.**

    If there are leaks, turn off the water, drain the valve, and resolder or glue the leaking joint.

17. **Install the escutcheon and control handles (see Figure 11-9).**

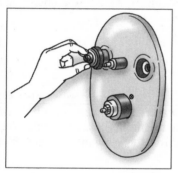

Figure 11-9: Installing the escutcheon plate and control handles.

Adding a hand shower bar

A hand shower is an easily accessible bathing aid that massages sore muscles with a spray of soothing warm water. Even the challenging task of bathing small children or large dogs can be easily handled with a self-directed hand shower. And for the more mundane chore of scrubbing and cleaning a tub and shower, it makes short work of rinsing off cleanser.

If the existing shower head is an old unit with the pivot ball as part of the shower arm, the arm needs to be replaced first, so that adds to the time and cost.

Most hand shower bars come with screws and anchors for a shower with tile walls. If your shower is fiberglass or acrylic, contact the manufacturer for what's required.

To install a shower bar, you need the following materials:

- ✓ ¼-inch masonry bit
- ✓ Adjustable wrench
- ✓ Electric drill

✔ Shower wall bar

✔ Silicone caulk or sealant

✔ Teflon thread tape

Follow these steps to install a shower bar:

1. **Hold the shower arm and remove the existing shower head by turning it counterclockwise with an adjustable wrench.**

2. **Thoroughly clean the threads on the existing shower arm.**

3. **Remove the decorative screw covers from the wall bar end pieces.**

4. **Position the bar so that the hand shower may be adjusted at a convenient height for household members.**

   Use a level to check that the bar is plumb.

5. **Mark the location of the mounting holes on the wall with a carpenter's level.**

   Be careful to not locate the wall bar directly underneath the shower arm and above the shower valve. A water line may be located there and may be damaged while you're drilling the mounting holes. If there is one, remove the access panel behind the shower valve and check the actual location of the pipes.

6. **Drill holes through the shower wall and install the anchors.**

7. **Use silicone caulk to seal the opening around the anchors.**

8. **Install the wall bar, using the hardware (screws and metal washers) that came with the wall bar.**

9. **Reinstall the decorative screw covers.**

10. **Wrap the shower arm threads with two or three layers of Teflon thread tape.**

11. **Screw the backflow preventer to the shower arm and then wrap its threads with thread tape.**

12. **Feed the hose through the hand shower holder.**

13. **Lower the hand shower until the hose end is seated firmly in the holder.**

Installing Grab Bars

Getting in and out of a shower isn't always easy even when you're fit and able, but if you have a sore knee or a sprained ankle, you may find it nearly impossible to safely maneuver without a secure handle. To prevent an accident, install a vertical grab bar inside a shower 18 to 24 inches from the shower head end for safe entry and exit. If you're installing a grab bar for someone with an injury or disability, get input from that person to decide the best location.

Inside a bathtub enclosure, position a grab bar horizontally, approximately 36 inches from the bottom of the tub, so that a bather can use the bar to help raise himself from sitting in the tub. For stepping into and out of a tub, consider installing a vertical bar at the tub edge as a convenient handhold as well.

Grab bars have prevented accidents, but the early ones didn't do much for the aesthetics of a bathroom. Today's grab bars are featured in the finest bathrooms of the plushest hotel suites, have evolved, and come in finishes and colors that make them much more appealing. Don't be tempted to buy a cheap one. Get the best quality you can afford and install it either with a blind fastening system or with blocking in the wall.

A new blind fastener, the WingIts system, can be used directly on wallboard without needing an attachment to structural support. The anchors flare out behind the wall to hold firmly (see Figure 11-10). The fastener should be installed only on a sound wall made of ⅝-inch-thick wallboard or tile over plaster, cement board, or ½-inch wallboard. The system exceeds all building code and ADA (Americans with Disabilities Act) specifications. The directions are for installing a grab bar on a tile shower wall.

Figure 11-10: Once behind the wall, the anchor expands and locks the mounting plate in position.

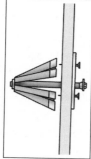

To install a grab bar with a WingIts grab bar system, you need the following:

- ✔ Electric drill with ⅛-inch masonry bit and 1¼-inch carbide-tipped hole saw
- ✔ Felt-tipped pen
- ✔ Measuring tape
- ✔ Rubber mallet or hammer

✔ Rubbing alcohol

✔ Screwdriver

✔ System with grab bar and fasteners

Here's how you install the grab bar:

1. **Locate the 1¼-inch mounting holes so the center of the grab bar fastener slides into the holes.**

2. **Measure from the inside of one bar flange to the outside of the other to find the center-to-center distance or the distance the 1¼-inch mounting holes should be spaced apart.**

3. **After making sure the wall surface is clean, mark the location of the mounting holes with a felt-tipped pen.**

4. **Use a masonry bit to drill a ⅛-inch pilot hole through the tile at these marks.**

5. **Hold the grab bar, with fasteners attached, to the wall to check that the pilot holes align with the center of the fasteners.**

6. **Use a 1¼-inch carbide-tipped hole saw to enlarge the pilot holes (see Figure 11-11).**

Figure 11-11: Use a carbide-tipped hole saw to bore the opening for a wall anchor.

If you hit a wall stud while drilling the holes, you can mount the grab bar directly to the wall stud with 2½-inch-long #12 stainless steel screws instead of the fastener.

7. **Use a screwdriver to back out the bolt of the fastener until the end of it is flush with the nut at the opposite end of the fitting.**

8. **Temporarily install the fasteners to the ends of the grab bar with the stainless steel screws provided.**

9. **Wipe the wall surface around these holes with rubbing alcohol so the tape will adhere.**

10. **Remove the paper that covers the adhesive on the faceplate.**

11. **Insert the fasteners into the holes in the wall while they're attached to the grab bar.**

12. **Press the grab bar tightly toward the wall for a moment so the fasteners can adhere to the wall in the correct position.**

13. **Remove the grab bar from the fasteners and use a screwdriver to firmly and quickly punch the head of the bolt toward the faceplate.**

    You can also hit the screw gently but firmly with a rubber mallet or hammer.

14. **Simultaneously, pull on the bolt and tighten it by hand.**

    Use a screwdriver to tighten the bolt very tightly.

15. **Attach the grab bar to the fasteners with the stainless steel screws.**

If you're remodeling and the walls are open, you can install blocking between studs to provide structural support. Doing this ensures that the grab bar will hold the weight of a bather.

To install a grab bar with blocking, you need these materials:

- Cold chisel and ball-peen hammer
- Drywall keyhole saw
- Grab bar
- Measuring tape
- Mesh wallboard tape
- Scrap 2-inch-x-10-inch lumber
- Stainless steel screws
- Wallboard joint compound

Follow these steps to install a grab bar with blocking.

1. **To make room for the blocking, first determine and mark the location for the grab bar.**

2. **Use a cold chisel and ball-peen hammer to chip away any tiles.**

3. **Use a drywall keyhole saw to cut out the wallboard surrounding the wall framing where the grab bar will be installed.**

    Allow for enough room to work on the framing where the blocking will be installed.

4. Cut a 2-inch-x-10-inch board to fit between the wall studs and screw it in place with stainless steel screws.

5. Cut and install a piece of new wallboard to fit the cutout.

6. Apply mesh wallboard tape and then joint compound to seal the joint around the cutout.

7. Let it dry and then sand.

8. Repeat Steps 6 and 7.

If the walls are tile, apply new tile to match.

Maintaining water temperature

The best protection against scalding is a special valve called a pressure-balance or antiscald valve, which maintains a constant water temperature, even if someone in the house decides to do a super-size load of laundry with a tub full of hot water.

Some of these devices are valves that sense changes in the water pressure and adjust the mix of hot and cold water. Others are electronic systems that remember the temperature of the last shower and deliver the same level of hot water until you or someone else resets them. More-elaborate systems allow you to program multiple water temperatures for the different degrees of hot water for the different people using the shower. Whether you're doing the bathroom yourself or hiring a contractor, arrange for a licensed plumber to take care of this particular job.

Now if you want an easy add-on valve (about $20) for your shower head, get a scald-guard device that shuts off the water if the temperature gets too high. All you do is remove the shower head, screw in the device, and replace the shower head. If you have a bit more money to spend but don't want to replace your existing shower valve, you can plumb a pressure-balancing valve into the supply line right before the shower valve.

Incidentally, the Department of Energy suggests setting the temperature of your hot-water heater no higher than 115 degrees to provide a comfortable hot-water temperature for most uses.

Chapter 12

Bowled Over: Basins, Cabinets, Countertops, and Faucets

. . . .

In This Chapter

▶ Selecting bowls, basins, and beyond

▶ Putting in pedestal and wall-hung sinks

▶ Choosing and installing bathroom cabinets

▶ Mastering Faucetry 101

. . . .

Depending on what dictionary you read, a lavatory is either a built-in washbasin or a room having one or more toilets and washbasins, or both. So don't be confused when you order a sink and it comes in a box labeled "lavatory." What makes today's bathroom a little more interesting than your grade school lavatory is the choices you have when it comes to selecting a washbasin. Sure, you'll find the traditional sink sunken into a nice countertop and some replicas of the old pedestal sink that may have been in your school bathroom, but a whole new breed of basins where you can wash your face and brush your teeth is now available.

Looking at Types and Styles of Basins

Before you walk into a bathroom design center to look at basins and faucets, do some noodling about who uses the bathroom, what the priorities are, how often it will is used, the style you like, and how maintenance friendly you want the room to be. Yes, a snappy red pedestal sink would be a knockout, but in a family bathroom, a better choice is a countertop sink with a vanity for storage in a light color that doesn't show soap scum and is easy to clean.

The range of styles of basins is matched by their prices, so the options are wide and varied. For example, a 19-inch diameter sink made of vitreous china, which is fired to a hard nonporous surface, sells for less than $100, and a cast-iron basin with a porcelain glaze goes for about $150. The price goes up to $1,000 if you want a fanciful pottery sink or glass vessel that sits above a counter or in a metal bracket mounted on the wall. For a granite or marble bowl, the prices go into the $1,600 range.

Both cast polymer and solid surface sinks are sold as one unit, called an integral sink, combining a sink and a countertop that you can install easily on top of a vanity base cabinet. They come in a range of sizes, from 25 to 49 inches wide, and are designed to fit the most popular size of vanity cabinets. The seamless design of these units makes them easy to clean and eliminates the need for caulk to seal a joint between the countertop and basin. A 36-inch-wide cast polymer countertop and sink, made of polyester resin and granite or crushed marble, costs under $350. For under $700, you'll get a solid surface unit with color throughout its thickness, a popular choice for shaped and contoured edges.

If you choose either a free-standing or wall-hung sink, make sure that you increase storage space in the bathroom because neither of these styles has it.

Picking a Pedestal Sink

What it lacks in storage space a pedestal sink makes up for in good looks and high style. The small-bowl pedestals are a good choice in a powder room because they take up little floor space, and the wider console styles with a basin ledge for toiletries make a handsome addition to anyone's bathroom. Assuming you're replacing a wall-mounted sink, installing a pedestal sink is relatively easy. You can hook the new sink up to the old plumbing.

The old pipes that may be hidden inside a vanity are exposed under a pedestal sink, so if the pipes are rusty, consider replacing the short sections of pipe with new chrome pipes and a new trap assembly. You can save some money by cleaning up the pipes and painting them. At the same time, appraise the condition of the wall and make any necessary repairs, because it will be clearly visible, no longer hidden by the old sink.

Before you purchase a new pedestal sink, you'll want to remove the old sink and measure the location of the plumbing lines so that you can choose a new pedestal sink that matches up with them. To get these rough-in dimensions, make a sketch of the wall and note the following measurements:

- Distance from the floor (or wall) to where the drain enters the wall (or floor)
- Distance between the floor and water supply pipes
- Distance right to left from each water supply pipe to the drain

Sit on the floor with the sketch in hand and try to visualize how the back of the pedestal sink matches up with the supply lines. Also, check the specifications and rough-in dimensions for the sink. One way to do this is find some sinks that you like at a bath center; note the manufacturer, style, and model number; and then visit the manufacturer's Web site. Most manufacturers provide specifications and rough-in dimensions online for you to access, so making the decision of what fits and what doesn't is easy.

Of course, a knowledgeable salesperson in a bath center or a plumber can help you do the same thing, assuming that you have your sketch with you and your measurements are correct.

How a pedestal sink is installed varies by its style and manufacturer. Some use a wall bracket, and others are secured directly to the wall with lag screws or toggle bolts through holes in the back of the bowl. Most rest on the pedestal but get major support from the wall mounting. The instructions in the following sections are for installing a pedestal sink with a mounting bracket. The project involves completing several individual tasks and then connecting everything together. The faucet, drain, and pop-up assembly are purchased separately. Before you install the pedestal sink, preinstall the drain, the pop-up assembly, and the faucet.

Installing the drain and pop-up assembly

The following steps are generic directions to install a typical assembly. Carefully read the directions that come with the unit you buy so that you're familiar with the parts and where and how they fit together. Figure 12-1 introduces all the major players in this process.

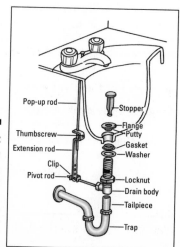

Figure 12-1: The main parts of a typical lavatory's drain assembly.

Pop-up rod
Thumbscrew
Extension rod
Clip
Pivot rod

Stopper
Flange
Putty
Gasket
Washer
Locknut
Drain body
Tailpiece
Trap

To install a drain and pop-up assembly, you need the following:

- ✔ Groove-joint pliers
- ✔ Plumber's putty
- ✔ Screwdriver

Installing the drain

The drain consists of the pipes that attach to the sink and lead to the trap. The following installation instructions describe where the different metal and rubber washers go.

1. **Thread the large locknut on to the drain body.**

2. **Slip the flat washer and finally the wedge-shaped rubber gasket onto the drain body.**

3. **Place a thin bead of plumber's putty around the underside of the drain flange.**

4. **Push the drain body up through the hole in the bottom of the sink.**

5. **Thread the drain flange into the body of the drain.**

6. **Turn the drain body so the opening for the pivot rod mechanism faces the back of the sink.**

7. **Using the pliers, tighten the locknut on the drain from the underside of the sink until the plumber's putty is compressed and the flange looks and feels tight.**

Assembling the pivot rod

The pivot rod operates the mechanism that opens and closes the drain. Most units have a rod with a ball on it that operates the drain plug. To assemble this mechanism, follow these steps:

1. **If the retaining nut is screwed on the valve body, remove it and the washers. If not, skip this step.**

2. **Slide the washer seal over the short end of the pivot rod.**

3. **Insert the short end of the pivot rod into the drain body.**

4. **Thread on the nut.**

   Don't tighten it yet.

5. **Insert the pop-up rod through the hole in the faucet's body, which is already installed.**

6. **Push the pivot rod all the way down.**

7. **Connect the extension rod (the short arm through which the pivot rod extends) by placing the pivot rod in the first or second hole of the extension rod and sliding the pop-up rod into the extension rod (refer to Figure 12-1).**

8. **Pull the rod all the way down and tighten the thumbscrew.**

Installing a pedestal sink

Before a pedestal sink takes its place, the wall behind it needs to be shored up to hold its weight. Then the installation goes easy.

To install a pedestal sink, you need the following material:

- ✔ Adjustable wrench
- ✔ Electric drill
- ✔ Hacksaw
- ✔ Measuring tape
- ✔ Pedestal sink with mounting bracket
- ✔ P-trap, tailpiece, and slip-nut fittings
- ✔ Ratchet with sockets
- ✔ Scrap plywood or 2-x-10 for blocking
- ✔ Wood screws

Shoring up the wall

To provide a solid surface for mounting the sink, reinforce the wall with wood blocking, which we describe in Steps 1 through 6 of the section, "Installing a Cast-Iron Wall-Hung Sink," later in this chapter.

Mounting the sink to the wall

After the wall is reinforced and repaired, the sink can be installed. Some sinks require a separate bracket that is installed first, but others mount directly to the wall. These directions are for a sink with a bracket. You can skip those steps if the sink you're installing doesn't have a bracket. Figure 12-2 shows a typical installation.

1. **Position the bracket on the wall and use the bracket as a template to mark the location for the mounting lag bolts.**

   To find the exact location of the mounting bracket, consult the roughing-in dimensions provided by the manufacturer.

   Make sure the bracket is level.

Figure 12-2:
Pedestal
sinks are
hung on a
wall bracket
or secured
directly to
the wall and
supported
by the
pedestal.

2. **Drill pilot holes through the layout marks on the wall into the wall reinforcement.**

   Make the holes about ⅛ inch smaller than the lag bolts supplied by the manufacturer. *Lag bolts* are large screws with a square or hex head.

3. **Install the bracket with the lag bolts.**

4. **Hang the basin on the wall bracket and then install the additional mounting screws to hold the sink to the bracket and wall.**

   If the sink doesn't have a mounting bracket, install it directly to the wall with the fasteners provided by the manufacturer.

5. **Test-fit the pedestal, mark its location, and then move it safely out of the way.**

Installing the P-trap

With the sink on the wall, you can now install the P-trap. The *P-trap* is the pipe that connects the sink to the house drain. The U-shape of this pipe is the trap that retains enough water to prevent sewer gases from entering the bathroom. The P-trap is adjustable and can slide up and down on the pipe leaving the sink drain. The other end of the P-trap can also slide in and out of the fitting on the wall.

To install the P-trap, you may have to cut the tailpiece that protrudes from the pop-up assembly if the P-trap doesn't align with the drain that comes out of the wall.

Referring to Figure 12-3, follow these steps to install the P-trap:

1. **Slide the short side of the P-trap onto the tailpiece that drops down from the sink drain. Move the P-trap up or down to align the trap arm with the opening in the wall.**

   Use a hacksaw to cut the tailpiece shorter whenever the P-trap can't be moved higher up the tailpiece and the trap arm is below the wall drain fitting. Purchase a longer tailpiece whenever the P-trap is above the wall drain fitting when attached to the end of the tailpiece.

2. **Take the lower part of the P-trap apart and insert the trap arm into the wall drain fitting as far as it will go.**

3. **Pull the trap arm out of the wall fitting until it aligns with the top U-shaped portion of the trap.**

   If the trap arm comes completely out of the wall before it can be attached to the trap, purchase a longer trap arm. If the trap arm is in the wall fitting as far as it will go and extends past the U-shaped part of the trap, cut it shorter with the hacksaw.

4. **Insert the trap arm back into the wall drain, move it into alignment with the trap, and thread on (but don't tighten) the slip nut.**

5. **When the trap parts are joined together, tighten the slip nuts on the tailpiece and the wall drain fittings.**

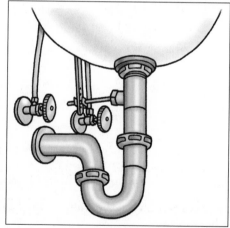

Figure 12-3:
The P-trap and riser tubes.

Attaching riser tubes to the faucet

After the P-trap is installed, you can turn your attention to attaching the riser tubes (supply lines) to the faucet tailpieces, using the compression nuts that came with the faucet. See Figure 12-3.

The riser tubes connect the faucet to the stop valves. Here are a couple of pointers for attaching the tubes to the faucet:

✔ Snug up the nuts by hand.

✔ Bend or loop the riser tubes so that they fit between the stop valves and the wall before tightening them with a wrench.

Finishing up

The moment of truth has arrived; you have to turn on the water at the shut-off valves and the faucet and test for leaks in the supply lines and fittings leading to the faucet and in the drain lines and fittings. When everything is drip free, you can install the pedestal by simply positioning it properly beneath the sink and securing it to the floor with a wood screw (see Figure 12-4).

Don't overtighten the pedestal mounting screw because doing so may crack the pedestal base.

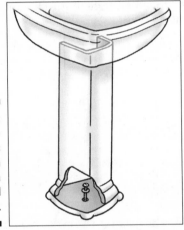

Figure 12-4: The pedestal is held in place with a wood screw.

Last, you can caulk any gaps or voids between the wall and the basin and remove any excess caulk with a wet rag.

Installing a Cast-Iron Wall-Hung Sink

Wall-hung sinks that are mounted on the wall can be customized to the height of the user. It's a nice way to personalize a bathroom for someone particularly tall or short. A sink mounted on the wall also is ideal for anyone in a wheelchair because there's access underneath it; however, be sure to slip an insulated cover over the trap so that this pipe, heated by hot water passing through, doesn't burn the legs of the person in the wheelchair. A wall-mounted sink also takes up less space in a small room than a traditional vanity with sink.

To install a wall-hung sink, you need these materials:

- ✔ Adjustable wrench
- ✔ Drill
- ✔ Green board and wallboard tape and joint compound
- ✔ Hammer
- ✔ Level
- ✔ Nails
- ✔ Saw
- ✔ Scrap 2-x-4s
- ✔ Scrap 2-x-10 board
- ✔ Scrap piece of ¾-inch plywood
- ✔ Screws
- ✔ Tape measure
- ✔ Wood chisel

Cast-iron sinks are very heavy. Get help lifting the sink and follow wall reinforcement instructions to the letter.

Preparing the supporting wall

When you're going to install the sink in an existing bathroom, you have to remove the drywall in the area behind the sink to add blocking to provide the support that's needed for the sink. The wall has to be opened to expose at least two studs, neither of which can be located directly behind the sink. If a wall stud happens to be centered directly behind the sink, then you need to open the wall to three studs: the one behind the sink and the studs on either side of it. Both ends of the blocking must be supported by a stud. Follow these steps to provide the necessary support:

1. **Cut a 2-x-4 into two 36-inch-long pieces.**

2. **Rip (cut lengthwise) these two boards to a 2¾-inch width.**

3. **Cut a notch that's 1½ inches deep and 9¼ inches high in these boards.**

Position the notches 23⅞ inches from the ends of the boards, as shown in Figure 12-5.

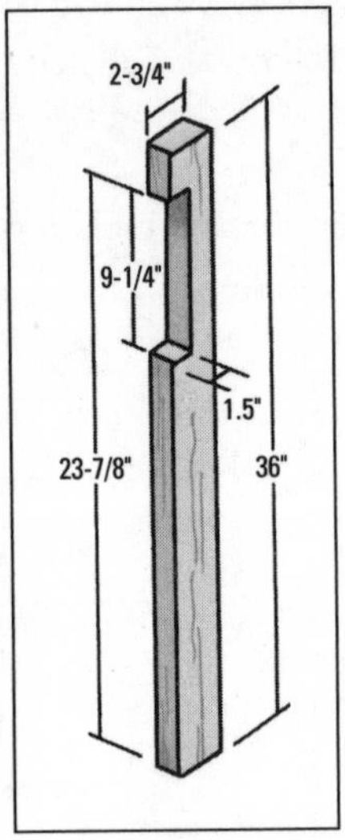

Figure 12-5:
These are the dimensions of the side braces that are cut from 2-x-4 lumber.

4. **Nail the boards to the studs.**

5. **Cut a piece of 2-x-10 lumber to fit between the notches and studs, as shown in Figure 12-6.**

If the 2-x-10 board spans a center stud, you must notch the stud to accept the board.

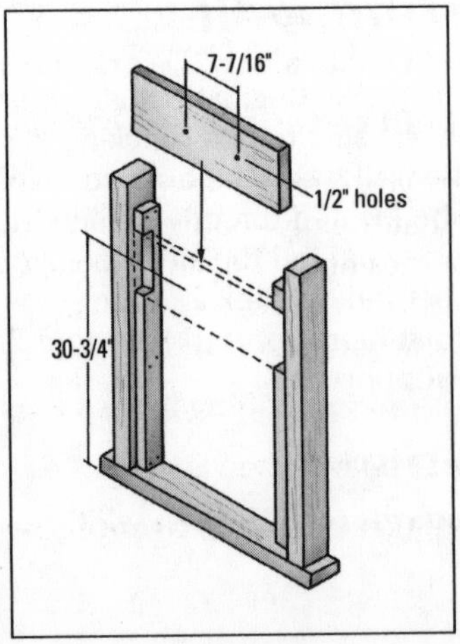

Figure 12-6:
Screw 2-x-10 blocking to the side braces to support the sink.

Setting the mounting bolts

Next, you need to set the mounting bolts into the support brace in the wall.

1. **Mark the location of the mounting bolts on the 2-x-10 board.**

   The bolts are located 30¾ inches from the floor and 7⁷⁄₁₆ inches apart. The bolts must be placed behind the sink, but they may not line up exactly in the center of the 2-x-10 brace.

2. **Remove the 2-x-10 board from the wall and drill ½-inch holes through the layout marks.**

3. **Insert the mounting bolts.**

4. **Install the threaded inserts to hold the bolts in place (see Figure 12-7).**

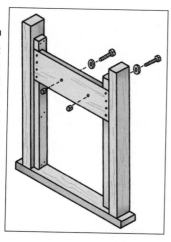

Figure 12-7: The mounting bolts are held in place by threaded inserts that are supplied with the sink.

5. **Fasten the 2-x-10 brace to the wall studs using 2½-inch screws.**

6. **Cut a piece of ¾-inch plywood to fit between the wall studs.**

   If the opening is three studs wide, you must remove ¾ inch from the front edge of the center stud so that the plywood can be installed flush with the wall studs on the outer sides of the opening. When this is the case, make several ¾-inch-deep cuts in the edge of the center stud and use a wood chisel to knock off the wood between the cuts.

7. **Drill holes for the mounting bolts and plumbing pipes in the plywood.**

8. **Screw the plywood to the support boards (see Figure 12-8).**

9. **Apply moisture-resistant drywall (green board) to cover the opening.**

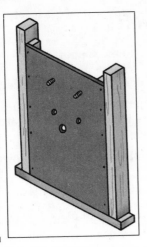

Figure 12-8:
Plywood filler is screwed to the side braces and must lie flush with the front of the studs so it can be covered with drywall.

10. **Tape and mud the joints between the existing wall and the new drywall with joint compound.**

11. **Sand the joints smooth and paint the wall.**

Bolting the sink to the wall

The last step is mounting the sink on the wall; it's heavy, so get help. After it's in place, see the earlier section about installing the drain and P-trap and the section later in the chapter about installing the faucet.

1. **Lift the sink onto the mounting bolts.**

2. **Slip on the washers and thread on the nuts (see Figure 12-9).**

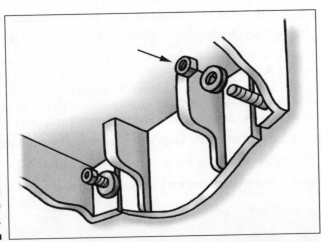

Figure 12-9:
Two large bolts hold the wall-mounted sink to the wall.

3. Use a carpenter's level to position the sink so that it's level.

4. Tighten the bolts with a wrench.

You're So Vain: Vanity Cabinets and Furniture

A vanity cabinet is like any piece of furniture in that the price goes up as the quality improves. You'll find in-stock factory-made vanities in a range of sizes and styles, meaning that you can simply walk into a store and leave with the vanity of your choice. Or you can order a semicustom vanity that is factory made and customized the way you want it, with specialty finishes and handy options such as a pull-out tray, bins, and shelves that make it uniquely your own. At the high end is a custom-made cabinet designed by you or a designer to exact specifications not available in stock or semicustom cabinets. Although a custom piece can be pricey, it may be a design solution that makes the most of a cut-up floor plan or takes advantage of confined space. A custom cabinet is available wherever you buy cabinets, but remember that you need to allow extra time if you're ordering a vanity that's made to order.

You get what you pay for when it comes to construction of a vanity. You should find that better-quality pieces have backs made with tongue and groove construction, a solid face frame, full-depth drawers, and thick shelving. Notice whether doors have substantial hinges that open and close easily and whether drawers glide on their tracks.

Standard widths of vanity cabinets are 18, 24, 30, 36, and 48 inches.

A vanity cabinet used to be an entity in itself, but today a vanity can be part of a suite of bathroom furniture. Yes, furniture for your bathroom. These modular components, also used for built-ins throughout the house, include shelving units, linen towers, open or closed wall and base cabinets, and filler pieces, all designed in various sizes that can be configured to create a custom bathroom. The pieces are ideal for storing towels, linens, and toiletries and for adding a rich custom look to a room.

Vanities are shorter than kitchen cabinets, which may work for kids and shorter adults, but you may get tired of bending down to wash your face. Manufacturers are now making taller vanity cabinets, or you can use kitchen cabinets as a base to create a higher vanity, and make a new kickboard (the board under the front of the cabinet to cover the platform).

When you have good cabinets but they're out of style, call a cabinet resurfacing company. For a fraction of the cost of replacing them, these specialists can resurface the cabinets with an updated look.

Looking at your options

The traditional vanity cabinet, which offers the most counter and storage space, is used with a single basin or pair of basins and is installed by fastening it to the wall. Several types of basins are available, and the methods of installing them vary:

- **A self-rimming sink** is dropped into a cutout in the countertop, and its rim overlaps the surface, forming a seal.

- **A flush-mount sink** is installed so that it's level with the surface of the countertop. It's also called a tile-in installation because the sink is designed to fit flush with a tiled countertop.

- **An above-counter basin,** also called a vanity top installation, is used for basins or vessels that are installed to rest on top of the counter.

- **An under-counter sink mount** is used with stone or solid surfacing countertops, so the rim slips beneath the countertop and creates a seamless appearance.

Converting furniture to a vanity cabinet

Make a bathroom an original by reinventing an old dresser or cabinet into a vanity. The front of the furniture can remain intact, but the back needs to be cut to make room for plumbing pipes. You cut another hole in the top for the basin. Plan to refinish or paint it and give it a topcoat (or three) of polyurethane to make the surface water resistant. Use the following tips to turn Aunt Suzie's dresser into a one-of-a-kind vanity.

- If the furniture has a drawer at the top, take the drawer apart and make a false front. It won't close properly with the top drawer left in because it will hit the bottom of the basin and plumbing pipes.

- Nail the drawer front to the sides so it's permanently installed. It will look like it opens, but it won't.

- Take careful measurements of the rough-in location for the pipes where they come out of the wall. Then mark the location for a hole large enough for the plumbing pipe to fit through and cut the hole.

- Carefully measure the cutout in the surface for the basin and faucets and install them before fastening the cabinet to the wall.

Every vanity needs a countertop, and some of the most common countertop materials include the following:

- **Laminates:** Laminates can be bought ready made in stock sizes or ordered in an endless number of colors and patterns.

- **Solid surface:** Solid surface, also available in colors and patterns, is another man-made material. Pliability is its unique feature, so it can be shaped in configurations that make it more versatile than laminate, particularly when edging details are the look you want.

- **Tiles:** Ceramic, stone, slate, and marble tiles are installed over a base and then laid in intricate patterns on a counter surface or as a solid design. Along with solid surfaces, these materials make ideal backsplashes, wallcoverings, and countertops in a bathroom. When installed over a base cabinet, the tiles are installed on a base of plywood and backerboard with thinset mortar and then grouted.

Installing a vanity

Carefully unpack the vanity from its box, recheck that its measurements are correct, and move it into position where it will be installed.

To install a vanity, you need the following:

- Carpenter's level
- Drywall screws
- Electric drill with bits
- Electronic stud finder
- Marking pen
- Measuring tape
- Shims
- Silicone caulk
- Utility knife

Make sure the floor is level so that the new vanity will be installed on a sound level surface. You may need to adjust the vanity slightly by using a shim.

When leveling and installing the vanity, removing the drawers and doors is a good idea that provides you with easier access and handling. Use a carpenter's level to determine whether the floor is level. If it is, proceed with the installation. If it isn't, then you must do the following:

1. **Find the high point by measuring the height of the cabinet and then marking this point on the wall, and marking the same measurement up from the high point if there is one. You can then use the high-point mark and the level to draw a horizontal line on the wall.**

2. **Use the level to draw a vertical layout line where the edge (or edges) of the cabinet will be located.**

3. **Slide the vanity in place and align it with the horizontal and vertical lines on the wall.**

   Drive tapered wood shims between the floor and the base to adjust and level the vanity (see Figure 12-10).

Figure 12-10:
Wood shims level the cabinet.

Finding wall studs located behind where you're placing your vanity also is important. You can use an electronic stud finder to accomplish this task. The studs probably were used to secure the old unit, so the screw holes from where you removed it may also point to the studs.

Besides using shims to level the vanity, if the wall behind it isn't flat (plumb), then you may need to insert shims in any gaps between the vanity back and the wall at each stud location. If you don't place shims here, the screws will pull the vanity frame rail to the wall and rack the cabinet out of square. Here's what to do to finish the installation:

1. **Use long drywall screws to fasten the vanity to the studs (see Figure 12-11).**

Figure 12-11:
Fasten the cabinet to the wall with screws driven through the back frame into the wall studs.

    2. Cut off any shims that show with a utility knife.

    3. Caulk small gaps between the vanity and the floor and wall.

Topping your vanity with stone

One of the hottest new looks in bathrooms is a granite countertop on a wood vanity cabinet. A rich-looking countertop of stone — a high-style material that's durable and resistant to everyday use — is often all that you need to update the cabinet. At home centers, you'll find a range of colors and sizes available. Typically, stone countertops come in widths of 25, 31, 37, and 49 inches, with a separate backsplash and separate bowl that you glue to the underside of the countertop before fastening it to the vanity base. The countertop is conveniently predrilled with three holes on either 4-inch or 8-inch centers, for a faucet.

To install a stone countertop and sink, you need these materials:

    ✔ Epoxy

    ✔ Marking pen

    ✔ Metal can

    ✔ Scissors

    ✔ Silicone caulk

Positioning the sink

The stone countertop comes ready for the sink to be installed.

1. **Lay the countertop polished side down on top of the vanity cabinet.**

2. **Unpack the sink and place it upside down over the sink hole in the countertop.**

3. **Line up the back edge of the sink so that it sits between the faucet holes and the inner edge of the sink hole in the top.**

   Make sure the sink is placed in the center of the sink hole. Feel around the edges underneath the countertop to be sure the sink is centered. It's okay if the front and back edge are not perfectly even, but the left and right sides should be as close to even as possible.

4. **With a marking pen, draw a line all around the sink on the bottom of the countertop.**

5. **Make alignment marks on the front and back of the sink and countertop.**

   Begin the line on the sink and continue it onto the countertop. After removing the sink, you can replace it in the exact same position by matching the lines on the sink with those on the countertop.

Sticking the sink to the stone

The sink is attached to the underside of the stone countertop with epoxy (see Figure 12-12). Don't worry — this step isn't difficult, but you must set the sink in the right place. After the epoxy cures, you can't change your mind! Here's how you glue the sink to the countertop:

Figure 12-12:
The sink is installed with epoxy applied around the perimeter of the sink opening.

1. **Lift the sink off the vanity top and set it down within easy reach of the countertop because you won't have much time to position the sink after you pour the epoxy.**

2. **Mix the epoxy following the directions on the epoxy packet that was supplied with the countertop.**

   To activate epoxy, you usually have to knead both sides of the packet together by hand or by sliding the packet up and down along the edge of the countertop to mix it thoroughly. Continue kneading the epoxy packet against the countertop edge until it begins to feel warm to the touch (takes about three minutes).

3. **When the epoxy feels warm, immediately cut off one corner of the packet with scissors and squeeze the contents quickly and evenly onto the countertop around the inside of the line you drew.**

   Work quickly! After the epoxy begins warming up, it continues heating up and hardens quickly. When finished (or if the epoxy gets too hot to handle), place the used epoxy packet in a metal can or on a nonflammable surface.

4. **Quickly place the sink back on the underside of the countertop inside the outline you drew, making sure that you place the back of the sink toward the faucet holes and line it up exactly with the front and back alignment marks you made.**

   Epoxy cures very fast, so place the sink in the circle carefully but quickly.

5. **Move the sink back and forth for about five seconds, being sure that it's within the layout circle.**

   Doing so ensures that the epoxy is spread around as much as possible between the top and sink.

Installing a sink and countertop on your vanity

After the epoxy has dried for about 45 to 60 minutes, check whether the sink is properly adhered to the countertop by carefully lifting up the sink a few inches by the bottom drain hole. If the vanity top lifts with the sink, you're ready to continue installing the vanity top to the cabinet.

Run a bead of silicone caulk around the top edge of the vanity and carefully lower the top in place and center it over the vanity base (see Figure 12-13). Clean up excess caulk with a damp rag.

Figure 12-13:
Run a bead of silicone caulk around the top edge of the cabinet to hold the countertop in place.

Finishing up

Clean the surface of the stone countertop and sink thoroughly, let it dry, and then apply a stone sealer. Finally, with the countertop in place on the vanity, install the faucet according to the manufacturer's directions.

Topping your vanity with tile

The selection of ceramic, slate, stone, and marble tiles for a bathroom countertop is vast indeed and limited only by your imagination. The choice of colors, textures, and patterns of ceramic tiles is awesome, and their hard finishes and durable quality make them good choices. Similarly, you may also want to consider slate, stone, and marble tiles, which offer that same durability in more natural shades and appeal.

Tile comes in many shapes and sizes but the specially shaped trim pieces are what make using tile so versatile. Finishing off the edge of a counter or navigating an inside corner are made possible by these preformed pieces. Here is a short list of trim you can find at most outlets:

- Edging or bullnose tiles with one rounded edge
- Inside-outside corners with four edges rounded
- Inside and outside corner caps
- V-cap for edging
- Bead for straight edges

You can transform a bathroom with a new tile countertop and add years of service to an existing vanity or replace it with a new one. The emphasis here is on the countertop, so choose your tiles with that in mind. For inspiration, visit a tile center or retailer, where you'll find the widest selection and displays of tile countertops. Bring along a sketch on graph paper with dimensions of the vanity cabinet, including the wall backsplash area behind it.

The old saying "Measure twice and cut once" certainly holds true for tiling. Before ordering the tile or making your first cut, take these tips to heart.

- Buy more tiles than you need to allow for miscuts or tiles that break when you cut them.

- Double-check your measurements and ask the tile dealer to check your dimensions so that you order the correct amount of tile and material.

- Before beginning the job, open all the cartons and make sure that the tiles are the right size, color, and design.

The best type of sink for a tile countertop is a self-rimming sink because it's installed after the tile is set and the joint between the sink and tile is easy to seal with caulk.

To install a tile countertop, you need these materials:

- ¾-inch exterior plywood
- ¼-inch square-notched trowel
- Backerboard
- Carbide-tipped scoring knife
- Caulk gun
- Epoxy grout
- Float
- Jigsaw
- Latex-modified thinset adhesive
- Self-rimmed sink
- Tape measure
- Tile cutter
- Tile nipper
- Tiles

Building the underlayer

The first stage in putting in a tile countertop is preparing a sturdy, level surface to lay the tiles on. Before you can start, however, you need to measure the length and width of the vanity cabinet and build a backing made of ¾-inch exterior grade plywood and cement board. If you're replacing an old countertop, use it as a template to cut the backing and cement board (see Figure 12-14). Otherwise, cut the plywood and cement board 1 to 2 inches larger than the cabinet (depending on how much overhang you want).

Figure 12-14:
The cement board and plywood form a sturdy base for tiles.

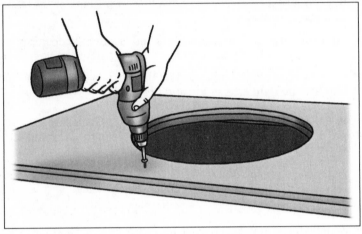

1. **With the template that came with the sink, trace the outline for the cutout where the sink will be located onto the plywood and cement board.**

2. **Drill a starter hole in the plywood so you can use your jigsaw to cut the hole for the sink out in the plywood.**

3. **Using the plywood as a pattern, transfer the location of the sink to both sides of the backerboard by scoring (cutting the surface) it with the scoring tool.**

   If the sink isn't centered in the countertop, remember to flip the plywood when you mark the other side of the backerboard.

4. **Knock out the waste piece (where the sink goes) with a hammer.**

5. **Place the plywood on the cabinet and drive screws through the cabinet's corner blocks up into the plywood to secure it to the frame.**

6. **Spread thinset adhesive on the plywood and comb with the notched edge of the trowel. Lay the backerboard in the thinset and secure with backerboard screws or roofing nails.**

7. **Fill joints between backerboard panels (if any) with thinset and mesh tape.**

   The sink cutout should line up exactly on both pieces.

Placing the tile

Plan the layout of tiles by arranging them so that they form an attractive pattern with as little cutting as possible; try not to cut any to less than half its size, except where necessary, and plan to put any rows of cut tiles at the edges or back of the counter.

Begin the layout at the middle of the front edge of the plywood backerboard base, dry-fitting the tiles to find the most pleasing placement and marking reference lines on the cement board as your guide.

Most tiles have built-in lugs on the side for spacing. If your tiles don't, use plastic spacers so that they're aligned properly.

1. **After the front to back spacing is decided, lay the tile dry along the width of the counter.**

   Shift the tiles right or left to produce the largest tiles at the ends.

2. **Mark the location of the center row of tiles on the backerboard and draw a straight layout line along the edge of the tile row.**

   Do the same with the tile row running across the counter. Use these two lines to start the first row of tiles.

3. **Begin work in a small area close to the layout lines and apply thinset adhesive to the cement (backer) board up to the layout lines with the smooth side of the trowel.**

   Then use the notched side of the trowel to comb the thinset.

4. **Lay down the full tiles along the layout lines using spacers (if necessary) between them.**

   Push the tile down to ensure full contact with the adhesive (see Figure 12-15).

5. **When the full tiles are in place, cut the border tiles and fit them into place before moving on to the next section of the counter and beginning the process again.**

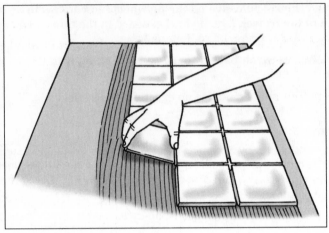

Figure 12-15:
Lay the tiles flat on the adhesive and then push them down to assure full contact with the adhesive.

6. **When all tiles are in place, allow the adhesive to cure overnight before grouting.**

Grouting the tile

Read the grout manufacturer's instructions for an overview of applying grout. Then follow these easy steps:

1. **Spread the grout over the entire tile surface with a rubber float, making sure the grout gets pushed into the spaces between the tiles (see Figure 12-16).**

Figure 12-16:
Using a rubber float, push the grout between the tiles.

2. Remove excess grout using a wet grout sponge and then let the grout dry.

3. Follow the tile and manufacturer's instructions about whether and when to use a sealer.

Dropping in the sink

With the tile in place and grouted, the sink goes in next.

1. **Place a bead of silicone caulk along the underside of the sink's rim.**

2. **Lower the sink into the sink cutout and secure it with the mounting hardware provided by the manufacturer.**

3. **Hook up the drain and pop-up assembly and the faucet. (See sections about "Installing the drain and pop-up assembly" and "Attaching riser tubes to the faucet," earlier in this chapter, and "Putting in an easy-install faucet," later in this chapter.)**

Much Ado about Medicine Cabinets

There's no better place to store medicines, toiletries, and other personal grooming products than right where you need them: in a convenient cabinet in the bathroom. Yes, you'll still find boring antiseptic metal boxes faced with a mirror, but you'll also see inspired and appealing designs with intricate beveled glass and mirrors and colorful whimsical designs.

Considering sizes and styles

Standard-size medicine cabinets come in a variety of shapes and sizes, with one, two, or three doors. You can choose square, rectangular, round, or oval shapes, and some have arched tops. Others feature built-in lighting, a design solution where space is at a premium. They are approximately 30 inches high and 4 to 6 inches deep and available in widths of 22, 28, 34, and 48 inches. Medicine cabinets were traditionally installed on the wall above a vanity, but now you'll also find them recessed in side walls of a shared bathroom, especially when a mirror is used over a vanity.

A good-quality medicine cabinet has a ¼-inch-thick mirror and at least ½-inch shelving and a mirror on the back of the cabinet door for added convenience and visibility. Some have the option of a lock, a nice feature if you have prescription drugs you want to keep safely stored. Many are designed as reversible mounting so that you can install them with a right- or left-hand opening, whichever is the most convenient for the cabinet's location. Some cabinets are ready to install, and others require assembling the pieces first.

A cabinet is installed either surface mounted and secured with anchors directly on the wall or recessed in a cutout in the wall and screwed into the wall framing. A recessed installation is more difficult but well worth considering for its streamlined appearance.

The specifications for a medicine cabinet help you decide the features and size you want. For example, the specs for a cabinet that's 15 inches wide by 25 inches high indicates those measurements as overall size dimensions. The specs also indicate the wall or rough-opening dimensions are 1 inch smaller. In this case, the rough-in dimensions needed to recess the unit in the wall are 14 x 24 inches.

Hanging a surface-mounted medicine cabinet

A medicine cabinet is sold preassembled except for the door, with drywall anchors to fasten it to the wall. Because of its weight, the best location is on the wall with a wall stud behind it. You don't want it falling off the wall, so fasten it securely to the wall framing, which is much more secure than the wallboard alone. Because most wall studs are usually 16 inches on center, meaning that there is a space of 16 inches between the centers of two studs, and a cabinet is at least 15 inches wide, you should be able to adjust the position of the cabinet to center one of the mounting holes over the wall stud.

To hang a medicine cabinet on the wall, you need the following items:

- Carpenter's level
- Electric drill
- Electronic stud finder
- Screwdriver
- Shims
- Wall-mount medicine cabinet with wall anchors

Follow these directions to hang a medicine cabinet.

1. **Locate at least one wall stud within the mounting area of the cabinet with a stud finder.**

2. **Mount the medicine cabinet to the wall by driving a screw through the back of the cabinet into at least one wall stud.**

   If another stud is not located behind the cabinet, use a plastic wall anchor. Follow the specific directions that come with the medicine cabinet to make sure that it doesn't require a different kind of mounting process.

Whenever you need to install a wall anchor, check the installation instructions. Depending on the type of anchor, you may need to drill a hole and install the anchor before you put the cabinet in position to hang it.

Replacing a recessed medicine cabinet

The best strategy is choosing a replacement cabinet that is the same or close to the same size of your original cabinet so that it fits in an existing wall cavity. Another good bet is to get a larger cabinet, which you can install after enlarging the opening. It's relatively easy to measure the additional space needed and then enlarge the opening by cutting the wallboard with a drywall saw.

If you have a large hole left from an old recessed cabinet and choose a smaller cabinet, the job is more complicated. You have to apply new wallboard, tape, and compound; let it dry; and then finish the wall with another application followed by sanding.

If you must cut a stud, install additional short pieces of 2-x-4 lumber at the outside of the cutout to support the cabinet (see Figure 12-17).

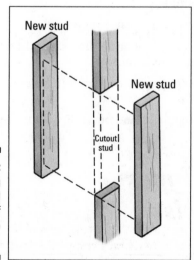

Figure 12-17: Adding additional support if you have to cut a stud.

To replace a recessed medicine cabinet, you need the following items:

✔ Drywall saw

✔ Recessed-mount medicine cabinet with fasteners

✔ Shims

Follow these steps for professional-looking installation:

1. **Take the old cabinet apart by removing the door and finding the fasteners that hold the cabinet in the wall cavity.**

2. **Remove the fasteners and pull out the old cabinet.**

3. **If the new cabinet came with the door attached, remove it, following the instructions from the manufacturer.**

   Carefully store the door so it's protected to prevent damage to the mirror.

4. **Test-fit the cabinet body in the wall cavity.**

   The cabinet should be square.

5. **Remove the cabinet from the cavity and make adjustments to the cavity by cutting the wallboard with a drywall saw and filling in voids with shims if necessary.**

6. **Reinsert the cabinet into the wall opening.**

7. **Check again to ensure that the cabinet is level and square.**

8. **Insert the mounting screws in the mounting holes in the cabinet body, following the manufacturer's instructions, and tighten the screws to secure the cabinet in the opening.**

   If the cabinet comes with screw covers, snap them in place.

9. **Install the hinge mechanism for the door on the cabinet body and position the door so that it's properly aligned.**

10. **Position the shelf brackets where appropriate for items and set the shelves on top of the brackets.**

11. **Check the door for proper alignment and make any adjustments.**

Getting a Handle on Types of Faucets and Controls

When you're selecting a faucet, make sure that it's compatible with the sink you choose. Lavatory sinks are drilled for faucets with a distance of 4 inches (center-set) or 8 inches (widespread) between the hot and cold faucet handles. A single hole accommodates most single-control faucets. Many sinks are also available with centered single holes, and some have no drillings for faucets mounted directly on the countertop or on the wall.

When it comes to faucet controls and handles, some single-handle faucets have the handle mounted directly behind the spout, which can limit the space around the spout, making it challenging to keep clean. You'll notice that short spouts don't take up much room, but they also don't always deliver water where you want it in the basin. The bottom line is to decide whether you're happy with the faucet control and handles of the faucet you have, and then choose a new one based on that decision. Many people wouldn't consider a two-handle faucet because they enjoy the ease of operating a single-lever control, especially comfortable for someone with a sore wrist or chronic arthritis.

Others swear that a pullout spout with a push-button spray in the bathroom is the handiest convenience because they like to wash their hair in the sink. Only you know what type of faucet and control gives you the convenience and comfort you want from a faucet.

Finishes come in basic chrome alone and brushed with polished brass and other finishes, including stainless steel, nickel, black, white, and new accent colors and patterns. For design direction, consider choosing your bathroom fixtures and fittings from a manufacturer's collection of products, which are all coordinated, but from different price categories, and which can be stylishly used together.

Putting in an easy-install faucet

Many of today's faucet manufacturers have a line of easy-to-install single-control faucets designed specifically for do-it-yourselfers. The reason that it's easy to install is it's accessible almost entirely above the countertop. No more lying on your back cramped into a dark cabinet. The manufacturers have figured out a way to preassemble the unit, which alone is revolutionary. Just knowing that you're not going to face a bag of strange-looking unfamiliar parts and the challenge of installing them correctly makes the unit a godsend for DIYers.

Choosing riser tubes

The thin flexible tubes under a sink are called *supply tubes* or *riser tubes* because they direct water from the main water valve to the sink. The ones we prefer are made of stainless steel mesh and have a polymer lining. They are sold in a variety of lengths and don't rely on compression nuts. They attach directly to the tailpiece of the faucet and stop valve to form a strong and flexible connection.

The nastiest part of this job is emptying the stuff under the cabinet so you can reach inside to hold the faucet while you tighten it. You need only two tools to install the faucet:

- ✔ An adjustable wrench
- ✔ A screwdriver

The directions that follow are for installing a quick-install type faucet.

1. **Drop the flexible supply lines through the holes in the sink.**

2. **Align the center toggle with the center hole in the sink and push the valve body down to force the toggle through the hole.**

3. **Use a standard screwdriver to tighten the setscrew in the back of the faucet body (see Figure 12-18).**

   You may have to hold the toggle that is now underneath the sink to keep it from turning.

Figure 12-18:
This faucet has pre-installed supply lines and installs with a screw-driver.

4. **When the toggle reaches the underside of the sink, firmly tighten the screw to lock the faucet in place (see Figure 12-19).**

5. **Thread the caps of the flexible supply lines onto the stop valves and tighten them with a wrench.**

Don't forget that whenever you thread fittings on to a pipe, you should apply Teflon plumber's tape to male threads and pipe dope to female threads to help seal the joint and reduce the chance of leaks. Compression fittings used to connect copper riser tubes don't require tape or pipe dope.

Installing a two-handle faucet

The hardworking bathroom faucet doesn't have to be ordinary, but it does have to be properly installed. Many of today's faucet manufacturers have taken the challenge of demystifying the installation process of the two-handle faucet, too. Some faucet designs use a rubber gasket to seal the joint between the base of the faucet and the sink. Others require a bead of plumber's putty placed around the perimeter of the faucet's base. (See Figure 12-20.) The new designs of these two-handle faucets make installing one of them easier than it's ever been.

Look, Ma, no hands!

You know how handy it is to wash your hands at the airport washroom? Well, we think it is, too. It won't be long before the price of those electronic "hands-free" faucets will come down in price and become a popular choice in today's busy family bathrooms. Maybe the cost of water will have something to do with it too, because these faucets are very thrifty. The least expensive one we found costs about $300 (by Delta Faucets), but it's not that easy to install. One of the advantages to the no-hands electric faucets made for residential use is that you can change the water temperature. You can't do that with commercial models, which are set at a fixed temperature. Remember that you heard it here first: Electronic faucets will be playing in your neighborhood soon.

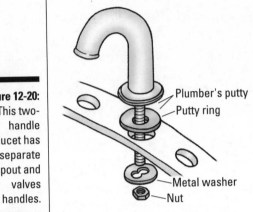

Figure 12-20:
This two-handle faucet has a separate spout and valves handles.

Plumber's putty
Putty ring
Metal washer
Nut

To keep the process simple, whenever possible, install the faucet before the sink is put in place so that it's easier to work on. This is especially true if the sink or countertop will sit on the vanity cabinet, where working in a dark, tight spot makes installation difficult, not to mention uncomfortable.

To install a two-handle faucet, you need the following:

- ✔ Basin wrench
- ✔ Groove-joint pliers
- ✔ Plumber's putty
- ✔ Screwdriver

A wide selection of two-handle faucets is on the market. They all install in basically the same way, but be sure to follow the specific instructions that are included with the unit. Generally, here's what involved.

1. **Unpack the faucet and check that it:**

   - Is the model you want
   - Fits the sink holes
   - Comes with all the parts that are needed for installation

2. **Follow the manufacturer's directions and install the gasket or apply the plumber's putty.**

   Many faucet designs have a rubber gasket that goes between the base of the valves and spout assembly and the countertop. Others require a bead of plumber's putty to be applied to the underside of these units.

3. **Place the faucet spout on the sink or countertop.**

   If the spout has riser tubes already installed, align them with the hole in the sink and lower the spout body into place.

4. **Place the faucet valve assemblies (hot and cold) into the holes in the countertop.**

   If these valves have riser tubes already installed, thread them through the holes in the countertop.

   If the faucet isn't equipped with built-in riser tubes, thread them onto the valve tailpieces and then jump ahead to Step 8.

5. **From the underside of the sink, tighten the hold-down bolts.**

   Some models have large washers and nuts that screw on the valve tailpieces, and others are held in place with brackets that bolt to the underside of the valve body.

6. **From under the sink, connect the flexible hoses from the hot and cold valves with the spout (see Figure 12-21).**

Figure 12-21:
The separate valves and spout allow this faucet to fit a wide variety of sinks. The valves are connected to the spout with flexible tubes.

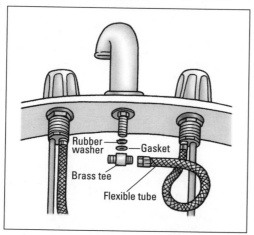

Rubber washer — Gasket

Brass tee

Flexible tube

7. **Connect the riser tubes from the hot and cold valves to the stop valves on the wall.**

8. **Turn on the water and look for leaks.**

9. **Remove the aerator screen from the spout and run water through the faucet to flush out any debris that may be in the pipes.**

10. **When the water runs clear, replace the aerator.**

Showdown at the shut-off valves

A shut-off or stop valve controls the water flow to your faucets, so it's a good idea to have them installed for every faucet (one for the hot water and one for the cold). Many homes have them, but surprisingly not all of them do. The valve is important because it stops water supply lines so that when you need to fix a leak, you don't have to shut down the water supply to the entire house. It's a safety precaution too, so if there's an overflow, you can stop the flow of water to the faucet.

The two styles used at sinks are a right-angle stop valve for when a water pipe enters through a wall, and a straight stop valve for when water enters through the floor. Before you buy one, you should know what valve style you're replacing and what type of water pipes you have: plastic, copper, or galvanized. For this job, you use basic plumbing tools: a basin wrench, an adjustable pipe wrench, and, of course, a bucket.

Part IV
Winning Ways with Walls, Windows, and More

The 5th Wave   By Rich Tennant

KERM BROS. SERVICE STATION

"Faux wood grain towel dispensers, matching toilet plungers, herb scented urinal cakes, where's it all end, Stan?"

In this part . . .

In this part, we discuss the basics of covering walls, finishing floors, and choosing windows to make your bathroom the best it can be. In addition, we offer the latest lighting ideas and suggestions on ways to ventilate your bathroom.

Chapter 13

Walls and Ceilings Finished to Perfection

. . . .

In This Chapter

▶ Preparing the surface

▶ Releasing the power of paint

▶ Getting the hang of wallpaper installation

▶ Creating a country atmosphere with beadboard

▶ Walking the plank on the ceiling

. . . .

*B*athroom walls can be boring or beautiful, but whether in a small hall bathroom or an expansive luxury spa, they're a critical element of the room. Just change the color from beige to blue, and the entire room takes on a new look and feel. You can expand the feel of a small dark bathroom with an airy, open-pattern wallpaper, just like you can unify the cut-up floor plan of a master bath with a warm monotone design.

Traditionally, bathroom walls have been painted, wallpapered, or tiled, but today the walls are clad in paneling, wainscoting, and solid surface. Whatever the style of fixtures and cabinetry you choose, there are wallcoverings to enhance the style. Because all budgets and bathrooms are unique to their owners, you'll find projects for both the frugal and fanciful to tempt your creative spirit.

Taking On Surface Preparation

Although you'll probably derive no real joy in the process of preparing the walls and surfaces in a bathroom for a new finish, you certainly need to do that job. A coat of paint needs a clean solid surface to adhere to, and wallpaper should be applied to clean, flat walls. Any material such as tile or paneling needs a sound surface as well. So take on this task with the smug assurance that only you will see the perfect condition of the walls behind the finish.

Cleaning with gusto

Haul out the vacuum cleaner and use its crevice tool to remove cobwebs and dust in the ceiling corners, on the tops of windows and door casings, on baseboards, and anywhere else you find them.

Wash any dirty or dusty surfaces, including the ceiling, walls, doors, and woodwork, with detergent and water. (Before washing, protect the floor with a dropcloth.) Complete the job by rinsing the surfaces with clear water and letting them dry.

The small black spots that don't easily wash off may be mold or mildew stain, which is a common problem in bathrooms that don't have enough ventilation. To kill mildew, use a solution of one part household bleach to three parts water applied with a sponge. It may take more than one application. Let it sit for 15 to 20 minutes before rinsing the surface with clean water. If you're planning to paint the walls, wipe them down with water to stop the bleaching action. You also can use mildew cleaning solutions that are on the market.

Household bleach is strong stuff, so wear old clothes, rubber gloves, and eyeglasses and provide plenty of ventilation. Bleach can burn your lungs and aggravate asthma. Remember to never mix bleach and ammonia.

Repairing small holes and cracks

Remove pictures and wall hangings and any fixtures and cabinets that will be replaced, along with their fasteners. Doing so will probably expose pin holes, gaping holes, and holey holes, but thoroughly repairing the surface of the walls is a task that you can't skip.

To repair small holes and dings, get a small container of patching compound and apply it with a putty knife. When dry, sand the patch smooth with fine sandpaper on a sanding block or an electric pad sander. The compound shrinks as it dries, so you'll probably need to add another coat.

Filling in larger holes

To fill larger holes revealed when a wall-hung sink or toilet is removed, or to patch a hole that the doorknob bashed into the wall, make a wallboard repair patch by following these easy steps:

1. **Use a drywall saw to enlarge the hole and a square to square off the edges (see Figure 13-1).**

   Measure the hole and add 2 inches to the length and width to determine the size of the patch.

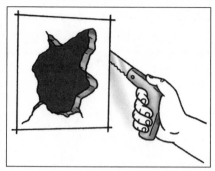

Figure 13-1:
Enlarge the irregular hole by cutting away the damaged wallboard.

2. **With a utility knife, cut a piece of drywall to use as a repair patch.**

   Use the measurement from Step 1.

3. **Place the drywall repair patch with the face (paper side) down on a table and draw straight lines 1 inch in from the edges of the patch to form a square 1 inch smaller than the patch.**

4. **With a utility knife, cut along the lines to penetrate into the gypsum core of the repair patch.**

5. **Without cutting into the paper facing, carefully score the patch with the knife, and break off the outer section of core.**

6. **Peel off the gypsum core and leave the paper backing attached.**

7. **Score the patch along the other lines and remove the 1-inch piece of core from around the perimeter of the patch.**

8. **Spread drywall compound evenly on the back of the paper facing that you just exposed by cutting away the core.**

   Make sure that you spread the compound on the edge of the gypsum core.

9. **Place the repair patch into the hole in the wall and use a putty knife to smooth the paper edges, squeezing out the excess drywall compound.**

10. **Spread this excess drywall compound evenly over the patch.**

11. **Apply another thin coat of compound over the patch edge, feathering the coat several inches beyond the outline of the patch (see Figure 13-2).**

12. **Let the compound dry overnight and then apply a second coat in the same way.**

13. **When dry, sand the repaired area so that it's smooth and even with the surface of the wall.**

Figure 13-2:
Apply a thin coat of drywall compound to the perimeter of the patch to cover the paper edges.

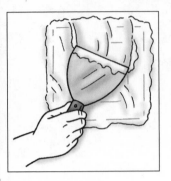

Fixing popped nails

If you come across some popped nails, those crescent-shaped indentations or dimples in wallboard, they're easy to fix. Here's how:

1. **Secure the wallboard to the studs with a new nail or drywall screws above and below the popped nail.**

   Drive the nail or screw so it's just below the surface of the wallboard but doesn't break the wallboard's paper facing.

2. **Use a nail set to drive the loose nail tight against the stud.**

   Give several good hammer taps to the nail set to drive the popped nail all the way through the wallboard core and tight against the stud.

3. **Finish up the repair by applying two or three coats of joint compound to conceal the area, and let it dry.**

4. **Sand the area smooth with fine sandpaper or a sanding block.**

5. **Repeat Steps 3 and 4 if necessary.**

Fixing sagging ceiling plaster

Sagging is a chronic problem with loose ceiling plaster. To beat it, we recommend securing the loose plaster to the lath with plaster washers and then covering the entire surface with thin $3/8$-inch wallboard panels. We've used this technique in several rooms, including the bathroom.

1. **Fasten the loose plaster to the lath behind it with plaster washers, small metal discs fastened with four $1^5/8$-inch drywall screws (see Figure 13-3).**

Figure 13-3:
Plaster washers used with drywall screws pull any loose plaster tight against the lath.

2. **Cover the ceiling with new ⅜-inch wallboard.**

   Use at least 2-inch drywall screws to penetrate through the wallboard and plaster and reach the ceiling joists.

3. **Finish it with drywall tape and compound and then sand it smooth.**

Removing electrical covers

Before finishing the walls, use a screwdriver to remove any light fixtures and switch and outlet covers. Cover the switches with blue painter's tape with the light switch in the "off" position.

Use a neon circuit tester, an inexpensive device found in the electrical section of home centers and hardware stores, to verify that there is no power to exposed wires.

Prime-Time Painting

Why paint? A can of paint is the best bang for your decorating buck because it's the fastest and cheapest quick fix that will transform any bathroom, no matter how humble or grand. We suggest you use a mildew-preventive paint or a mildewcide additive in the paint you use to combat the growth of the nemesis of all bathrooms: mildew. But before you pick up the paintbrush, take the time to assess the condition of the surfaces and make any repairs that are needed. The more time spent smoothing, sanding, and cleaning the walls, ceiling, and woodwork, the better the paint job.

At the Dutch Boy Web site (www.dutchboy.com), you'll find an interactive Project Planner that provides a dramatic way to change the look of a room with paint. Starting with the Product Selector, the four-part Project Planner guides you through your project — coordinating colors, selecting primers and paints, giving you tips, and calculating the right amount of paint. Then you can print out a Project Companion with all the product and how-to information you need. Ain't technology great?

Removing old paint

Many old bathrooms have windows and trim laden in layers of paint that you should remove before repainting. You have a choice of using a chemical gel-type stripper or a heat gun. Neither is fun, but the results are worth the effort. For either process, you need the following materials:

- Dropcloths (the heavy plastic variety)
- Dust mask
- Paintbrush (an inexpensive one is okay)
- Paint scrapers
- Putty knife
- Respirator
- Rubber gloves that are chemical resistant
- Safety goggles

Don't sand or scrape lead paint, because the dust is toxic and, unless carefully contained, it will migrate to other parts of the house. Also don't use a heat gun to remove lead paint because it can vaporize the lead and breathing the vapors is just as much a health hazard as ingesting or inhaling the dust.

If you're not sure what kind of paint is on the window, test it with an inexpensive lead-paint kit. For information about dealing with lead paint, check with the National Lead Information Clearinghouse (800-424-LEAD).

Using a chemical stripper

When using a paint stripper, in addition to the materials in the previous list, you also need an after-wash product and steel wool. Using a paint stripper can be messy, but it's not hard to do.

1. **Apply the paint stripper with a disposable paintbrush.**
2. **Wait for it to lift the paint.**

3. **Scrape the paint off the wood.**

   Paint scrapers work for flat surfaces, but steel wool works best to lift the softened paint from contoured surfaces.

4. **Use a clean brush to apply the after-wash to remove any residue.**

5. **Dry the wood with a rag or paper towels.**

6. **Sand for a smooth finish.**

Using a heat gun

If you use a heat gun to remove paint, you need a putty knife to scrape off the paint after the gun melts and softens it. Sanding and smoothing the surface are the last steps.

Putting on new paint

In a bathroom, we recommend using latex (water-based) paint. Applying latex paint is easy, even for a first-time painter, and in a matter of hours can dramatically transform a bathroom. The bonus is that you can wipe away drips with a water-dampened rag and clean up brushes and rollers with water, making it the easiest paint to work with.

Many people prefer an eggshell, low-luster, or satin finish that has a slight sheen. If the bathroom will be used often and by many members of your household, consider a semigloss, which will be more durable and scrubbable than an eggshell finish. And if you want the walls to have a high-tech shiny sheen, go with a semigloss or high-gloss finish.

Take a trip to the paint department of any hardware store or home center or go to a paint retailer and get advice from the pro at the paint counter about paint for your bathroom. Several types of primers are available to help the paint bond on certain surfaces, such as unfinished wood or walls with stains and mildew. Several paint manufacturers have a paint with mildewcide, such as Perma-White, that comes with warranties against mildew growth. Spend some time asking questions of the pros so that you choose the best paints for the different surfaces in your bathroom.

The best sequence for painting is to start at the top and move downward. We recommend painting the ceiling and walls first and then the woodwork, because the paint roller always splatters a mist of wall paint on the trim. It's easy to swipe the splatter with a damp rag.

You need the following tools and materials to apply paint:

- 2- or 2½-inch sash brush
- Dropcloths

- ✔ Paint
- ✔ Paint paddle for stirring
- ✔ Paint roller with a ½-inch nap
- ✔ Roller pan

Before you get started, here are some tips to make the job easier:

- ✔ Protect the floor and fixtures with dropcloths and assemble the paint and equipment.
- ✔ Stir the paint according to the directions on the paint can and pour the paint into a roller pan.
- ✔ Use a paint roller with a ⅜- or ½-inch nap roller and pan to apply paint to the wide surfaces of the ceiling and walls.
- ✔ Paint out of the can with a 2-inch-wide angled sash paintbrush for outlining or cutting in the paint at joints and around woodwork.

Painting the ceiling

The key to a professional-looking ceiling is to go slowly, work in one small area (6 to 8 square feet) at a time, and overlap all previously completed areas.

1. **Cut in the ceiling joint where it meets the wall.**

   Use a 2- to 2½-inch brush to apply paint into the corner. Run the ceiling paint ½ inch or so onto the wall to be sure to cover the old wall or ceiling color.

2. **Start painting with a roller along the area that you first cut in, going slowly and as close to the wall as possible.**

3. **Continue painting small sections at a time, rolling your way across the ceiling until the entire ceiling is covered.**

   As you go, remember to overlap the previously painted area.

Paint with plenty of light and inspect your work for drips, ridges, or missed spots as you work.

Painting the walls

Paint the walls with the same smooth roller motion that you use on the ceiling.

Use an extension pole for both ceilings and walls. It screws into the end of any paint roller and lets you spread paint high on the wall without using a ladder.

1. **Cut in around the corners of the room and around the woodwork and trim with a brush.**

2. **Using a roller and starting in an upper corner of the wall, spread the paint evenly, feathering the paint into the wet edge of the cut-in paint, and then moving to the area below it.**

3. **Blend the top and bottom sections with light, floor-to-ceiling strokes before moving to the next area.**

   As you complete each floor-to-ceiling area, blend it with the adjacent one.

4. **Keep a lookout for drips (clean them up with a rag) and missed spots (fondly referred to as *holidays*) and go over these areas again with the roller.**

5. **Clean up the paint applicators, put the paint away, and let the paint dry.**

If you have to stop in the middle of a painting project, wrap the brush or roller in plastic wrap and put it in the refrigerator. Before using it again, let it return to room temperature so you don't thin your paint with condensation.

Painting woodwork: Trim, doors, and cabinets

For hard surfaces such as woodwork and cabinets, we recommend an alkyd (oil-based) paint, which provides a tough, durable finish that can be washed frequently. Alkyd isn't as clean-up friendly as latex paint because you use mineral spirits or paint thinner to clean up drips and clean out brushes and rollers, but we think the long-lasting quality is worth it.

Latex paints have gotten so good that more and more people use latex on woodwork. A good-quality 100 percent latex acrylic gives a smooth, easy-to-maintain finish. Latex enamels dry faster than alkyd-based paints and are a bit more difficult to work with to get a smooth finish free of brush marks. A paint conditioner like Flotrol can extend the wet edge time of latex paint and make it easier to handle.

Do the math: Calculating how much paint to buy

To figure out how much paint to buy, find the square footage of the bathroom and divide by the number of square feet covered by a gallon of paint (approximately 350 square feet). For example, suppose that you have a 10-x-12-foot bathroom with an 8-foot ceiling. Because the room has two 10-foot walls and two 8-foot walls, you count each wall twice when calculating how much paint you need. The math looks like this: 10 x 8 x 2 = 160 and 12 x 8 x 2 = 192; 160 + 192 = 352 square feet. About a gallon of paint will paint the room, with some left over for touch-ups. The square footage of a 10-x-12 ceiling is 120, so a gallon of paint will be plenty. Actually, you can probably do it with two quarts, but ceiling paint is most commonly sold by the gallon and quarts are so expensive that, if you buy two, you've almost paid as much as for an entire gallon.

You can definitely spend more time preparing these surfaces for paint than actually painting them. To recoat painted wood, patch any holes in the surface with wood filler and let it dry before sanding it smooth. Use a stain killing primer such as B-I-N on any water-stained wood. By spot priming trouble areas before painting the finish coat, you're improving the bond of the topcoat to the surface, giving you a better paint job.

You'll get the best-looking paint job by preparing the surface first by sanding with medium-grit (80–100 grit) sandpaper. Then use fine (150-grit) and very fine (220-grit) sandpaper, sanding only as needed to dull the existing finish, smooth repairs, or sand out any scratches. You can use a rubber sanding block or a finishing sander on the flat surfaces and a sanding sponge on contoured surfaces. Sand the entire surface until it's uniformly smooth.

If the woodwork or trim is new, unfinished wood, sand it first and then apply a primer that you brush or roll on before the final sanding.

An alternative to sanding previously painted surfaces is to use a chemical deglosser, which you brush on shortly before you're ready to paint.

Depending on the preparation needed, the process of painting woodwork and cabinets can involve several applications, with drying and sanding in between. You'll get the best results by applying a primer followed by a split coat of a 50/50 mixture of primer and topcoat and a final coat of topcoat.

Paint the woodwork and trim in a room before hanging wallpaper so that you don't risk getting paint spills or drips on the wallpaper. If you can schedule the work to give the paint job a few days to dry and harden, you'll be guaranteed a nice, tough surface.

Starting with primer

When the surface is clean and dry and the sheen has been removed by sanding, it's ready for the primer coat. Use masking tape and plastic dropcloths to protect surfaces and fixtures and protect the floor with a dropcloth.

To paint windows and doors, use an angled sash brush and an inside-to-outside approach with the primer coat. In other words, begin on the sashes of a window and work your way out to the casing. When painting a paneled door or cabinet, use the same approach: First paint inside the panel and then work to the outside. As you paint, hold the brush loosely and dip into the paint no more than halfway up the bristles. Tap the brush on the edge of the can to remove the excess paint.

If you're painting a cabinet, paint detailed areas first and then the flat surfaces, brushing with the wood grain. Brush out of corners, not toward them, to avoid dragging your brush across edges, which leaves too much paint in the corners.

Painting with paint

When the primer coat has dried, sand with 220-grit sandpaper to remove any roughness, brush marks, and imperfections. Then apply the first split coat in the same manner as the primer coat. Let the first split coat dry and repeat with a second application.

Painting tiles

Yes, you can paint plastic or ceramic wall tile, as long as the tile is sound and not in direct contact with water, like inside a shower or bathtub. This is a no-brainer for a do-it-yourselfer because of the low investment and high payback: new wall tiles in any color you want. It's a real saving compared to the alternative of removing the tile, resurfacing the wall, and installing new tile, and is the answer to changing the look of a bathroom without breaking the budget. However, painted tile isn't as durable, and eventually it will show some wear.

Follow these steps for painting tiles:

1. **Wash the surface with a 50-50 solution of household ammonia and water to remove soap film from the tiled walls and then rinse with plain water and let them dry.**

2. **Scrub the grout lines with a stiff toothbrush to remove dirt and mildew.**

   Allow the tile to dry before you use bleach to kill any mildew on the grout.

3. **Let the tiles and grout dry.**

4. **Lightly sand the tiles with a medium-grit sandpaper for better paint adhesion.**

5. **Apply a shellac-based primer, such as B-I-N, to coat and bond the surface.**

6. **Apply two coats of alkyd paint, letting each coat dry between applications (see Figure 13-4).**

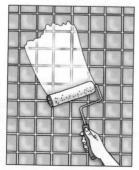

Figure 13-4:
Apply paint
to tiles with
a roller.

Two light coats are better that a single heavy coat. Use an angled sash brush to cut in a 2-inch-wide border of paint around the perimeter of the tiled surface. Then apply paint inside the border with a paint roller. Be careful to blend the top and bottom sections with light strokes before moving to the next area and roll the paint out in one direction until it's evenly spread. Lightly apply your final strokes with a nearly dry roller and overlap the previously completed area.

As you work, periodically shine a work light on the fresh paint to check for drips, ridges, or missed spots.

Use painter's masking tape to protect the surround surfaces, cabinets, fixtures, or anything else that you don't want to paint.

Stenciling for a fast and fanciful fix-up

To transform ordinary painted walls in a bathroom, add a light touch with a decorative stencil design. In no time at all and with very little money, you can change the room's personality. Pick up a precut acetate stencil design, a stencil brush, and some acrylic paints (which are easier to use if you pour out a small amount into a small container) at a paint or craft store, and you're good to go.

The stencil has registration holes used to align the repeating pattern as you reposition it along the wall. You'll need a pencil, string, and a level to lay out the design so that it's level. Use spray adhesive or low-tack painter's masking tape to attach the stencil to the wall (see Figure 13-5).

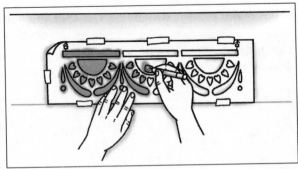

Figure 13-5: Painter's masking tape keeps the stencil in place as you work.

Follow these easy stenciling instructions:

1. **Beginning at a corner of the bathroom, measure down from the ceiling to the point where you want the top or bottom of the stencil and pencil a tick mark at this point.**

2. **Use a level to draw a level guideline around the room.**

3. **Starting in a corner, align the top or bottom of the stencil, depending how you drew the layout line.**

4. **Use tape or spray adhesive to hold the stencil in place.**

5. **Dip the stencil brush into the paint, blotting it first on paper toweling to remove the excess.**

6. **Dab the paint inside the cutout of the design, working your way around from its edges and filling the center of the design last.**

   Because most stencil patterns use more than one color, do one color at a time. Put masking tape over the unused cutouts so you don't get confused (and so you don't get paint in places where you don't want it).

7. **Pencil a mark in one of the registration holes and use it as an easy reference point as you walk the stencil around the room (see Figure 13-6).**

Figure 13-6:
Use the
registration
marks on
the stencil
to maintain
pattern
alignment.

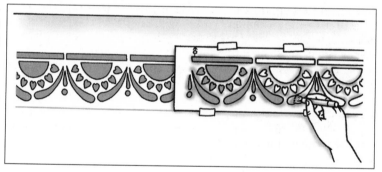

8. **Make your way around the room, applying the first paint color in the cutout and peeling the acetate from the wall as you go, being careful not to smudge the fresh paint.**

9. **When the paint is dry, erase your pencil lines and marks.**

We feel compelled to tell you we also wrote *Painting and Wallpapering For Dummies* (published by Wiley), which goes into greater detail and can answer any questions you have about painting and wallpapering.

Working with Wallpaper

There's no two ways about it. Either you hate a wallpaper pattern and can't wait to get it off the walls or you're enchanted with its color and design and can't wait to hang it. Whether it makes you crazy or makes your day, wallpapering is one of the most popular home decorating projects.

Removing wallpaper: Cheap therapy

Need to blow off some steam? Feeling stressed out? There's no better time to remove old wallpaper than when you want to release tension and stress. It can be therapy for your soul. Removing wallpaper is the epitome of grunt work that anyone can succeed at, and it feels so good when it's over.

Paint over wallpaper? Yes, you can, but we won't tell you how because you'll never be able to forgive yourself when you see how lousy it looks. And if you sell the house, the new owners have a legal right to come after you. Just kidding.

Here are the tools and materials you need to get stripping. If you don't have them, look in the wallpaper section of a paint or home center.

- Abrasive pad
- Bucket and sponge or paint roller tray and roller
- Gel-type wallpaper remover
- Masking tape
- Old towels
- Plastic dropcloths
- Single-edge razor blade
- Wallpaper scraper
- Wheeled scoring tool

First, you need to find out whether the paper is dry-strippable: Loosen the paper at a corner with a single-edge razor blade and then pull slowly at a low angle. If the wallpaper doesn't strip off, or if only the decorative facing comes off, leaving behind its paper backing, you'll need to take the leap and strip it off. We make this process as painless as possible in the following steps:

1. **Turn off the power to the bathroom at the main panel to prevent getting a shock from the exposed wiring in the electrical boxes.**

2. **Remove the electrical outlet and switch plate covers with a screwdriver and cover the outlets with masking tape.**

3. **Use plastic dropcloths and masking tape to protect the floor and fixtures (see Figure 13-7).**

4. **Perforate the face of the old wallpaper with a wheeled scoring tool so that the wallpaper remover can penetrate it and soften the adhesive holding it on the wall (see Figure 13-8).**

   Scoring is particularly necessary for vinyl, vinyl-faced, or other non-porous wall coverings. Roll the tool all over the surface to make hundreds of little cuts through the paper.

Figure 13-7: Catch the soggy wallpaper with a plastic dropcloth taped to the baseboard.

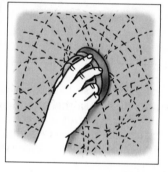

Figure 13-8: Perforate the surface of the wallpaper so that wallpaper stripper can soak behind the paper faster.

5. **Pour a gel-type wallpaper remover into a bucket or paint roller tray and apply it to the wallpaper with a sponge or paint roller.**

   Work slowly from the bottom up to minimize the amount that rolls down the wall. To start, apply the gel in two 3- to 4-foot-wide, floor-to-ceiling wall sections. Don't go overboard wetting the wallpaper.

6. **Scrape the wallpaper when it turns a dark color or starts to bubble.**

   Follow the directions on the wallpaper remover can. Use a wallpaper scraper designed to remove the wallpaper without damaging the surface beneath it.

7. **Reapply remover in the areas where the paper doesn't come off.**

   Just rewet the remover and wait for it to work.

8. **While the adhesive residue left on the walls is still soft, wash the walls with clean, warm water.**

   Use a sponge or an abrasive pad where needed. Work quickly on drywall to avoid overwetting the surface.

9. **Have a helper follow immediately with a towel to dry the surface.**

Wallpapering a bathroom

In Chapter 5, we discuss choosing wallcoverings for a bathroom and suggest that vinyl-coated, fabric-backed, prepasted ones are the best. Now we're down to the brass tacks of hanging it.

To determine how much wallpaper to buy, calculate the area you plan to paper and divide that number by the usable yield per roll of paper. As you're making your selection, ask a store employee to look at your numbers. Tell the clerk the square footage of the room and the number of doors and windows, and he can calculate how many rolls you need based on the area of the room and the pattern on the paper you've chosen. The larger the size of the repeat, the more waste.

The wallpaper goes up last, after you've painted the ceiling, woodwork, and trim and after you've applied a wall sizing designed to seal the wall surface and make it easy to reposition the paper while you're installing it. Sizing is easy to apply with a paint roller, and it's well worth the added effort.

Hanging wallpaper in the bathroom is not a two-person sport, or at least it's not for us. The small confines and intricate cuts make this a challenging project, so don't even think about doing it in a hurry. Bathrooms are usually small spaces and sometimes even setting up a ladder can be a challenge. So allow plenty of time to do the job, turn on the radio, and unleash your creative talents.

Gather the following tools and materials to hang wallpaper:

- 6-inch broad knife
- Carpenter's level
- Dropcloths
- Paint roller and pan
- Razor knife and blades
- Scissors
- Screwdriver
- Wallpaper brush
- Wallpaper sizing
- Wall sponge

Before you can hang the paper, you have to remove all wall decorations, towel bars, and wall accessories and patch any holes in the walls with spackling compound. Lay down dropcloths to protect the fixtures, cabinets, and floor.

Don't forget to remove the switch plate covers from the electrical outlets in the walls and turn off electricity to the room so that you don't risk getting shocked if your razor knife happens to hit a "live" wire in an electrical outlet or lighting switch. No kidding — that happened to a friend of ours, and he landed in the hospital.

Follow these steps to hang wallpaper:

1. **Use a paint roller and pan to apply a wallpaper sizing to the walls so that it's easy to slide the wet wallpaper around on the wall as you position it.**

   Allow the sizing to dry before hanging the paper.

2. **Follow the instructions on the wallpaper packaging about wetting the wallcovering to activate the adhesive on the back of it.**

3. **Find a starting point in the room — the corner in the back is usually a good place — and, using a carpenter's level, draw vertical lines at the top, middle, and bottom of the wall.**

   The lines will be the location for the first strip of wallpaper (see Figure 13-9).

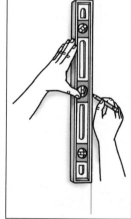

Figure 13-9:
Use a level to draw a vertical line on the wall to align the first sheet of wallpaper.

4. **Unroll the wallpaper and reverse it so the top of the pattern is at the top of the roll.**

5. **Rough-cut the first strip.**

   Hold the roll on the wall and, allowing for an excess of about 3 inches at the top and the bottom, cut the first strip.

6. **When the adhesive on the back of the first strip is ready to hang, fold the paper without creasing it with the wet back sides together.**

This technique is called *booking the paper*, and it keeps the adhesive moist.

7. **Unfold the top of the first strip, align it with the vertical lines at the starting point, and position the strip so you have about 3 inches above the ceiling joint.**

8. **Use a wallpaper brush to smooth the strip all down the wall, working your way from the center of the strip toward the edges of the paper, removing creases or bubbles with the brush.**

9. **Use a sharp razor knife and trim guard to cut excess wallpaper at the top and bottom of the wall, making a clean, decisive cut through the wallpaper (see Figure 13-10).**

   Use a 6-inch broad knife as a guide to push the paper tight against the trim before cutting it.

Figure 13-10:
Cut wallpaper with a
very sharp
razor knife.

10. **Remove excessive adhesive with a wet sponge.**

11. **Unfold the next strip, aligning it with the first one and matching the pattern, allowing about 3 inches at the top and bottom.**

12. **Join the strips together at a butt seam and smooth and seal them with a small hand-held seam roller.**

Papering around obstructions

As you work your way around the room, you'll meet electrical outlets, windows, doorways, and fixtures. Simply make relief cuts around them. The cuts can be simple right angles cut around an electrical outlet or more free-hand cuts around ceiling fixtures. Smooth the paper as close as possible to the obstruction, hold the razor knife firmly in hand, and make a clean sharp cut.

Another technique involves creasing the wallpaper around the obstructions, peeling it back gently, and using a pair of scissors to make the cut along the crease.

Papering a corner

To make cuts at an inside or outside corner, use a wrap and overlap technique to double-cut the wallpaper, creating a nice, clean seam.

1. **To hang a strip into a corner, measure and cut the strip lengthwise so it will meet the corner, wrapping around the corner about ½ inch.**

2. **Hang the strip, but peel it back from the corner a few inches, about ⅛ inch farther from the corner than the narrowest width of the cutoff.**

   Use a carpenter's level as a guideline.

3. **Apply the next strip on the adjacent wall and wrap the corner, making sure that the pattern matches.**

4. **Smooth the second strip in place and trim with the razor knife guided by a long metal straightedge (see Figure 13-11).**

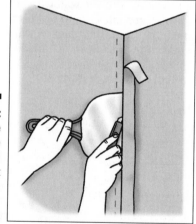

Figure 13-11: Overlap the paper in the corner and then cut through both layers.

5. **Remove the trimmed area and peel back the wallpaper from the corner so you can reposition the first strip.**

6. **Smooth both in place with the seam roller.**

7. **Continue around the room until reaching the starting point, using the same double-cutting technique we explain in Steps 4 and 5 to fill in the gap between the first and the last strips, if the last strip doesn't fill exactly.**

8. **Reinstall the switch plate covers, and you're done.**

For an almost instant face-lift for a bathroom, apply a prepasted or adhesive-backed wallpaper border. You'll find them in 15-foot-long rolls in a wide selection of styles and sizes for upwards of $8 a roll.

Adding Beadboard Wainscoting

In a bathroom, which has so many hard surfaces, wood can soften the look, adding a natural warmth and appeal. Beadboard, which is a wood panel with vertical grooves, is an old material given new life in today's homes. You'll see it everywhere, but it's especially popular teamed with a chair rail and used as wainscoting. Whether used in a small half bath or an expansive master bath suite, beadboard wainscoting adds charm and character that few other materials can.

Beadboard is sold in 4-foot-wide panels that come in an 8-foot length to cover walls and ceilings and also as 32-inch-high precut panels specifically for use as wainscoting. It comes in unfinished pine and in various woods and finishes. You'll also find beadboard made of polystyrene that's perfect for painting.

Wainscoting is installed by gluing and nailing it to the wall with adhesive and capping it with a chair rail molding. You'll see intricate to ordinary rail moldings with beadboard finished with paint or stain. You paint or wallpaper the top two-thirds of the walls where wainscoting has been installed.

To install beadboard wainscoting, you need these materials:

- Beadboard wainscoting panels
- Chair rail molding
- Chalk line
- Circular saw
- Construction adhesive
- Hammer
- Line level
- Measuring tape
- Miter saw (or miter box)
- Nail set
- Pencil
- Putty knife
- Saber saw
- Safety glasses

✔ Sandpaper

✔ Stud finder

✔ T square

Follow these directions to install wainscoting:

1. **Beginning in a corner, make a mark on the wall 32 inches up from the floor.**

2. **Drive a finish nail through the mark and hook the end of the chalk line over it.**

3. **Stretch the chalk line to the opposite corner.**

   Make sure the line is level.

4. **When the line is level, make another mark on the wall and drive a nail through the mark (see Figure 13-12).**

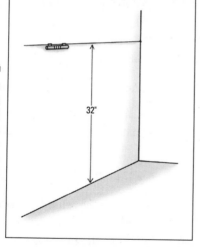

Figure 13-12:
Use a chalk line and line-level to establish a level line around the perimeter of the bathroom.

32"

5. **Measure the distance from the mark you make in Step 4 to the floor.**

   If it's over 32 inches, this is the low side of the room and you can continue around the room with the line.

   If the line you mark in Step 4 is less than 32 inches, start at the other end of the room (the high side) and mark a level line around the room.

6. **From the high side of the room, continue the level line around the room.**

   The line should be 32 inches above the highest point of the floor.

This way, the top edge of the beadboard can be installed on the level line without having to cut any panels. Molding will cover the gap at the floor.

7. **After you have the layout line established, use the stud finder to locate the wall studs and mark their location on the layout line and on the floor.**

    These marks will allow you to nail the panels and trim moldings to the studs. The floor marks will come in handy when you install the floor moldings.

8. **Beginning in a back corner, lay out the panels along the walls to see where the joints fall.**

    Arrange the panels so that you will not have a narrow piece in one of the corners or against a door or window.

9. **Run a line of construction adhesive in vertical lines about 4 inches apart on the wall and place the first panel into position.**

10. **Make adjustments so that the panel is level, press it firmly in place against the adhesive, and nail it into place.**

    Nail through the panel into the wall studs and use a nail set to drive the nail heads below the surface of the panel.

11. **Continue this process around the room.**

To fit a beadboard panel around a window, door, or cabinet, you need to do some careful measuring and cutting. For panels that will go around doors and other simple shapes, just transfer the profile of the door molding (or whatever object you're paneling around) to the panel and then use a saber saw to trim the panel.

Installing wainscoting around a window is a little trickier. Follow these steps:

1. **Measure the distance from the last panel to the window jamb and cut the panel to that width.**

2. **Measure down from the top of the panel to the top of the sill and mark this on the edge of the panel.**

3. **Measure from the top of the panel to the lower edge of the sill and mark this on the panel.**

4. **Measure the projection of the sill past the jamb and mark this on the panel.**

5. **Use the outline as a guide to create the shape of the sill and cut it out with a jigsaw (see Figure 13-13).**

Measure twice and cut once. Continually test-fit the panel to avoid miscutting the panel. Use the same technique of measuring and test-fitting the panel to make cutouts for electrical outlets or other obstructions.

Partitioning off the toilet area

To create a sense of privacy in a bathroom that has many users, divide the toilet area from the rest of the room with a full, three-quarter, or half-wall partition. Using framing and wallboard is one way, but also consider using a glass or acrylic block system to divide the space. You can configure the systems in a variety of shapes and sizes. You can find more about working with these systems in Chapter 11. Keep in mind that the suggested clearance requirement for a toilet enclosure is at least 36 inches wide and 66 inches deep.

Figure 13-13:
Trim the wainscoting to fit around window and door trim.

When all the panels are installed, install the chair rail and base moldings. Use a miter box to make miter cuts at the corners.

Hanging a Laminated Plank Ceiling

To create a classic country or cottage look in a bathroom, consider adding a laminated plank ceiling that's designed for a do-it-yourselfer to install. On any ceiling, planks are a definite attention getter, and on a less-than-perfect ceiling, they're a good coverup, too.

Look for planks designed to resist humidity — a good choice for a bathroom.

The interlocking tongue-and-groove planks can be installed in several ways, but in a bathroom, they're attached to two crisscrossing layers of furring strips, creating adequate air space above the planks. The planks are held up with a series of metal clips, which are slipped into the edges of the plank and screwed in place (see Figure 13-14). The clips and screws are concealed as the next plank is installed. Instead of using clips, you can staple the planks in place.

Figure 13-14:
The easiest method to secure the planks to the furring is with clips.

When you're planning the job, think about the directions you want the planks to run. Keep in mind that the planks run opposite the direction of the furring strips they're attached to.

The planks are ⅜ inch thick. Add that to the depth of the two layers of furring strips to determine how much ceiling height the plank ceiling will take up. If the room has a ceiling light fixture or vent, plan to mount the electrical boxes so that they're ⅜ inch lower than the furring strips. To prevent discoloration of the planks, choose a light fixture that will not raise the temperature of the planks above 230 degrees.

A day before you plan to install the planks, unpack them in or near the bathroom so that they can acclimate to the room.

To install a laminate plank ceiling, you need the following materials:

- 1-x-3 furring strips
- 2½-inch wood screws
- Chalk line
- Circular saw or jigsaw
- Cordless screwdriver
- Electric drill
- Handsaw
- Laminate ceiling plank system with installation kit

✔ Measuring tape

✔ Pencil

Fastening furring strips to the ceiling

To install a laminated plank ceiling, follow these steps:

1. **Decide which direction the ceiling joists run and snap a chalk line perpendicular to the joists every 16 inches across the ceiling.**

2. **Fasten a 1-x-3 furring strip to the ceiling along the chalk line, using 2½-inch wood screws.**

   Be sure to attach furring around the perimeter of the room. Use two nails or screws at each joist to keep the furring flat. When necessary, shim the furring strips to ensure a flat installation of the planks (see Figure 13-15).

3. **Repeat the process, installing another row of furring strips that criss-cross the first row.**

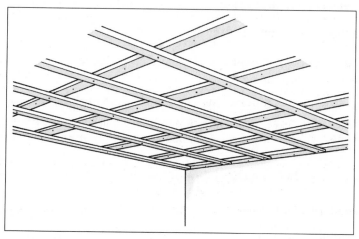

Figure 13-15:
A double grid of furring strips is required in a bathroom because of the high moisture.

Installing the planks

To have a balanced appearance of the planks, you have to do a little math calculation and determine the size of the first and last rows of planks so they're even. With accurate calculation, you're ready to install the planks.

1. **Find the width of the first row of planks by measuring the room in inches.**

2. **Measure across the room parallel with the strips and convert the dimension into inches.**

3. **Divide that number by 5 inches (the width of the planks) to find out how many planks you need.**

   For example, if the room measures 11 feet 4 inches, change it to 136 inches. Divide that amount by 5 inches and you get 27 planks with a remainder of 1 inch. Add 5 inches to the remaining 1 inch, which equals 6 inches. Divide 6 inches in half and get 3 inches. This is the width of the first row of planks. You will have 26 rows of full-width planks, with the first and last rows 3 inches wide.

4. **Rip (cut lengthwise) the planks to the proper width for the first row.**

   Be sure to cut off the tongue edge of the plank. If it's a little rough, that's okay because it will be covered by molding.

5. **Decide the starting point for aligning the first row of planks by measuring from the starting wall at each end of the room and marking the distance equal to the width of the starting plank plus ½ inch.**

6. **Snap a chalk line on the marks so you'll be able to align the planks.**

7. **Hold the first plank so that its grooved edge is on the chalk line and it's about ½ inch away from the wall (so it can expand).**

8. **Insert one of the metal clips into the groove that's milled in the edge of the plank and drive the screw into the furring strip.**

9. **Fasten the edge of the plank nearest the wall by screwing through the face of the plank.**

10. **Continue this process, putting one clip into each furring strip.**

    As you proceed, make sure that all the end joints fit together tightly. Check that the tongue is fully seated in the groove and the ends butt tightly together.

11. **To begin installing the full-width planks in the second and subsequent rows, choose random-length planks and stagger them.**

    This arrangement creates the most natural and pleasing appearance. When necessary, cut the planks.

12. **Continue this process, working your way across the ceiling and always screwing one metal clip at every furring strip.**

13. **Cut the last row of planks to width.**

    They should be the same width as the first row (see Steps 1 to 3).

14. **Slip them in place and screw through the faces of the planks as close to the wall as possible to secure them.**

15. **To finish the installation and conceal the gap around the perimeter of the ceiling, install a ceiling molding.**

Chapter 14

Floored by the Choices

- -

In This Chapter

▶ Choosing your flooring material

▶ Inspecting the subfloor

▶ Getting the subfloor ready

▶ Installing the floor

- -

Did you know that a floor accounts for about one-third of the space you see in a room? So no matter what size bathroom you're planning, the flooring material you choose packs a wallop of an impression. Do you want the floor to be the focal point of the room or provide a neutral backdrop for the fixtures and furnishings? If you have a plain-Jane bathroom that can use some visual interest, an oh-my-gosh tile floor may be a tremendous improvement. But if the new wallpaper and cabinets you plan shout, "Look at me!" perhaps a more neutral or subdued flooring is the best choice.

Sure, its visual impact may be powerful, but the comfort a floor creates and the care it requires are just as important. Keep in mind that the type of floor you choose should be determined by the bathroom's function, your taste and budget, and the maintenance it requires. Ebony floor tiles are indeed a dramatic choice, but remember that anything dark will show every speck of dirt and dust, not to mention talcum powder.

Selecting Your New Flooring Material

Today's flooring materials for a bathroom offer many choices in styles and textures, and many are surprisingly easy to install. Vinyl tiles range from 40 cents to $4 a square foot, while ceramic tiles are from $2 to $10 a square foot.

You'll find the greatest selection at a flooring retailer, where you can make arrangements to take samples home. Some stores charge a small rental fee that's applied to the purchase of the material; others trust you to return them like a library book. Take advantage of the opportunity to bring samples home and lay them on the floor to help you visualize how the pattern will look in your bathroom.

Most flooring retailers offer to install the materials they sell, so you can easily find out the cost of installation compared with doing it yourself. Keep in mind that the more expensive the material, the greater the risk of doing it yourself. By that, we mean if you make a mistake on inexpensive floor tile and have to buy more tiles, it isn't going to break your budget. But a mishap with top-of-the-line materials is going to cost you big time. We know many contractors who consider do-it-yourselfers their best customers. The pro gets called in whenever the do-it-yourselfer botches the job and turns to the pro to make it right. So put the cost of the materials and your time and talents in the equation when you're making the decision whether to do it yourself.

We explain how to install four different flooring materials in this chapter. Each one has its advantages and disadvantages, and the material you decide to use depends on many factors. Here's what to look for.

- **Ceramic or stone tiles:** Ceramic and stone floor tiles offer you an endless number of choices in their size, style, and colors, not to mention how you choose to lay them out. For safety's sake, those with a matte finish offer the best footing. Also keep in mind that the larger the tiles, the faster the installation.

- **Laminates:** While laminates were first introduced as wood look-alikes, today you'll find laminates that look like tile, quarried slate, and many variations and shades of different woods. The planks lock together like tongue-and-groove wood flooring. Some laminates are glued together, and others lock together with metal edges. They lie on a thin foamlike sheet of underlayment. A laminate floor can be installed over almost any subfloor. It is durable and resists stains and surface moisture, so it's a good choice for a bathroom.

- **Sheet vinyl:** When you want one dramatic pattern to cover your floor, sheet vinyl is a durable and long-lasting choice that offers variety and ease of use. Installation requires careful cutting and then laying the flooring over a layer of adhesive.

- **Vinyl tiles:** Embossed vinyl tiles are tough-working, no-wax surfaces. Some are self-sticking, with adhesive on the back of each tile, so you simply press them in place. Others are designed to be set into a bed of adhesive, adding a step to the installation process. Either type of tile is a good choice for a fast fix-up.

Before choosing one type or brand of flooring over another, find out whether there are any special considerations for using it in a bathroom.

Don't be afraid to ask questions and get advice from the retailer about ordering the correct amount of flooring for the job. Even when you're on an exploratory trip, have an accurate drawing of the floor with dimensions so that you can get an idea of the size and scope of the project. You'll quickly see that each type of flooring material comes in a range of prices, so look for a style that's within your budget. If you have an idea for a complex tile pattern, take a picture or a drawing of the design so you can estimate the different tiles you'll need.

Raves for radiant flooring

Tile is a great floor for any bathroom, but one of its drawbacks is obvious when your bare feet hit cold tile. The best solution to this chilling experience is installing an electrical radiant floor warming system before you install new floor tile. In fact, several manufacturers make low-wattage electric resistance mats that can be installed under just about any flooring material.

Some systems are designed to be imbedded in the thinset mortar bed under tile. Other systems can be installed under carpeting, laminate, or vinyl floors. If you have access to the underside of the floor, some systems can even be installed under an existing floor.

The electric heating coils are installed on the underlayment and then covered with thinset mortar and tile. These mats are efficient and consume about 12 watts per square foot of heated area. If you team this flooring with a smart thermostat programmed to turn the heat on during peak-use periods, this level of luxury is truly affordable.

See the flooring material calculators on the Cheat Sheet in the front of this book to estimate how many tiles you'll need.

When you're selecting material, make sure that it's available in the quantity you need. Although this advice may sound obvious, we know too many people whose remodeling or building projects have been halted because the flooring material was a no-show. Unless the flooring is laid, vanity cabinets can't be installed, and consequently, neither can countertops. So confirm that the material you choose is available in the quantity you need so that no snafu halts the progress of your remodeling.

On a more practical note, don't forget about making a bathroom safe by choosing surfaces prone to safe footing. Water makes polished surfaces such as marble and high-gloss tiles slippery, so if you choose them for flooring, use them as an accent, not directly near a bathtub or shower. Better choices are unglazed porcelain tiles and flooring with a textured surface, both of which are more resistant to slipping.

What Lies Beneath: Checking Out the Subfloor

A good bathroom floor begins beneath it at the subfloor level. It's sort of like the old saying, 'Behind every great man, there's a woman pushing him." Only when it comes to flooring, the saying goes, "Beneath every great floor, there's a structurally solid subfloor topped by a smooth layer of underlayment." You get the idea.

The easiest way to get an idea of what's under your floor is to remove a heating register in the floor and look at the exposed layers of flooring. You can also remove the door threshold, the metal or wood strip at the entrance to the room, to expose the joint between the floor in the bathroom and the other rooms. If you find several layers of flooring, remove the old floor down to the subfloor.

Floors in bathrooms are subjected to moisture, and through the years, even small amounts of water can cause the underlayment to rot, swell, or delaminate. In this case, both the floor and underlayment must be replaced.

Removing old flooring

Take it off. Take it *all* off. We're talking about the flooring material that you've determined is necessary to remove. We're always amazed at what we find under layers of old flooring. Yes, it's the typical ugly moss green and gold vinyl from the 1960s, but we've also found outdoor carpeting, ceramic tile, and old sheet vinyl that's stained or damaged. You need to get rid of it so you can take a good look at what lies beneath.

Some asbestos can be found in vinyl and linoleum flooring and mastics made before 1978. Asbestos is hazardous when it's disturbed so it's usually better and safer to cover an old floor (which may contain asbestos) with underlayment instead of tearing it out. If it has to be removed, call your local health department or state environmental agency to find a certified professional to test the material and remove it. Don't do it yourself.

Removing the molding

Before you can remove the existing flooring, you have to get the molding out of the way. To do this, you need these tools:

- Broad knife
- Hammer
- Marker
- Pry bar
- Thin piece of wood or shim

Start by removing the *base shoe* (piece of molding nailed to the baseboard molding to hide the gap at the floor) and the baseboard molding, which is nailed directly to the wall. The new material will butt up directly to the wall with a ¼-inch gap that allows for expansion.

To remove the base shoe, loosen it first with a broad knife and then use a pry bar (with the broad knife behind it to avoid marring the baseboard) to pull the base shoe from the baseboard. The pry bar's design gives you leverage to slide one end in between the molding and wall, while you use the other end to force the molding away from the wall. When the base shoe is off the wall, set it on a sturdy work surface and remove the nails with a hammer.

Remove the baseboard in basically the same way. First insert the broad knife between the wall and molding and then force the pry bar between the molding and broad knife. Loosen the baseboard in small increments (see Figure 14-1), prying the molding an inch or so from the wall at each nail and then repeating until all the nails are loosened before you remove the molding. When it's loose from the wall, insert a thin piece of wood between the baseboard and wall to protect the wall and give you better leverage with the pry bar.

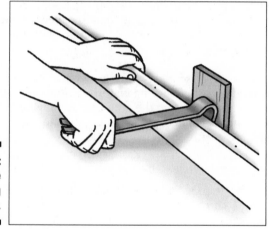

Figure 14-1:
Remove
the molding
carefully.

When the molding isn't covered in layers of paint, plan to reuse it and re-install it after the new flooring is laid. Use a marker to identify the location of the molding so you'll know where to reinstall it. For example, write something like "back wall behind toilet" on the back of the molding as soon as you remove it.

You may prefer to install new molding so that it's as shiny and new as your floor. You'll find new pine base shoe and baseboard molding sold at any lumberyard and some home centers. Measure the lengths of all the walls and then add about a quarter more so you'll have enough.

To install new base shoe molding, use a miter box and handsaw to make miter cuts at the outside corners and coped joints at the inside corners. Where the base shoe molding joins a door casing, smooth the junction and bevel the end with a block plane. Use 2-inch finishing nails to reinstall it. Use a nail set and hammer to drive the finish nails into the molding, and fill the holes with putty. Let it dry, and then sand and paint the molding.

Priming and sanding molding is much easier when you do it before installation. Then you can touch up any dings you make during installation, fill the nail heads with putty, sand, and apply a topcoat of paint.

If the molding is a simple rubber cove base, removing it is easy. Just use a broad knife or kitchen spatula and slide it down behind the cove base to break the seal of the adhesive holding it to the wall. Pull the rubber base away from the wall and remove the residue left with the putty knife. You may need to use a mastic remover if you can't scrape off the residue.

Peeling and prying off the old floor

Trial and error is the best advice we can give about removing an existing floor. You may get lucky and find that the adhesive under the floor is pliable and that you can easily peel off the floor — making the job a piece of cake. Or, you may find that the adhesive is like cement or is cement and nothing short of dynamite will dislodge the flooring.

For about $20 you can buy a *floor scraper,* a broom-size tool with an angled steel head used to strip off layers of flooring material. Often the tool is useful for dislodging the flooring material from the adhesive. Removing adhesive from the underlayment can be a challenge. Try softening the adhesive with a heat gun and then scraping it with a wide putty knife.

Removing tile

Removing tile isn't an easy project, and it's very labor intensive (expensive to pay someone else to do), so it pays to rip up old tile yourself. Be sure to protect yourself during the battle — wear safety glasses and heavy, preferably leather, gloves. The edges of the tile can be very sharp, so work carefully.

To remove tile, you need these tools and materials:

- ✔ Cold chisel
- ✔ Floor scraper
- ✔ Hammer
- ✔ Kneepads
- ✔ Leather gloves
- ✔ Safety glasses
- ✔ Small sledgehammer

If the tiles you're removing were set in mastic and not mortar, you're lucky — a floor scraper will do the job. However, if the tiles were set in mortar, follow these steps for getting it out of there:

1. **Break up the first tile by hitting it in the center with a hammer.**

2. **Place the cold chisel in the grout line at the edge of the tile and start chipping it out.**

3. **Repeat Steps 1 and 2 until you've removed several tiles.**

4. **Start breaking up several tiles at a time and removing them with the floor scraper.**

5. **Remove the mortar from the underlayment by hammering on a 2- to 3-foot-square section of the floor to smash up the remaining mortar, and then use the floor scraper to scrape the broken pieces of mortar off the underlayment.**

   If this doesn't get most of the mortar up, it's probably going to be easier to replace the underlayment.

Removing carpeting

Removing carpeting is much easier than removing tile. The following steps tell you how to do it:

1. **Remove any door thresholds or moldings that hold the carpeting in place and then choose a corner to start removing the carpeting.**

2. **Use a pry bar to lift one corner of the carpeting.**

   It may be installed on carpet strips, with tacks, or with adhesive. With carpet strips or tacks, be careful of the tacks around the edges because they're sharp. With glued-down carpet, you may have to use the floor scraper to loosen it and remove the mastic from the underlayment.

3. **Pull and then roll the carpeting up, along with any padding that may be there.**

4. **Remove all the material and then pull up any carpet strips, tacks, or adhesive until the floor is completely bare.**

   Getting down to the bare hull of the floor is crucial for installing a new one.

5. **If you find an uneven surface, sand the floor with an electric sander to make it smooth and blemish free.**

6. **If there are holes in the floor, apply a floor patching compound or resurfacer to fill in the voids.**

Removing vinyl flooring

Depending on how the floor is installed, removing vinyl tile and sheets can be easy or just about impossible. Some vinyl sheets are stapled or only glued around the perimeter, and they come up easily. Vinyl tile is always glued down and a real challenge, but newer self-stick tiles don't leave behind gobs of hard-to-remove mastic.

Follow these steps to remove newer vinyl sheet flooring:

1. **Use a sharp utility knife to cut vinyl sheets into 2-foot-wide strips.**

2. **If the floor is stapled or glued around the edges, pull up the edges, roll up the strips, secure them with heavy twine, and cart them away.**

3. **Remove any remaining backing or adhesive with a floor scraper.**

If you're removing vinyl tiles, follow these steps:

1. **Use a sharp utility knife to cut through the face of a tile.**

2. **Push the blade of a putty knife under the tile and pry it up.**

3. **When all the tile is removed, use a floor scraper to chip away at any remaining backing stuck to the floor.**

 To get rid of vinyl floor that is glued down, set the blade depth on a circular saw to cut through the vinyl and underlayment, but not into the subfloor. Cut the floor into manageable-sized pieces, pry them up, and cart both the underlayment and floor out together.

Assessing the subfloor

Damage to the subfloor will affect the look and longevity of your new flooring. One problem area is around the toilet, which can sweat during the summer, causing water to fall on the floor, work its way down to the underlayment and subfloor, and cause them to deteriorate. This happens over time, so the process usually goes unnoticed.

To assess any damage, you have to remove the toilet (see Chapter 9) and flooring. The damage will be evident around the area directly under the toilet, but you have to remove the underlayment surrounding the toilet to see whether the subfloor is also damaged. To make any necessary repairs to the subfloor, see the steps in "Replacing a damaged subfloor," later in this chapter.

Using the Existing Floor as a Base

In many cases, you won't have to do anything but install the new floor. Sheet vinyl can be installed over most old flooring materials if it's in good condition, and ceramic tile can go right over old tile. Most laminated wood products can be installed over just about any structurally sound surface.

But what if someone has already beaten you to the punch and installed a second or even a third layer of flooring? In this case, you'll have to come clean and rip out the old before you install the new.

Another consideration in adding a new layer of flooring to the existing floor will affect the tub, sink, and toilet. If these objects weren't removed when the new layers of floor were installed, the build-up around them creates an unsightly problem. Remember that the head room in the bathroom shrinks as the thickness of the floor grows.

Here is a rundown of existing floors that will work under a new floor:

- ✔ **Existing tile:** Ceramic tile that is properly installed is a very durable floor and can be used as a subfloor for just about any new floor. If the floor has cracked and some tiles are loose, you can remove them and fill the depressions with a floor patch. As long as there is no movement in the floor around the cracked areas, the floor can be patched. If there is movement between the cracked sections of the floor when you step on the crack, the supporting structure under the tile may be failing. In this case, breaking up the tile and removing it is better than trying to repair it.

- ✔ **Existing vinyl flooring:** In most cases, you should plan to remove the old vinyl floor, especially if it's the cushioned type or highly embossed, because the pattern will *telegraph,* or show through the new floor. A single layer of vinyl over a plywood or particleboard underlayment can support another vinyl floor, but vinyl isn't hard to remove (see the section "Removing old flooring," earlier in this chapter) and you'll get a much better job by starting with the underlayment.

  If the existing floor is an old vinyl floor, use a floor resurfacer to fill in the embossed patterns and make it level. To install sheet vinyl over a ceramic tile floor, make sure that the surface is level and patch where necessary. Follow the manufacturer's directions about applying a primer to the existing surface. Do not install vinyl directly over ceramic tile, because the irregular surface will telegraph through.

- ✔ **Concrete:** Many types of flooring can be installed over concrete. Houses built on a slab may have the bathroom floor laid over the concrete. As long as the cement is smooth without major cracks, it makes a good base for just about all types of floors. If your bathroom has a concrete floor with an uneven surface, apply a self-leveling epoxy floor resurfacer to create a uniform surface before adding a new floor. The material is applied with a trowel and bridges gaps and holes so that new flooring has a sound, level base.

Preparing the Subfloor

The foundation of a bathroom floor is its subfloor, so replacing a damaged one is key to having all the fixtures soundly installed and operational. The process is straightforward, and even though the flooring material will cover it, you'll enjoy a sound bathroom floor for years to come.

Replacing a damaged subfloor

You need these tools and materials to replace a damaged subfloor:

- ¾-inch plywood to fit
- 2-inch all-purpose wood screws
- Circular saw
- Construction adhesive
- Safety glasses
- Scrap pieces of 2-x-4 lumber

Follow these steps to replace a damaged subfloor:

1. **Using a circular saw, cut away the subfloor on each side of the toilet up to the floor joists that are not under the damaged area.**

2. **Inspect the floor joists.**

   A really bad leak can rot them, too.

3. **Nail a 2-x-4 to the joists on each side of the toilet to act as a ledge for the new subfloor to rest on.**

4. **Measure and cut a piece of ¾-inch plywood or match the thickness of the existing subfloor.**

5. **Run a bead of construction adhesive on the 2-x-4 ledges.**

6. **Screw the subfloor in place with 2-inch all-purpose screws.**

Installing underlayment for vinyl floors

Plywood is the underlayment of choice for most vinyl floors. This material is inexpensive and easy to work with, and ⅛- or ¼-inch sheets are usually adequate if the subfloor is at least ¾-inch thick. The major drawback is that both plywood and particle board are not moisture resistant. A more waterproof underlayment, called Fiberock, is available from United States Gypsum Company, and it's easier to install than cement board but just as durable. Check to see whether the flooring manufacturer has guidelines for specific underlayment recommendations.

To install underlayment, you need these tools and materials:

- 6d ring shank nails
- Belt sander
- Circular saw

- ✔ Compass
- ✔ Floor leveling compound
- ✔ Jigsaw
- ✔ Pencil
- ✔ Straightedge
- ✔ Underlayment material
- ✔ Utility knife

Whatever type underlayment you choose, install it using this technique:

1. **Carefully inspect the subfloor for any high spots, proud fasteners that protrude above the surface, or other imperfections.**

   At this point, all baseboard and trim should have been removed, and old underlayment should be gone.

   The underlayment will bridge minor imperfections, but you must fix major problems like rot, loose boards, and major high or low spots before installing the underlayment. See "Replacing a damaged subfloor," earlier in this chapter, for more information.

2. **Fill low areas with floor-leveling compound.**

   Minor high spots can be leveled with a belt sander before installing underlayment.

3. **If the open floor space of the bathroom is less than one full 4-x-8 sheet of underlayment, cut the sheet into smaller sections, keeping them as large as possible to avoid joints.**

   Place the large sheet in the center of the room.

4. **Cut ⅛-inch plywood underlayment by scoring its face several times with a sharp utility knife and then breaking the sheet along the score line.**

   Use a circular saw to make straight cuts in particleboard and thicker plywood, and use a jigsaw to cut the sheet into irregular shapes.

5. **Place the first sheet in position and then fasten it in place with 6d ring shank nails.**

6. **Place the fasteners on 2-inch centers around the perimeter of the sheet and on 6-inch centers in the center of the sheet.**

7. **Cut the border sheets to fit around the perimeter of the room.**

   Measure the distance from the installed sheet to the wall and subtract ¼ inch for expansion; then cut a sheet of underlayment to this dimension.

8. **Use a compass to transfer the profile of any irregular shapes, such as door trim, to the underlayment panel.**

Place the point of the compass along the wall, and move the compass over the molding or whatever shape you want to transfer to the underlayment. The compass point moves along the contour of the molding, while the pencil on the other arm of the compass transfers this movement to the underlayment (see Figure 14-2).

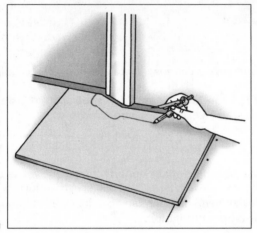

Figure 14-2:
Use a compass to transfer the contour of irregular shapes to the underlayment.

9. **Cut the profile with a jigsaw and then replace the sheet ¼ inch from the wall and mark the overlap with the straightedge (see Figure 14-3).**

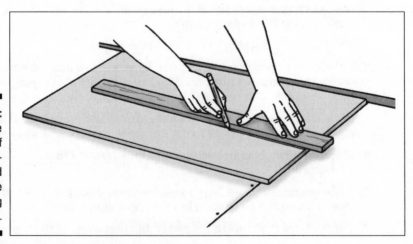

Figure 14-3:
Mark the overlap of underlayment and then cut the sheet along this line.

10. **Remove the sheet and cut.**

11. **Fasten the sheet with nails or screws.**

Installing underlayment for tile floors

Cement board, also called cement backerboard, is the preferred underlayment for tile. It's a little harder to work with than plywood, but it isn't bothered by moisture and makes a very solid base for the tile.

As good as the cement board is, it must be installed over a sound subfloor. A ¾-inch plywood or OSB (orientated strand board) subfloor is adequate; anything less should be beefed up. Many houses have a ½-inch plywood subfloor covered by ⅝-inch particleboard. In this case, if the underlayment shows any signs of water damage, remove the particleboard and replace it with ⅝-inch plywood. In all cases, the subfloor should be screwed to the floor joists with drywall screws placed on 6-inch centers.

To install cement board underlayment, you need the following tools and materials:

- ✔ Broad knife
- ✔ Carbide cutter
- ✔ Cement board underlayment
- ✔ Circular saw and abrasive masonry or diamond blade
- ✔ Fiberglass tape
- ✔ Leather work gloves
- ✔ Notched trowel
- ✔ Respirator
- ✔ Safety glasses
- ✔ Screws or galvanized roofing nails
- ✔ Thinset adhesive
- ✔ Utility knife

Cement board is difficult to handle, so wear heavy work gloves to protect your hands. Also wear safety glasses to protect your eyes when cutting it. Allow a ¼-inch gap around the perimeter and ⅛-inch gaps between the panels.

To cut and install cement board, follow these directions:

1. **Cut and fit the cement board to the room.**

   Cut the cement board by scoring it on both sides with the carbide cutter and then breaking the board with a short snapping motion. Kneel on the panel near the score line and use your weight to lift the edge up to snap it. If the board has a mesh backing, cut it with a utility knife.

If you cut cement board with a circular saw equipped with an abrasive masonry or diamond blade, the saw will raise clouds of fine dust, so wear a respirator.

2. **Mix thinset adhesive according to the manufacturer's directions and allow it to *slake* or set for 5 minutes or so.**

3. **Use the smooth edge of the ¼-inch square-notched trowel to spread the thinset. Then rake the notched edge over the adhesive to leave the correct amount of material on the underlayment.**

4. **Place the board in position on the thinset adhesive.**

5. **Screw the cement board to the underlayment with cement board screws or galvanized roofing nails spaced every 4 inches.**

6. **Install the other panels in the same way.**

7. **Cover the joints with fiberglass tape.**

8. **Use a broad knife to spread a thin coating of adhesive, forcing it into the gaps between panels.**

9. **Smooth the thinset several inches on each side of the joint.**

Laying out layout lines for tile floors

Any tile floor requires establishing a layout line or a beginning point on the subfloor. The layout lines are two perpendicular lines that intersect in the center of the room and that you use as a guide for laying down the tiles. You make the layout lines with a chalk line and then place the tiles along the edges of it.

Use the center of the room — not a wall — as a starting point because there's no guarantee that the walls in a bathroom (or any room) are actually square. The center of the room is the best starting point.

Follow these steps to establish a layout line:

1. **Find the center of the room by measuring two walls on opposite sides of the room and marking the center of each side.**

2. **Drive a finishing nail in the center of one of the walls.**

3. **Hook the clip end of the chalk line on the nail and line up the other end with the center mark on the opposite wall.**

4. **Snap a chalk line between the marks.**

5. **Repeat the process on the other two walls, creating a line perpendicular to the first one.**

6. **Use a framing square to confirm that the two lines create perfect 90-degree angles (see Figure 14-4).**

Figure 14-4:
Use a
framing
square to
make sure
the layout
lines are
perfectly
square.

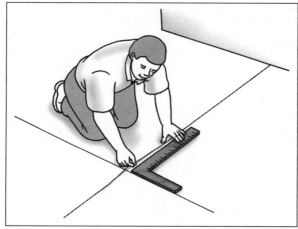

Getting Down to Business: Laying Your New Floor

Now for the moment you've all been waiting for — it's time to lay your new floor.

Preparing the room

No matter what type of flooring you plan to install, your job will be easiest if you get the room ready with a few simple steps.

1. **Remove the toilet, the pedestal sink (if there is one), and the door to the bathroom.**

2. **Use a handsaw to undercut the door casing so you have space to slide the new flooring underneath it.**

3. **Use a pry bar to remove the old base shoe molding, floor registers, or anything attached to the floor.**

4. **Use a vacuum to clean the floor, especially the joint along the walls and in corners.**

Laying a sheet vinyl floor

The prerequisite for doing this job yourself is finding a clean workspace where you can lay out the material and template (like an open floor area in a garage, basement, or other room in the house) where you can work on it. For an average-size bathroom, that shouldn't be too difficult; for a large one, it may be. If you do have a large bathroom, you may need to join two pieces of vinyl together because it's sold in 6- or 12-foot widths. When that's necessary, always plan to place the seam where it will be the least noticed.

Not all vinyl sheet flooring is installed exactly the same, so discuss the installation when you're at the retailer. Ask a lot of questions and go to the manufacturer's Web site to get the specific installation instructions. Take the time to download the file, print it out, and read the instructions so that you have a clear idea of what's involved before you buy the flooring.

Here are the basics of what's involved when installing sheet vinyl flooring with a paper template. Follow the suggestions at the beginning of this chapter about removing the existing flooring if necessary and choosing and preparing a subfloor suitable for vinyl flooring.

To install sheet vinyl flooring with a paper template, you need these tools and materials:

- Adhesive
- Carpenter's square
- Combination or framing square
- Compass
- Flooring knife
- Heavy paper for template or template kit
- Marker
- Masking tape
- Molding to fit the perimeter of the room
- Rolling pin
- Scissors
- Sheet vinyl flooring
- Straightedge
- Trowel
- Utility knife

Making a template

Take time to make a pattern for the floor, using a template of heavy paper. Some manufacturers include a template or template kit, and others suggest you get butcher paper. If the type of flooring you chose requires a ¼-inch gap to allow for expansion between the vinyl and the wall, make your template accordingly.

1. **Use masking tape to connect pieces of the paper to make a pattern of the floor (see Figure 14-5).**

   Trim individual pieces of paper to fit around cabinets and doorways and then tape them together. Continue around the perimeter of the room.

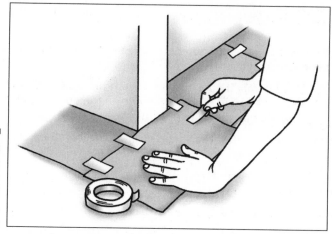

Figure 14-5:
Make
a paper
template of
the room.

2. **Cut holes in the paper so you can tape the template directly to the floor as you progress to assure that the template does not shift.**

   If the bathroom is large and requires seaming the vinyl, mark that on the template so you'll line up the pattern correctly.

3. **Use a combination or framing square to line up obstacles, such as a cabinet, and use a compass to accurately make a cutout for a pipe.**

4. **When the template is completed, reinforce the paper with masking tape.**

   Tape the large seams together before you pick up the pattern off the floor. Then starting at one corner, lift the template off the floor and carefully fold the template and remove it.

Laying the floor

Some flooring material is stapled around the perimeter of the room and doesn't require adhesive. The molding is installed with finishing nails spaced about 12 inches apart. It covers the staples. For that type of installation, follow Steps 1 through 8. Then paint the molding to match the finish on the walls. Other flooring material requires adhesive, which you find out about applying in Steps 9 to 15.

1. **Unroll the vinyl on a sheet of plywood with the pattern side up.**

2. **Position the template on top of the vinyl so that the design will be centered in the room.**

3. **Tape the template to the vinyl and use it as a pattern to cut the vinyl.**

   Use a ballpoint pen or marker to trace the outline of the template on the vinyl.

4. **Carefully remove the paper template from the vinyl and use the outline to cut the vinyl.**

   To make clean, straight cuts, use a flooring knife and a straightedge or carpenter's square. Hold the straightedge on the outline and press firmly into the vinyl, pulling the knife toward you.

5. **When the vinyl is cut to the shape of the floor, roll it up and put it in position on the floor.**

   Begin by sliding the vinyl beneath the door casing and then spreading it out into the room.

6. **Use the knife to make any short trim cuts.**

7. **If the floor is large and requires seams, match the pattern along the seam and overlap the second sheet on the first so the patterns align.**

8. **Cut both sheets at once.**

9. **If the vinyl requires adhesive over the full floor, roll back the floor about halfway and use a trowel to apply the adhesive.**

   Use the type of adhesive suggested by the flooring manufacturer and follow the directions for its application and drying time.

10. **Use a rolling pin to press the vinyl into the adhesive.**

11. **Repeat the process on the other half of the floor.**

12. **If the floor is perimeter bonded with adhesive, spread the adhesive around half the floor and then roll the flooring on the adhesive and press in place with the rolling pin.**

13. **Do the same to the other half of the floor.**

14. **Go over the entire floor again with the rolling pin to force out any air bubbles and assure complete contact between the new floor and underlayment.**

15. **If the vinyl floor is stapled around the perimeter, roll the flooring out on the entire floor. Push the flooring tight into the corners and staple.**

Some manufacturers recommend rolling the floor with a 100-pound roller after installation. You can rent one at a rental center or from the retailer who sold you the flooring material. Because it's hard to get the large roller close to cabinets, especially under kick spaces, also rent a J roller, which is used to fabricate countertops, to reach close to the wall and around tight areas.

Laying vinyl tiles

One of the easiest ways to transform a bathroom is with vinyl tiles that you can lay down and install easily. They are lightweight enough to cut and create an almost instant face-lift for a bathroom.

You need these tools and materials to install vinyl floor tiles:

- ✔ Adhesive
- ✔ Chalk line
- ✔ Compass
- ✔ Notched trowel
- ✔ Pencil
- ✔ Rolling pin
- ✔ Scrap piece of cardboard
- ✔ Self-stick vinyl tiles or dry-back vinyl tiles
- ✔ Straightedge
- ✔ Utility or floor knife

Follow these steps to install vinyl tiles:

1. **Chalk layout lines according to the instructions in the section "Laying out layout lines for tile floors," earlier in this chapter.**

2. **Dry-fit the tiles to see how they line up along the edges of the room.**

   Leave a ¼-inch gap around the perimeter. The idea is to avoid a narrow strip of cut tiles outlining the room. Start at the center of the room where the layout lines intersect. Check to see that, when the tiles reach the wall, they won't require cutting to less than half of their width. If the tiles need to be cut more than that, adjust the chalk lines and go back and do another dry layout of the tiles.

3. **Remove the backing from self-stick tiles or, if using adhesive, spread it on the floor in a 2- or 3-square-foot area along the layout lines with a notched trowel.**

If you're using self-stick tiles, be careful when you remove the paper backing on the tiles. It's very slippery, so don't let it get scattered around the floor. Instead, stash it in an empty tile box so that no one slips and falls.

4. **Starting in the center of the room, begin to lay all the full (also called field) tiles.**

Set the tiles along the edges of the chalk line and apply pressure so that they're firmly seated on the floor. Many tiles have a pattern direction. Look for arrows on the back of the tile or the paper backing sheet and make sure the tiles are oriented in the same direction.

5. **Continue laying the tiles along the layout lines toward the walls.**

This will give you a straight square reference. Don't cut the border tiles now.

6. **Spread adhesive over small areas and fill in the tiles between the layout lines.**

Form a series of steps as you work from one layout to the adjacent line.

7. **Begin spreading the adhesive in another quarter of the room. Install the tiles along the layout lines to the walls and then fill in the remaining tiles.**

8. **Repeat this process for the remaining areas of the room.**

9. **When all the full tiles are laid, continue by cutting the outline tiles around the border of the room (see Figure 14-6). Here's how:**

   1. Lay a full tile face up and centered over the last full tile that you laid.

   2. Take a second tile and position it on top of the first tile, with the back edge of the second tile ¼ inch from the wall.

   3. Mark the first tile with a pencil, using the edge of the second (top) tile as a guide.

   4. To cut the tiles, place a straightedge on the cut line and scribe with a sharp utility knife.

      After several cuts, the tile will break evenly when bent. The portion of the first tile that was not under the second tile is the border tile.

Figure 14-6:
Border tiles
should be
as large as
possible.

10. **To cut around corners or other obstructions, first make a cardboard template and use it as a pattern to cut a tile.**

    Alternatively, you can use a compass to transfer the shape of the object to the cardboard or directly to the tile.

11. **Rent a floor roller or get down on your hands and knees with a rolling pin to apply pressure on the tiles.**

Laying ceramic and stone tiles

Laying a tile floor involves several steps, but the end result is one of the best-looking surfaces you'll ever find. Just like with other flooring materials, the initial layout is important to create a tile surface that will last a very long time.

Practice making cuts using a tile cutter and nippers on scrap pieces of tile. That way, when you're installing them, you'll be familiar with how to operate them. Don't use good tiles. Look in the sale bin for ugly leftover tiles that are the same size and type you're using. Practice makes perfect cuts.

To lay a ceramic tile or stone floor, you need these tools and materials:

- Ceramic or stone tiles
- Chalk line
- Electric drill with mixing paddle
- Grout

✔ Grout sponge

✔ Pencil

✔ Rags and bucket

✔ Rubber grout float

✔ Thinset mortar

✔ Tile cutter

✔ Tile nippers

✔ Trowel

Laying tiles

Start tiling in the center of the floor, using full tiles and working out toward the edges, where you'll need to cut tiles to fit.

1. **Make the layout lines on the subfloor (using the information in the earlier section "Laying out layout lines for tile floors") and use them as a guide to lay the tiles down dry.**

   The goal is to use the most full-size tiles as possible, which will look the best and require the least amount of cutting. Also adjust the layout lines to provide the largest border tiles possible.

2. **Follow the manufacturer's directions for mixing thinset mortar, using a mortar paddle attachment on an electric drill.**

   A five-gallon bucket is a good size container to hold and mix the mortar.

3. **Beginning at the center of the room and following the chalk lines, spread mortar on the floor with a trowel, working at a slight angle.**

4. **Comb the mortar with the notched-teeth edge of the trowel.**

5. **Set a tile in place and press it down firmly to seat it in the mortar, using a slight twisting and turning action.**

6. **Work your way along the center line, carefully placing the tiles.**

   Use spacers between the tiles to make sure the tiles line up evenly.

7. **When you're finished with a section, remove the spacers if you used them.**

Never walk on freshly set tiles. Plan your installation carefully.

Cutting border tiles

Unless you're extraordinarily lucky and the tiles fit perfectly in your bathroom, you have to cut tiles for the borders. Here's how it's done:

1. **Lay a full tile on top of the last full tile. Place another tile on top of it and move it to the wall, leaving a ¼-inch gap and space for the grout line next to the last full tile between the wall and the tile.**

2. **Mark the first tile with a pencil, using the edge of the second (top) tile as a guide.**

3. **Align the tile in the cutter so the cut line is under the cutting wheel, raise the bar, and pull the bar toward you to engage the cutter.**

4. **Release the cutting wheel, lower the pressing tee, and snap the tile at the cut line.**

   To cut irregular shapes, use the tile nippers. Draw the shape of the cut on the tile and then begin taking small bits at one end of the cutline. If it's a curved cut line, work from both ends into the center.

5. **Clean up any mortar from the face of the tiles with a rag and let the thinset cure, following the time requirements of the manufacturer.**

6. **Clean excess mortar from between the tiles to allow room for grout.**

Finishing up

Use grout to fill the joints between the tiles. It's a messy job, but somebody's gotta do it.

1. **Using a rubber grout float held at an angle, push the grout into the joints between the tiles.**

   Use a wide sweeping motion as you spread the grout, making sure to press the grout into the joints. Raise the grout float on edge to scrape off excess grout when the joints are packed full.

2. **Clean off the grout residue left on the face of the tiles with a damp grout sponge.**

   This may require several wipe-downs.

3. **Remove the haze with a dry rag first, followed by a damp one.**

4. **Finish by using a clean, dry rag to buff the tiles.**

   If necessary, follow the grout manufacturer's directions about misting or applying a sealer.

Laying a laminate floor

Get ready to see a major improvement in the floor when you install a laminate floor in the bathroom. The new surface has transforming powers you'll notice almost instantly.

A laminate floor can be installed over almost any subfloor. It's durable and resists stains and surface moisture, so it's a good choice for a bathroom. Before choosing one brand over another, find out whether it is recommended for use in a bathroom and whether there are any special considerations.

Stack the unopened packages of flooring material in flat rows in the bathroom two days before installing it so it can adjust to the room temperature.

To lay a laminate floor, you need these tools and materials:

- ✔ Damp cloth
- ✔ Floor-leveling compound
- ✔ Foam underlayment
- ✔ Handsaw or circular saw
- ✔ Laminate flooring planks with glue
- ✔ Scissors
- ✔ Straightedge or try square

Use a handsaw to undercut door molding or casing. Lay a loose plank (of your new flooring) upside down against the door casing over a piece of the underlayment and saw off the bottom of the casing. Doing so enables you to slide the new planks underneath the casing. Fill any low spots in the underlayment (greater than ⅜ inch) with floor-leveling compound.

Dry-fitting the planks

Working with laminate flooring is like putting together a puzzle, and you'll have to figure out where the pieces go before you start gluing them into place. Carefully read the instructions from the manufacturer. You can also ask for installation directions where you bought the flooring. Before you get started, unroll the foam underlayment on the floor and cut it to fit with scissors. Now you're ready to dry-fit the planks, following these steps:

1. **Dry-fit the planks by installing the first three rows of planks, working from the center to the wall, with the groove toward the wall.**

   To maintain the necessary expansion space, use the spacers, which provide a ¼-inch expansion space between the plank edges and the walls or other fixed surfaces.

2. **When you reach the last plank at the end of a row and it must be cut to fit, turn the plank 180 degrees.**

3. **Place this plank with its tongue against the tongue of the last installed plank.**

4. **Slide the end of the last plank to be cut to the wall and then back off ¼-inch or place a spacer between the end of the plank and the wall.**

5. **Use the end of the abutting installed plank as a reference to mark the cut line on the plank.**

   Use a straightedge or try square to draw a straight line on the plank.

6. **Using a handsaw, cut the plank with the finish side up.**

   If you're using a circular saw, cut the plank with the finish side down.

7. **Use a pull bar to fit the last plank's groove tightly over the tongue of the plank it butts up against (see Figure 14-7).**

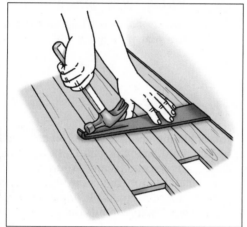

Figure 14-7:
Use a pull bar to force the planks together.

When possible, use the piece that is left over from the previous row to begin the next row.

8. **Repeat this process until three rows of planks are fitted and you're convinced that your layout plan is going to work.**

Installing the planks

You're just a few steps and a lot of adhesive away from having a new laminate floor.

1. **When you've laid out and cut the first three rows of planks, carefully lift them up and begin gluing them together, following the same order the planks were dry-fitted.**

2. **Fill the plank groove with glue.**

   Some glue should squeeze out along the entire length of the plank when the planks are joined together. If you don't get squeeze-out along the entire joint when you snug up the plank, you haven't used enough glue.

3. **Assemble the planks on the floor.**

   Some floor systems use straps and tapping blocks to pull the planks together.

4. **Remove any excess glue with a damp cloth before it dries.**

5. **Let the first three rows dry for an hour before continuing.**

6. **Continue gluing the remaining planks, working from left to right, row after row.**

   One end of the plank has a tongue, and the other has a groove. Apply glue to the groove and then push the planks together.

7. **Follow the manufacturer's instructions about how long the glue should dry before removing the spacers and installing the base shoe molding.**

Adding a transition strip

A door threshold does the job of joining unlike surfaces, such as hall carpeting and bathroom flooring. A threshold, made of wood, marble, or metal, provides a transition between flooring types and rooms. Wooden thresholds, installed with finishing nails and metal strips that come with screws, are sold in home centers in the door hardware section. At tile and stone specialty centers, you'll also find a selection of marble thresholds designed for use in a bathroom.

Chapter 15

Getting Creative with Doors and Windows

In This Chapter

▶ Choosing and installing doors for tight spaces

▶ Making a window the focal point

▶ Skylighting a bathroom

*I*f you haven't given much thought to the doors and windows of your new bathroom, think again. A door is more than a way to get in and out of the bathroom; it just may be a design solution if your floor plan is tight on space. For example, special hardware allows standard bifold doors to open and fold flat against the wall instead of taking up precious space in the door jamb. Attractive new pocket doors don't need to swing out into the room and take up valuable space.

Many innovative styles and new materials can make a window the focal point of your new bathroom. Sure, a window is a necessary part of a bathroom, letting in daylight and opening up the room to fresh air. But a window can be much more. A decorative window can become a dramatic focal point, and skylights — distant cousins to the window — can visually open up a small bathroom with daylight. Doors and windows are necessary parts of a room, but they can be a solution that makes a bathroom more functional, more accessible, and, yes, more beautiful.

You'll find a wide selection of specialty doors, the related hardware, and windows sold at home centers and lumberyards; many are in stock, but others require a special order. As you're working on your floor plan, consider all your options for doors and windows — they can be more than just an ordinary element of the room.

Using Specialty Doors and Hardware

As you're designing your new bathroom, consider how much space the swing of the door into the room requires. If you relocate the door on a different wall, will that open up the space in the room? Or if you use the existing door but rehang it on the opposite side of the jamb, will that make for a more pleasing floor plan?

If you have a good solid bathroom door that just needs a fresh coat of paint to make it fit in the new decor, definitely reuse it, but consider changing the doorknob, lock, and hinges to give it a new and fresh look to match the finish on the accessories.

If you're replacing the door with a new one, invest in a solid core door that shuts out sound and offers privacy to those inside (making the noise) so those outside the bathroom can enjoy peace and quiet.

Know-when-to-fold-'em doors

Bifold doors are frequently used in bathroom storage closets or as a way to conceal a clothes washer and dryer when the bathroom does double duty as the laundry room. The trouble with the track hardware of most traditional bifold doors is that it folds the four panels of the doors into the jamb, taking up valuable space. The two door panels on each side take up almost 12 inches, limiting the access and usability of the closet. Full-access folding door hardware, which is installed as a hinging mechanism so the door panels can lay flat against each other, is a better choice. The panels fold outside of the jamb against the wall, giving you easier access to the closet or laundry equipment.

Here are the directions for installing the hardware kit for a full-access folding door made by Johnson Hardware, which is the type we've installed. If you're using another brand, follow the manufacturer's directions. The steps that follow give you an idea of the work involved:

1. **Lay out the position of the hinges on the door.**

   Measure 7⅛ inches down from the top of the jamb and mark the edge of the jamb. Make a second layout mark 3 inches down from the top hinge and another mark 31 inches down from this mark.

2. **Mount the hinges on the door jamb.**

   Align the hinge so that the top edge of the hinge is on the layout line with the front of the hinge flush with the jamb casing, and mark the location of the mounting screws on the jamb. Drill ⅛-inch pilot holes for the mounting screws and then install the hinges with the screws provided. Install the hinges with the pin side of the hinge facing up.

3. **Lay out the position of the hinges on the door.**

   On the edge of the bifold door that faces the jamb, make layout lines 7 inches from the top of the door, 31 inches down from this mark, and another 31 inches farther down the door.

4. **Install the other half of the hinges so the holes for the hinge pins are facing down and the bottom edges of the hinges are aligned with the layout marks and flush against the face of the door.**

5. **Hang the door and test its fit.**

6. **Install the hinges on the other jamb and door if you're hanging four doors.**

7. **Remove the doors from the jamb hinges.**

8. **Place the doors face side down on a flat surface and align the doors at the top and bottom.**

9. **Mark the location of the mounting screws, drill pilot holes, and mount the hinges with the screws provided.**

   Locate the door hinges 6 inches from the top of the doors and then every 31 inches (see Figure 15-1).

Figure 15-1:
Hardware
layout
diagram.

10. **Rehang the doors and check their movement.**

11. **Install the control arm bracket on the back of the outer bifold door so that it's flush with the outer edge of the door.**

    If the jamb has a headstop, measure its thickness and add 1 inch to this measurement to calculate how far down from the top of the door to mount the control arm bracket. If there is no stop, mount the bracket 1 inch from the top.

12. **Attach the arm to this bracket and then open the doors so that they fit flush against the wall.**

13. **Adjust the length of the control arm so that it's ¼ inch less than the width of one door.**

14. **Screw the other end of the bracket to the jamb or to the doorstop.**

Handy-as-a-pocket doors

A pocket door slides into a metal and wood cage that is installed as the walls are framed (see Figure 15-2). In some older homes, a sliding pocket door was used to create privacy and separate a living room from a parlor or dining room. The door disappeared into the wall when it wasn't being used but was convenient to pull out when needed. The clever design of a pocket door continues to be a space-saving solution in today's homes, especially in a small bathroom where a hinged door swing takes up too much floor place. The framing hardware within the cavity of the wall allows the door to slide in and out of the wall, a solution in a room where floor or wall space is at a premium.

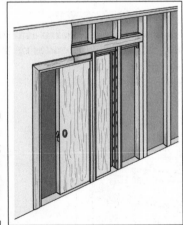

Figure 15-2:
A pocket door stores itself inside the wall cavity.

A pocket door is also a good choice for a bathroom for someone who uses a wheelchair or walker because it's easy to open and close.

Although the hardware can work on any type of door — solid or hollow core or flat or paneled — it's a good idea to buy a pocket door hardware system that includes the door. For a bathroom, consider a door with a mirror on one or both sides, which is a convenient and useful choice.

You'll find a pocket door frame hardware system for doors 1⅛ inches to 1¾ inches thick by 6 feet 8 inches high. The hardware is an improvement over the old-fashioned door in the wall because it can't stick or come off its track. The system is made of wheel assemblies that roll in boxed tracks that prevent the doors from derailing, floor anchors that maintain proper distance between the jamb studs, and door glides that center the door as it glides into the open position. Pocket door locks, available in several styles and finishes, are designed with a recessed handle that folds flat against the edge of the door when it is in the recess.

Before you begin, read the directions for the pocket door kit you're installing to get an overview of the process and what's involved. All pocket door systems are installed in basically the same way, but the manufacturer's directions should give you the best advice for installing that particular product.

1. **Construct the rough opening or modify the existing wall to fit the rough opening dimensions for the door jamb supplied by the manufacturer of the hardware.**

   Make sure that all studs are plumb (perfectly vertical) and the header is level.

2. **Follow the manufacturer's instructions and cut the pocket door header-and-track assembly to length with a hacksaw.**

3. **Install the header-and-track assembly on the top jamb with the fasteners and brackets supplied with the door. Nail the end plate to the wall studs (see Figure 15-3).**

   Check that the track is level so that the door rolls easily.

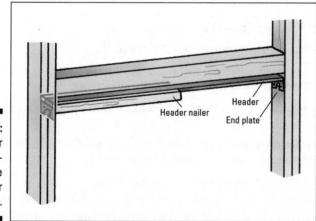

Figure 15-3:
The header track supports the door roller assemblies.

Header nailer

Header

End plate

4. **Attach the split jamb stiffeners to the floor bracket and then plumb them with a level and nail the brackets to the floor. Nail the split jamb to the header (see Figure 15-4).**

5. **Repeat for the second pair of stiffeners, installing them in the middle of the pocket.**

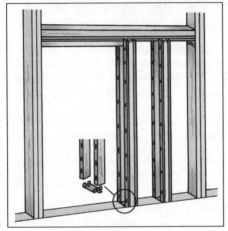

Figure 15-4:
Thin metal split jambs are installed between the header and floor.

6. **Paint or stain all edges and faces of the door to prevent it from warping.**

7. **Install hanging hardware on the top edge of the door according to the manufacturer's directions.**

8. **Slide the wheel hangers into the track and hang the door on the two hangers.**

9. **Adjust the hangers until the door is plumb.**

   You can also install the door handle/lock at this point.

10. **Remove the door and then install drywall over the door pocket, using construction adhesive and 1-inch drywall screws.**

11. **Finish the joints with drywall tape and several coats of drywall compound.**

12. **Reinstall the door and then install the door guides on the inside and outside of the door at the mouth of the pocket.**

    The guides, which are adjustable, should center the door in the opening and allow just enough clearance for the door to slide smoothly.

13. **Nail the two-piece side and head jambs on either side of the door so it is flush with the finished wall surface (see Figure 15-5).**

14. **Use screws to install one side of the head jamb so you can remove the door in the event of a problem.**

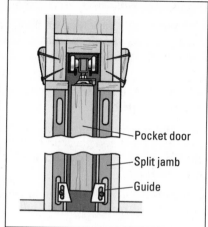

Figure 15-5:
The cross section of the pocket door shows the location of the major components.

Pocket door

Split jamb

Guide

15. **Install a full-width strike jamb on the opposite side.**

16. **Drill a hole and chisel a shallow mortise in that jamb for the strike plate, which the door latch engages.**

17. **Install door casing, nailing it to the jamb and to pocket door studs.**

   Use 6d finish nails to install the top and strike jamb casing. Use shorter nails to install the casing on the pocket side of the door jamb to prevent damage to the door.

18. **Apply a bead of construction adhesive to the back side of this casing to compensate for the short nails.**

Adding Style and Fresh Air with Windows

A window brings daylight into the room and has the pleasing effect of opening up the space. It's a natural attention getter in a bathroom, whether providing a view of treetops in a second-floor room or a glimpse of a colorful garden from the first-floor powder room. But a window isn't for aesthetics alone; it provides ventilation and fresh air, both key elements for a bathroom.

If you're redesigning your new bathroom around the existing windows, you probably already know how they function and enhance the room. But if you're adding a new window and have never given windows much thought, consider the fact that today you have many choices in styles, sizes, and materials:

- ✔ For ease of opening, choose a side-opening casement window.

- ✔ For a small, dark bathroom, a roof skylight or a tubular skylight finds light from high spaces. How about an acrylic glazed skylight, which disperses light through a room and is energy efficient at the same time?

- ✔ An octagonal, or stop-sign-shaped window, often used in a foyer, works nicely in a bathroom to let daylight inside and add an architectural feature on the interior and exterior of the house.

- ✔ Plant lovers often incorporate their passion for greenery in the bathroom with a greenhouse window, an insulated glass unit with a shelf that extends about 18 inches from the siding. What better place for plants than the moist conditions of a bathroom?

- ✔ Glass and acrylic block has long been a stylish solution for replacing old, rotten wood bathroom windows Today, ready-to-install units make the installation much easier.

When it comes to a bathroom, consider what the window will add to the interior and exterior (what it looks like) and what function it performs. Use your room sketch to determine an approximate window size so that when you're window shopping (not a pun), you'll be able to gauge how it will look. You'll find a selection of windows at window retailers, building suppliers, lumberyards, and home centers. Many such window displays feature windows in room settings, and others simply exhibit the window unit itself.

If lighting is a key issue in your bathroom, consider the possibilities of windows, and check out Chapter 16, which deals specifically with lighting.

Blocking the view with a block replacement window

Anyone who has ever lived in a row house with side-by-side houses knows the importance of privacy. When your house feels like it's sitting on top of another one and you need to replace a bathroom window, get an acrylic or glass block window unit. The unit is prefabricated, so no individual mortaring is required and the window is ready to be installed in the opening. In one step you can replace an old rotten window with a new block unit that is fixed or opens, making it a popular solution.

You'll see some dramatic examples of block windows in the color insert of the book. Some are the focal point of the room; others provide privacy where it's needed but let the sunlight in.

The prefabricated glass block window requires a specific size opening. Consult the roughing-in dimensions provided by the manufacturer. If you're replacing an existing window, choose a glass block window that is smaller than the existing opening, because making a window opening smaller is easier than enlarging it, although you may still have to deal with patching in sheathing and siding on the outside of the house.

1. **Lift the glass block window into the opening.**

   If the window is large, you may need a helper for this — glass block is heavy. The prefabricated windows have a one-piece vinyl frame with a built-in flange for attaching the unit to the framing.

2. **Use a level to check the window's position in the opening.**

3. **If necessary, shim one corner up until it is level and then put a temporary nail through the flange into the wall framing.**

4. **Use wood shims inserted between the window unit and the wall framing to level the window.**

   If the gap is more than ¼ inch, use small blocks of wood to level the window.

5. **Drive nails through the remaining slots in the mounting flange.**

   Make sure that the nails penetrate into solid wood.

6. **Fill the gap between the new window's vinyl frame and wall framing with insulation.**

   If you use fiberglass insulation, don't pack it too tightly because doing so reduces its insulating value. If you choose an aerosol foam insulation, use a minimal-expansion type to avoid creating pressure between the glass block and the wood framing.

7. **Finish the installation inside, making sure that the inside edge of the window is flush with the surface of the wall.**

8. **Working from the exterior, install flashing, which deflects water from entering the gap between the window and jamb, in this order: first at the bottom of the window; then on the sides of the window, overlapping it over the bottom flashing; and finally at the top, overlapping it over the side flashing.**

   Installing the flashing in this order allows water to run off the top flashing over the side and bottom flashing.

9. **Before replacing the siding you removed to install the window, cover the bare wall surface with building paper (see Figure 15-6).**

10. **Replace the exterior molding around the window opening, and apply caulk between the molding and the siding to prevent water infiltration.**

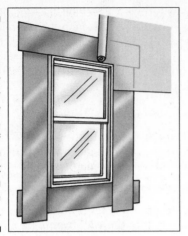

Figure 15-6: Flashing and building paper applied over the window on the outside of the house prevent water from entering the perimeter.

Calling attention to windows

If you're replacing a window, consider making the new one the focal point of the room. Make the replacement a showoff decorative window instead of an ordinary one to fill the opening left by the original. A decorative window, made of acrylic or glass block or stained glass, can be the attention getter in any room, and it's particularly effective in a bathroom, where it lets in light and at the same time provides privacy. Plus you don't need a window treatment because you don't want to conceal the design. These window units come in a range of sizes, shapes, and patterns, and some can be installed vertically or horizontally, thus offering some variety in placement.

Assuming the exterior of the house has wood, aluminum, or vinyl siding (not brick or concrete), the installation of a decorative window is similar to installing any window unit. It involves framing the rough opening to size as specified in the installation instructions, positioning the unit in place, using wooden shims to adjust and level the window, fastening it into the framing with wood screws, and caulking it to seal any openings around it. Many decorative windows are prefabricated with trim, so no carpentry trim work is required.

If the wall opening is the same size, installing the new unit isn't too difficult. If you need to make the opening larger, however, the job requires cutting into the exterior siding and interior wall. The worst case involves an opening larger than the new window; in that situation, the exterior siding has to be patched in with framing and siding, and the interior wall has to be framed and finished around the new unit. Replacing windows with units of the same size or smaller is the most economical approach.

Sill-y advice: Repairing a damaged window

If you don't want to replace an entire bathroom window just because the sill is rotten, you can use a two-part epoxy wood filler to restore the sill. Because removing a sill isn't easy, a wood filler does a good job of rebuilding the damaged wood and lets you shape and sand the surface so it conforms to its original appearance. The wood filler isn't a structural repair, but it's a good choice for any rotten wood trim.

In general, an epoxy wood filler system has two components: a liquid that's squeezed into the damaged sill to stabilize the wood and a two-part epoxy filler applied with a putty knife that hardens and conforms to the shape. When the filler is cured, you sand it smooth and add a coat of paint. Wood filler repair kits are sold at most hardware stores and home centers. Because they have their own specific requirements, follow the manufacturer's directions about applying them. Here are some general instructions for repairing a window sill with epoxy wood filler:

1. **Scrape out the rotten wood and old paint from the jamb and sill with a hook-type paint scraper.**

Remove as much bad wood as possible. You can find the rotten wood by pushing the blade of a screwdriver into the wood. If it goes in easily, the wood is bad and should be removed. You can use a chisel to gouge out any soft wood.

2. **After chiseling, use an electric drill to make $\frac{1}{8}$-inch holes to fill with the consolidant or stabilizer component of the wood filler.**

3. **When that component is dry, apply the filler with a putty knife to fill in the voids.**

Overfill them so that you can file and sand the repair area to the original shape of the sill or jamb.

4. **When the filler is dry, use a coarse file or rasp to shape the surface to the existing profile of the window sill.**

It may take several applications, with sanding in between, to rebuild the surface.

5. **Apply a top coat of a good oil-based exterior primer and enamel (instead of interior paint) to withstand the moist conditions of a bathroom.**

Opening the roof to open the room

When a bathroom is on the top floor, a skylight that opens up is a popular solution to bringing in daylight and ventilation, especially when wall space is at a premium. Today's skylights, whether they open or not, are better made than those of earlier years, and they're also better insulated and designed with bulletproof seals (a slight exaggeration) to prevent leaking. Many are engineered for easy installing, with no flashing, mastic, or sealants required.

Going tubular

Another relatively new way to bring natural light into a dark room is a tubular skylight. Here's how it works: The round skylight captures natural light through a roof dome and directs the light into the room through a reflective tunnel with a diffuser that spreads sunlight around the room. Many units come with an electric light so they can function as a ceiling light at night, and others combine an electric light with a vent fan.

Installing a tubular skylight involves working on the roof, cutting an opening and weather-sealing around the dome, cutting another hole in the ceiling, and assembling and connecting the components.

The following instructions are for installing a typical 10- to 14-inch-diameter tubular skylight. This size fits between the framing and doesn't require cutting into the floor joists or roof rafters with 16-inch on-center framing. The roof must have an adequate pitch (more than 4 inches of vertical rise per horizontal foot) for proper drainage. For other situations, refer to specific directions provided with the unit. Optional flashing collars are also available from the manufacturers for different types of roofs, such as Spanish tile or slate.

1. **After you choose the location you want for the interior diffuser end of the skylight assembly, tap the ceiling or use a stud finder to be sure you're not directly below wood framing.**

2. **Drive a nail or drill a small hole through the ceiling, stick a piece of wire up through the hole, and find the wire in the attic.**

   If the wire isn't directly between the ceiling joists, you must relocate the hole. The tube must be placed between the ceiling joists to provide adequate clearance. Clear away any insulation in the attic, and adjust the position of the hole if necessary.

   The ceiling opening doesn't need to be directly below the roof opening because the tunnel is adjustable (see Figure 15-7). Some units are designed with solid sectional tunnels that can be twisted into position, and others have flexible tubing that bends around obstacles.

3. **While you're in the attic, look for the most direct route for the skylight roof dome, which usually should not exceed 10 feet from diffuser to dome.**

   Remember that a shorter, straighter tube runs work better, and if you have a choice, always pick a southern location for the dome for maximum light.

Figure 15-7:
Light tubes
are easy
to install.

4. **Make a small hole through the roof, centered between two rafters, to mark the location for the dome, and insert a wire to help you find the spot when you go outside.**

5. **Use the diffuser frame or template, if one is provided by the manufacturer, to mark your cut line on the ceiling.**

   Make sure that the template or frame is centered over the locator hole you made in the bathroom ceiling.

6. **Use a compass or drywall saw to cut inside the line and remove the section of ceiling (see Figure 15-8).**

   Don't throw the ceiling section away; save it to use as a roof template.

7. **Install the bottom tube assembly into the hole.**

   You can install the rest of the light tunnel from the attic side after you complete the roof dome cutout.

8. **Find the locator hole, position the drywall circle from the ceiling directly over it, and mark the shingles; then use a razor knife to cut out the circle.**

9. **Use a jigsaw to cut through the roof decking inside the circle.**

10. **Carefully pry up the nails of shingles immediately above and next to the hole. Slide the roof dome's flashing collar into place (see Figure 15-9) under the top and side shingles and over the bottom shingles.**

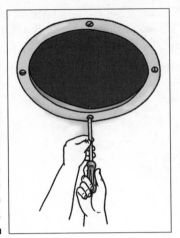

Figure 15-8:
Cut the hole
in the
bathroom
ceiling and
install the
frame to
hold the
light tube
and diffuser.

Figure 15-9:
Slide the
flashing
collar under
the top layer
of shingles.

11. Follow the manufacturer's directions for caulking and nailing the collar to the roof.

12. In the attic, connect the tube or tunnel to the ceiling collar section, and extend it up to the roof opening (see Figure 15-10).

13. Cut it to fit, if necessary, and attach it to the roof dome collar.

    Use the manufacturer's installation instructions to see how to fasten and secure the tube or tunnel.

14. When you have connected the tube at the top and bottom, tape all joints and seams and replace the insulation between the ceiling joists.

15. In the bathroom, place the diffuser lens into the ceiling trim ring, and snap or clip the ring to the ceiling frame.

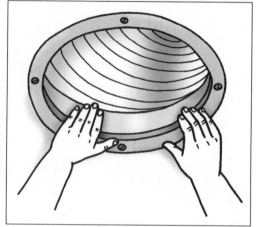

Figure 15-10: Install the light tube between the roof dome and the ceiling trim ring.

Chapter 16

Let There Be Light!

In This Chapter

▶ Getting the lighting right

▶ Lighting your bathroom from overhead

▶ Hanging the lights on bathroom walls

*N*o matter what its style, a bathroom should be well lit, well ventilated, and quiet, all qualities that make it a useful and peaceful place. Good lighting is important because of the many tasks — shaving, applying makeup, personal grooming, and reading — performed in a bathroom that require illumination. Proper ventilation is needed in every room of a house, but it's most important in a bathroom to prevent the growth of mold and mildew, which create harmful indoor allergens, not to mention stains on surfaces. (Check out Chapter 8 for more about ventilation.) And because no matter how humble, a bathroom is always a retreat, it should be quiet and restful, truly an escape from the rest of the house.

Most of the time you probably tend to take lighting for granted. In fact, if you notice the lighting, it's probably because it's problematic. If the area seems too bright with a lot of glare or not bright enough, the lighting plan can use some fine-tuning. To get the most out of any bathroom remodeling project, improving the lighting should be at the top of the list. Many homeowners feel comfortable doing electrical work, and it is allowed in many jurisdictions.

If your bathroom remodeling project involves new electrical lines, definitely hire an electrician to run them and install new fixtures. The electrical work must meet the building codes, so you want a licensed electrician or electrical contractor to guarantee that it's done safely and properly. But if you're replacing existing fixtures and you're comfortable working with electricity, you can replace an old light fixture with a new one.

Turning the Spotlight on Different Types of Lighting

The American Lighting Association says that a bathroom that incorporates overall and specific lighting fixtures makes the time spent there more enjoyable. The science of lighting has come a long way, and today lighting designers divide the needs of a bathroom into three basic categories: ambient, task, and accent. A lighting plan needs to address each of these categories to be successful.

Ambient

Ambient, or general lighting, provides the overall illumination of a room or area. It can take many forms, and at times, task lighting and accent lighting contribute to the ambient light. In most cases, the ambient light is provided by an overhead light fixture. Of course, the natural light coming in from windows and skylights is part of the ambient light during the day. See Chapter 15 for more about skylights.

Ambient light must be adequate to provide sufficient illumination for safety, cleaning, and moving about; it also balances the brightness of other fixtures. The ceiling fixture is the most common source of ambient light and can be combined with a vent and heat in small bathrooms. Strategically placed recessed fixtures can also provide ambient lighting.

Task

This category of lighting provides illumination to specific areas of the bathroom, such as the shower stall or bathtub area, toilet area, and sink and mirror. These fixtures provide task lighting:

✔ **Horizontal lighting strip or track above a double vanity:** A strip of horizontal vanity lights with tiny halogen bulbs ensures that those using the vanity will have sufficient light. Mount the strip 78 inches off the floor. However, having only overhead lighting at the mirror makes applying makeup more difficult because it casts shadows under eyes, nose, and chin. Combine it with vertically mounted lights on both sides of the mirror (like those noted in the next item) to create shadow-free light for grooming.

✔ **Theatrical light strips with globe-shaped incandescent bulbs:** These are mounted vertically at the edges of the mirror and provide plenty of light for shaving or applying makeup. A dimmer control enables you to adjust the lighting level.

- ✔ **Decorative wall sconces:** These lights, placed on both sides of a small medicine cabinet or mirror, provide even, shadow-free facial illumination for personal grooming. Mount fixtures at least 28 inches apart and at eye level or approximately 60 inches off the floor.

- ✔ **Tub or shower light:** This light should be bright enough for safe footing, bathing, shaving, and reading shampoo and soap labels. Choose a recessed downlight designed for use in a wet area. A shielded fixture will protect reclining bathers' eyes from glare. If you read while soaking in the tub, choose an adjustable accent light, aiming it from outside the tub for glare-free reading.

- ✔ **Recessed down light:** This light, placed above a toilet, provides light for reading. This fixture is especially essential if the bathroom has a separate toilet compartment.

Accent

Accent lighting highlights some architectural feature of the room or sets a mood. Examples include lights highlighting the base of the whirlpool or soaking tub. Track lighting systems with low-voltage halogen bulbs can be used to spotlight decorative objects and to create a relaxing mood. This lighting teamed with dimmer controls enables you to dial in just the right amount of light to fit the need of the moment.

Don't put any form of lighting within reach of someone in a bathtub or shower.

Don't forget to incorporate night lights into the lighting plan. Install them at the base of cabinets to provide illumination for those middle-of-the-night trips to the bathroom. Low-voltage linear lighting systems placed in the toe spaces beneath the vanity and cabinet are inexpensive to operate.

Dimmer switches on bathroom fixtures are another idea for night lighting and to create a mood. The ones with the slide next to the toggle switch are easy to operate and are unobtrusive. Use dimmer switches where you want to control lighting to soften a light or make lighting brighter for grooming or cleaning.

Shining the Light from Above

The most straightforward way to provide adequate lighting in a bathroom is to install an overhead light. Bathrooms must also have adequate ventilation (which you can read about in Chapter 8), so it makes sense to combine the light and vent in one unit, especially in smaller bathrooms. You can take this one step further and incorporate motion- and humidity-sensing circuitry to control the light and fan, giving you a completely automatic system.

Installing a dynamic duo: An auto-sensing vent and light

The Home Ventilating Institute (HVI) suggests that an exhaust fan should run at least 20 minutes after using the bathroom, but you don't need to leave it on all day or until you remember to turn it off. A "smart" unit senses when someone enters the room and turns on the light and monitors the humidity. It automatically turns on the vent fan if the humidity level rises and turns it off when the condition of the air returns to normal.

If you're replacing a stand-alone light or fan with a combination light and fan, you'll likely have to run new wiring if you want the choice of operating the light or fan separately.

If the room has an existing light or vent in the ceiling and you have experience with electrical projects, you can replace the old ceiling unit with a new sensing combination unit. If new wiring is needed, you can't get to the light vent from above, or there is no existing duct, this project is best left to a professional.

To install a light and fan fixture, you need these tools and materials:

- ✔ Drywall saw
- ✔ Duct tape
- ✔ Hammer
- ✔ Light and fan fixture
- ✔ Light bulbs
- ✔ Screwdriver

Assuming that no new electrical line is needed and the ductwork is already in place, you can do this job yourself. Because you'll be working in the bathroom and the attic, however, having someone to help you is more convenient. Before getting started, carefully read the instructions that come with the unit and identify the parts and hardware. If the unit is located in a bathtub or shower enclosure or within 5 feet of a shower head, the circuit must be GFCI-protected.

Before you begin, shut off the power to the bathroom at the circuit breaker or fuse panel.

Taking out the old unit

Follow these steps to remove the existing fixture:

1. **Double-check to make sure that the power is turned off at the main panel before starting this project.**

2. **Remove the grille of the old unit and disconnect the wiring.**

3. **If the fixture is attached directly to the joists, remove the nails or screws and then carefully pull the unit down through the ceiling opening (see Figure 16-1).**

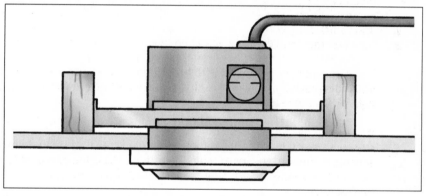

Figure 16-1:
A typical bathroom vent is mounted in the ceiling between the joists.

4. **Disconnect the duct from the fan, but leave it in place. The duct is the metal or plastic pipe that distributes the air from a fan, furnace, or air conditioning unit.**

   If you can't find the fasteners that hold it in place, look at the unit in the attic. It may be suspended from mounting brackets nailed to the joists. Be especially careful when you take out the last fastener.

   Disconnect the wiring and any ductwork, and lift or lower the fixture away from the opening.

5. **If the housing for the new fixture is larger than the old one, use the template supplied by the manufacturer to mark the new larger opening on the ceiling.**

   If there's not a template, trace around the fan housing itself.

6. **Cut out the opening with a drywall saw, being careful to cut within the lines.**

Putting in the new unit

Follow these directions to install the new unit:

1. **Position the unit so that its longer dimension is parallel with the joists, or the unit may not fit between the ceiling framing.**

   Disassemble the motor from the fan housing, which lightens the weight you have to hold over your head while you work.

2. **Fasten the fan housing in the opening and connect the wires to both the fan/light and switch.**

   Connect the wires according to the manufacturer's instructions for like-colored wires: black to black, white to white, and green or bare wire to the ground wire.

   The unit is likely to be installed in a switch loop. If that's the case, the white wire running between the switch and the unit is hot and should be marked at each end with black tape or marker to indicate that it's hot. Fan/light leads are likely to be colors like red or yellow — anything other than black and white.

3. **Permanently mount the unit in one of two ways (see Figure 16-2):**

   • Use the extendable mounting brackets (if provided) and attach them to the joists from the attic. Then crimp the guides that hold them to the housing.

   • If the fan is aligned next to a ceiling joist, some units can be fastened directly to the ceiling joists through the holes or slots in the housing. In this case, remove the brackets so they won't rattle when the unit operates. Double-check that the height is such that the edge of the housing is flush with the finished ceiling.

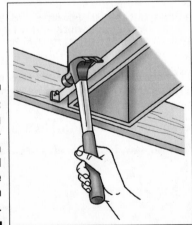

Figure 16-2:
Mounting
the com-
bination
light and
vent to the
joists with
brackets.

4. **With the housing securely in place, reinstall the fan motor and tighten all connections.**

   The unit has separate plugs on the housing for the fan and light (they're usually color-coded for easy identification) to connect them.

5. **Reconnect the ducting, being sure that the unit's damper moves freely and opens fully after you make the connection.**

6. **Wrap the joint with duct tape to ensure an airtight seal.**

7. **Install the grille and insert the bulbs and the light's diffuser.**

8. **Restore the power at the circuit panel and test all functions.**

   The unit's sensors are preset for sensitivity and timer duration at the factory, but you can readjust them to suit your lifestyle.

Recessed lighting

Another popular option for overhead lighting in a bathroom is recessed lighting. This style of lighting comes in many forms and can have incandescent, fluorescent, or halogen bulbs. Moisture-proof versions, which usually feature a glass or plastic lens over the can opening, are recommended for areas over bathtubs and shower stalls.

Recessed lights are economical and not too difficult to install. Some versions designed for remodeling projects can be installed through an existing ceiling.

If you're going to install recessed lights in an insulated ceiling, make sure that they're the insulation-compatible (ICAT) type, which is airtight and rated for insulation contact. The packaging of the light is labeled IC or ICAT.

If no power source is available (usually through an existing ceiling light) to tap into, hire an electrician to install the necessary switch and wiring to the light fixture.

To install a recessed light, you need these tools and materials:

- Coat hanger
- Electric drill and bits
- Electronic stud finder
- Jigsaw
- Recessed remodel light fixture with bulb

Follow these steps to install a remodel-type recessed light fixture, which is the type to use when there's no attic access to the joist cavity.

1. **Use an electronic stud finder to locate the joists that the recessed fixture will be installed between.**

2. **Use the fixture or the template supplied by the manufacturer to mark the opening on the ceiling.**

3. **Drill a ¼-inch hole through the center of the layout.**

4. **Push a piece of bent coat hanger through the hole and probe for hidden pipes or electrical wires.**

   You don't want to hit either of them. If you do, you have to relocate the fixture.

5. **Use a drywall or jigsaw to cut the opening for the recessed fixture between the joists.**

6. **Connect the wires.**

   The incoming power enters through the light's built-in junction box. The wires are easy to hook up by connecting the like-colored wires together: white to white, ground to ground (green or bare wire). The black wire is attached to the black or possibly red or other colored wire.

7. **Use a pliers to twist the wires together and then thread on a wire connector and twist tightly.**

8. **Disassemble the fixture according to the manufacturer's directions.**

   Most of these fixtures are designed to be inserted through the opening in the ceiling and then the mounting arms extended to engage the ceiling joists (see Figure 16-3). Some have tabs or fingers that engage the drywall and hold the fixture in place; others have brackets and clips.

Figure 16-3:
This recessed lighting unit can be installed from below by pushing it through the mounting hole and then securing it to the ceiling joists.

Some like it hot

A heat lamp is installed like a recessed light fixture in the ceiling and provides a direct source of heat to a room. Although it doesn't heat the entire room, its radiant heat warms objects, not the air, in a specific area, often above a vanity or the floor space outside the tub or shower. A heat lamp in the ceiling is a solution for a small bathroom where wall space for a heater is at a premium. You need an insulation-compatible type if the ceiling has insulation.

9. **Double-check that all electrical connections are in order.**

    Switch boxes should be closed, and connectors should be firmly in place.

10. **Screw in the light bulb, restore power to the circuit, and test the light for operation.**

11. **Install the trim ring and diffuser if the fixture has them.**

Using Wall Lighting

One of the fastest face-lifts for a bathroom is replacing an old medicine cabinet and the wall sconces on either side of it. If you've never done an electrical project and would like to try one, replacing a wall sconce is a doable job, even for a budding do-it-yourselfer. That's assuming that the same wires are in good condition and that all you have to do is remove the old fixture and replace it with a new one.

Definitely hire an electrician if a new electrical line is needed, which may also require adding a circuit breaker to the panel. These jobs should be left to a pro who's licensed and bonded to do the work.

To install a wall light, you need these tools and materials:

- ✔ Carpenter's level
- ✔ Light bulb
- ✔ Screwdriver
- ✔ Wall light fixture

Before you start, read the directions that came packaged with the new wall sconce and lay out the parts and identify each of them and how they fit together.

Even though the electricity is off, always connect the ground wire first, then the neutral (white), and then hot leads, just in case something funky has gone on and you're actually working with live wires. Follow these steps to install your new wall light:

1. **Turn off the power at the main circuit breaker or fuse panel.**

2. **Remove the old fixture from the wall by unfastening the mounting screws that hold it in place and pulling it away from the wall.**

3. **Disconnect the wires by removing the wire nuts that hold the wires together and untwisting their ends.**

4. **Depending on how the old fixture is mounted on the wall, you may be able to reuse the mounting strap. If not, remove it by loosening the screws that hold it to the electrical box.**

5. **Follow the manufacturer's instructions and attach the new mounting bracket to the electrical box with the screws supplied.**

6. **Connect the fixture wires to the wires in the electrical box.**

   You may have to strip off ¾ inch of insulation from the ends of the fixture wires.

7. **Twist the ends of the black wires together with pliers and attach a wire nut.**

   Always connect the wires in this order: ground, then neutral, and then hot leads.

8. **Twist the white wires together and the bare copper or green wire to the ground wire in the electrical box.**

   Some fixtures have a green screw on the fixture body to connect the ground wire from the electrical box.

9. **Twist on wire nuts and fold the wires into the junction box.**

10. **Use a level to make sure that the fixture is straight on the wall.**

    Place the fixture on the wall and align the mounting screws with the holes in the canopy and screw on the cap nut. Check the level and then tighten the screws.

11. **Install the decorative shade or glass and secure it with the socket ring.**

12. **Screw in the appropriate size light bulb, turn on the power, and turn on the wall switch.**

Part V
The Part of Tens

The 5th Wave — By Rich Tennant

"You did an excellent job, Dave. But two months seems a long time to paint the bathroom."

In this part . . .

*I*f you are short on time and don't like to waste it, this part is for you. Here's where you can get our top ten ideas for finding storage space in a bathroom. In addition, you can discover a treasure trove of ten tried-and-true, really easy, and inexpensive decorating ideas to dress up a bathroom. Finally, get our list of the ten best Web resources for information about remodeling a bathroom.

Chapter 17

Ten Ways to Increase Storage Space in a Bathroom

In This Chapter

▶ Stowing stuff in unconventional spaces

▶ Making the most of the space you have

▶ Practicing the art of decluttering and finding inner peace

For being one of the smallest rooms in the house, a bathroom is expected to have a whole lot of stuff. It's no wonder storage is always at a premium. Consider using these ideas to help declutter and take advantage of every inch of space you have.

Putting a Corner to Good Use with a Cabinet

You may have thought that corner cabinets were only for the dining room, but they're just as attractive and functional in the bathroom. Use them for storing toiletries and linens. You can find new ones at unfinished furniture stores and discount department stores and used ones at antique stores and architectural salvage suppliers. Either way, they expand the storage capacity of a bathroom while adding a custom built-in touch. The installation is easy; just attach the cabinet to wall studs and finish the floor with molding, if needed.

Using Ready-Made Storage Units

Bathroom storage units are available in many shapes, sizes, and materials. You'll find them made of plastic, wicker, chrome, brass, wood, and veneers in several wood finishes. They come as space savers and floor and wall cabinets, and many have coordinating hampers and wastebaskets. A space saver, designed to fit over a toilet to make use of the area above it, is usually about 25 inches wide, 10 inches deep, and less than 6 feet high. It has one open shelf above the toilet, a nice place for a decorative accent, and enclosed cabinets above the shelf for storing toiletries, tissues, and other less-attractive but necessary items. These units are installed as a free-standing piece of furniture, but many require some assembly.

You can also find wall-hung storage units that are designed to fit over the toilet and that you bolt to the wall studs. These items, sold in catalogs and at home, bath, and discount centers, are available in a range of prices.

Building Cubbyhole Shelves

You can use the empty space between wall studs as a cubbyhole for shelves. The depth of the shelves depends on what's behind the wall. For example, the space will be shallow, about 3½ inches deep, for a standard wall. Walls with plumbing are usually deeper, up to 6 inches thick. If the other side of the wall is in a closet and you're willing to give up some of this space, you can build a deeper storage area that goes completely through the wall.

The ideal time to build a wall cubbyhole is when you're remodeling and before new wallboard is installed. When you're planning a new bathroom, think about wall space that's not being used and incorporate a cubbyhole in your design. The wall cavity should be empty, without any plumbing or electrical lines, so framing won't interfere with them. You can build and paint the cubbyhole frame out of ordinary wood, but consider using a better grade of wood if you plan a natural finish for the shelves. If you're using wall tile in the bathroom, use it inside the cubbyhole and use decorative edge tiles for trim.

Showing Off Towels Like a Designer

The addition of a small wicker chair with a stack of fluffy towels gives even the most modest bathroom an elegant look. In addition, putting the towels on display brings color and texture to the hard surfaces of the room. Or instead of a wicker chair, how about reinventing a small wrought-iron table or footstool that you find at a yard sale as a place to display the towels? Choose a small piece of furniture you can tuck in a corner, where it's out of the way.

Getting a Peg Up

Add a row of Shaker pegs on the wall in a family bathroom to create space for towels for everyone in the house. The pegs take up less space than towel bars or rings, and they assure that everyone's towel has a place to hang. The inexpensive pegs are easy to install and create a clean, stylish look.

If you want more storage that looks good with the pegs, get a metal storage locker — yes, just like the ones you see in locker rooms — and paint it to complement the room. The straight lines and utility of the Shaker pegs and locker go together nicely to make a family bathroom both practical and stylish without breaking the bank.

Customizing the Vanity Interior

Plastic-coated wire shelving components, designed to fit inside cabinets, come in a variety of styles and sizes, so no matter how small or large your bathroom vanity is, one is sure to fit your space. With the plumbing lines of the sink concealed in the interior of a vanity, the space can be awkward, but adding a two-shelf storage bin doubles the space. These bins are easy to install with screws in the floor or on the sides of the cabinet, but either way, the components offer handy pull-out bins just right for storing extra soaps, toothpaste, and shampoo.

Make a rough sketch and measure the interior of your vanity and take it along when you're shopping for a storage component. A key measurement is the space below the plumbing lines because the new unit has to clear it.

Boosting Hanging Space with a Coat Tree

Reinvent a hall coat tree as a bathroom tree, and you'll have plenty of room to store towels, bathrobes, and clothes that find their way into the bathroom. Wood and metal ones are available for as little as $25 at discount stores, and you can find elaborate old-fashioned brass trees for $100. The floor space a coat tree requires is very small when compared to its holding power, so it's an especially good choice in a small bathroom.

Going High Tech for Low Price

For about $20, you can buy a metal utility shelf and put it to good use in a bathroom. Play off its bare-bones industrial look and add inexpensive plastic dishwashing tubs as drawers to store toiletries and supplies. It may not be pretty, but it's clean, basic storage at a bargain price.

You'll need to assemble the shelf, so don't be intimidated when you open the box and find what looks like hundreds of screws. An electric screwdriver will come in mighty handy and so will a helper when it's time to hold the shelves in alignment with the legs and rails.

 If you want, finish the shelf with a couple cans of spray paint that will liven up the original gray industrial finish. Or get some restaurant-style heavy-gauge wire shelves that come in chrome or black. No assembly required and they're not that much more expensive. You can find them at home centers and kitchen stores.

Getting Bulky Stuff Out

Just because it's toilet paper doesn't mean you have to store a jumbo 12-pack in the bathroom. Keep a few rolls handy in the bathroom, but find somewhere outside the bathroom to stow most of your supply. The same is true for extra towels, bath mats, and holiday linens that you use only once a year.

Ideally, you can find a storage place near the bathroom so that when you need something, it's an easy trek to retrieve it. The goal is to have what you need in the bathroom, but eliminate what you don't regularly need to make room for the necessities.

Corralling the Kids' Stuff

Rubber duckies, bath sponges, and toys for kids' bath time can take up a lot of space. Keep them in tow in a mesh laundry bag that you can hang from a hook, or stash them in a colorful storage bin.

Chapter 18

Ten Easy Bathroom Decorating Ideas

*T*ry some of these easy-on-the-budget and easy-to-execute ideas to give your bathroom that finished look that professional designers do so well — the results may surprise you. No, your bathroom probably won't be featured in *Architectural Digest,* but your family and guests will notice the improvement.

Making a Small Bathroom Feel Larger

Contrasting colors cut up space, so to make a space appear larger, use one color with variations of it to create an open and balanced feeling. Use a light color on the floor because it reflects light and gives the room an airy quality.

Fool the eye by calling attention to the ceiling with a wallpaper border to make the room appear higher and wider. The stencil-cut borders with adhesive on the back are the easiest to install and give a room an almost instant new look.

Borrow the color scheme and style of the room or hall next to the bathroom so they flow easily together. When the bathroom appears to be part of the larger room, it feels more open.

Using Color in Things You Can Change

A small bathroom with white fixtures and walls can be an ideal backdrop for a changeable and colorful decorating scheme. Complete the backdrop by covering the window in a white shade or shutter. Add a dose of color — bright, primary colors or subtle, subdued shades — in a rug, shower curtain, and towels. Presto — your bathroom has a pulled-together look.

Instead of decorating the little kids' bathroom with kid-specific wallpaper, choose a neutral pattern that will grow with them. Let them choose the towels and decorations that you can change as they grow up.

Adding Old-Fashioned Charm

Give a plain-Jane bathroom some personality with a feeling of old-fashioned charm. Cover the walls with painted beadboard wainscoting and a chair rail and then decorate the room with finds from a flea market. Instead of colored plastic accessories to hold soaps and toothbrushes, start a collection of vintage jars, vases, antique saucers, bowls, and other small dishes. Or use different sizes and shapes of baskets, including a large one to hold towels. Add a large antique mirror or a grouping of small ones for grooming as well as for enhancing the decor. Choose a braided rug to complete the scheme and provide a soft warm floor covering. If you have room for a plant, use a hanging or potted fern, which is sure to appreciate the warm, moist conditions of a bathroom.

Creating a Custom Wallpaper

Wallpaper a small bathroom with photocopies of family pictures, wine labels, or even comic book covers for a very customized bathroom. We saw this done with race ticket stubs from the Kentucky Derby in a Louisville home, and it was very attractive. You make your own wallpaper by using the photocopies, overlapping them slightly, and gluing them on the wall with wallpaper adhesive. For a nautical theme, use old navigation charts. For a musical theme, use old sheet music. You get the idea.

Applying a Decorative Finish to Plain Walls

If you want to liven up ordinary painted walls, you can apply a glaze coat over them, allowing some of the base coat to show through. This glazing process does a remarkable job of adding depth and gives a completely different feel to the room. You'll find special brushes and rollers for applying a decorative finish at paint stores. Before applying this finish on your bathroom walls, practice using them on a scrap piece of drywall or poster board to get a feel for the effect you want to create. Don't be intimidated if you're not artistic; a decorative finish is as unique as the person who applies it. That would be you.

Adding an Etched Glass Window Film

Do you need to cover up an old bathroom window in the bathtub wall for privacy but hate to block the daylight? Instead of using an old plastic curtain, get a decorative window film. The film looks like etched glass and comes in several frosted designs that you'll find at home improvement stores and decorating centers. Installing it is as simple as cleaning the glass, measuring and cutting the film, and then positioning it on the glass, using a squeegee to smooth it in place.

 Another way to create privacy in a bathroom window is to hang a stained glass panel inside the window so that it covers the glass. Or replace plain glass with antique ripple glass that provides privacy while letting sunlight inside.

Accentuating the Positive

Take advantage of tile — on the walls or on the floor — that's in good condition and use it as the basis for your color scheme. If the tile has more than one color, emphasize one you like by choosing towels and rugs in a similar shade. Let the tile colors dominate and use a plain white shower curtain as a backdrop.

Showing Off in the Powder Room

If you have a powder room for guests, consider adding open shelves to display a collection of colorful glassware or any collectible items. Even though most powder rooms are small, they usually have a wall where you can show off something special. Glass shelves make figurines and porcelain appear like they're floating, and heavier wooden shelves are a nice natural way to display shells or stones.

Taking Cues from the Pros

The next time you go shopping, notice how cleverly and creatively retailers display things, and use some of their ideas in your bathroom. Roll towels up and stand the rolls up in a basket or stack them in rolls on a shelf. After your shower curtain is dry, tie it back instead of letting it hang straight. Be on the lookout for some ideas from professionals who make their living from being creative. It's free and it's fun.

Remembering that Less Is Better

Make everything in a small bathroom have an important reason to be there, thus creating a clean, inviting overall appearance. To free up space, get rid of stuff that's not being used or is seldom used. Do you have to have the bathroom scale in the bathroom? How about moving it to the bedroom? How about relocating the clothes hamper to the hall outside the bathroom?

Minimizing what's in the room visually expands the feeling of space.

Chapter 19

Ten Great Remodeling Web Sites

In This Chapter

▶ Finding design help online

▶ Using visualization tools like the pros

▶ Buying or browsing on the Internet

*W*hen you need help planning a new bathroom, spend some quality time online. Many Web sites are worthy of a long visit. You can get help visualizing colors and styles and find design tools to create a floor plan that lays out the fixtures and furnishings. Many of these design tools are simplified versions of the software that professional designers use, and some are just fun to use because they're interactive and let you play around with different color schemes and palettes. If you have access to the Net, let your fingers do the walking — on the keyboard, that is. Visit these sites, and you'll come away with some good insights and ideas, along with printouts of floor plans or product spec sheets and shopping lists.

National Kitchen & Bath Association

The National Kitchen & Bath Association is a nonprofit trade association that has educated and led the kitchen and bath industry for 40 years. Use the Web site (www.nkba.org) as a resource for everything from finding a design professional in your area to obtaining information on industry trends, products, and services. The association will send you a free consumer workbook that offers remodeling tips and guides you through the process of redesigning your kitchen or bath from beginning to end.

Internet Wallpaper Store

The Internet Wallpaper Store (www.wallpaperstore.com) is an e-commerce site that makes it easy to peruse wallpaper patterns, styles, borders, and murals because, unlike in the store, you don't have to manhandle the wallpaper sample books. The site is well organized and convenient to use, and your selection appears quickly on the screen. Search by brand name, pattern number, or theme and topic, or make your own search criteria. For $2, you can get a sample of wallpaper sent to you, a nice feature that eliminates the temptation to clip a sample from the wallpaper books in the store. Because the image of the pattern was scanned and the colors may vary from monitor to monitor, a sample is the only way to see the exact colors of a particular wallpaper.

ebuild

If you're looking for a particular manufacturer or product for a project, the ebuild site (www.ebuild.com) is the ultimate reference. It's a massive database of manufacturers in the construction industry, so it's the ultimate resource that includes everything from descriptions, diagrams, and dimensions to installation instructions, reviews, and supplier locators.

Kohler

At Kohler's site (www.kohler.com), you'll find a dizzying array of its products, along with two interesting design tools you can use to generate some high-level floor plans. The Virtual Shower Planner and Virtual Bath Planner have Flash tutorials that explain how to use the design software. These are elaborate programs designers use, and they help you develop and create a specific design. Plan to spend time finding out how to use the tools and fine-tuning your design, and you'll come away with a bathroom floor plan that makes the most of your space.

American Standard

American Standard (www.americanstandard-us.com) is another large manufacturer with an extensive site, along with a Room Planner, a 2D planning tool to create a new bathroom. You place the products into a resizable and printable bathroom template that you can use to order products. Before you start designing, however, you should get an idea of how much your bathroom will cost. To do that, use the Project Estimator, a series of basic questions about the fixtures you're replacing, what you're doing about the walls and floors, and whether you plan to do it yourself or hire a contractor. The calculator generates a rough estimate that will be very useful in your planning.

GELighting.com

General Electric's Web site (www.gelighting.com) has a Virtual House that allows you to see the different effects of lighting in a bathroom (and many other rooms). You're given an image of a bathroom and then prompted to choose the type of fixtures — ceiling, recessed, vanity, or wall sconce — that you're considering. Then the bathroom is lit using the type of fixtures you chose. By repeating the process with a combination of different fixtures, you can compare how they work together to create the best lighting for your needs.

Baldwin Hardware

Visit the Baldwin site (www.baldwinhardware.com) if you're uncertain about choosing a style of hardware for your new bathroom (and all the rooms in your house). The site features the Architectural Style Guide to help you establish a theme for your home by using their categories of architectural styles and suggests using them as a guide to create your personal style. You find the architectural style you have and then look at the bath products to see what type of accessories will complement your home.

Dutch Boy

This paint manufacturer's Web site (www.dutchboy.com) helps you visualize different color schemes to use in your new bathroom with the Project Planner. You see palettes of colors and how they look together, which is a nice feature when you're deciding about a color scheme. Through a series of quick qualifying questions about the type and condition of the walls in the room, you create a bathroom that virtually paints the colors on the walls. This approach is much easier than actually painting the room forest green with taupe trim and then realizing that you hate it. But remember, the color you see on your monitor may be different from the actual paint color.

Armstrong

Armstrong's site (www.armstrong.com) has a design tool called Design A Room that takes you through the process of creating all the rooms in a house and seeing what different flooring materials would look like in that setting. Because the floor is such an important choice for a bathroom, you'll find it very useful to experiment and see whether vinyl, laminate, or tile would look best in your bathroom.

The Bathroom Diaries

The Bathroom Diaries site at www.bathroomdiaries.com is one we just couldn't resist including here. What a hoot! Here's the site you want to visit before traveling because it lists thousands of free, clean restrooms around the world. No kidding. You can even link it up to your PDA. We agree with a quote we found on the site that says, "The huddled masses deserve a clean place to sit."

Index

• **Z** •

FOR DUMMIES®

The easy way to get more done and have more fun

PERSONAL FINANCE & BUSINESS

Investing FOR DUMMIES
0-7645-2431-3

Home Buying FOR DUMMIES
0-7645-5331-3

Grant Writing FOR DUMMIES
0-7645-5307-0

Also available:

Accounting For Dummies
(0-7645-5314-3)

Business Plans Kit For Dummies
(0-7645-5365-8)

Managing For Dummies
(1-5688-4858-7)

Mutual Funds For Dummies
(0-7645-5329-1)

QuickBooks All-in-One Desk Reference For Dummies
(0-7645-1963-8)

Resumes For Dummies
(0-7645-5471-9)

Small Business Kit For Dummies
(0-7645-5093-4)

Starting an eBay Business For Dummies
(0-7645-1547-0)

Taxes For Dummies 2003
(0-7645-5475-1)

HOME, GARDEN, FOOD & WINE

Feng Shui FOR DUMMIES
0-7645-5295-3

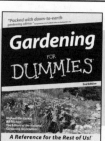

Gardening FOR DUMMIES
0-7645-5130-2

Cooking FOR DUMMIES
0-7645-5250-3

Also available:

Bartending For Dummies
(0-7645-5051-9)

Christmas Cooking For Dummies
(0-7645-5407-7)

Cookies For Dummies
(0-7645-5390-9)

Diabetes Cookbook For Dummies
(0-7645-5230-9)

Grilling For Dummies
(0-7645-5076-4)

Home Maintenance For Dummies
(0-7645-5215-5)

Slow Cookers For Dummies
(0-7645-5240-6)

Wine For Dummies
(0-7645-5114-0)

FITNESS, SPORTS, HOBBIES & PETS

Fitness FOR DUMMIES
0-7645-5167-1

Golf FOR DUMMIES
0-7645-5146-9

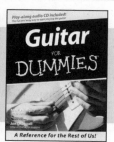

Guitar FOR DUMMIES
0-7645-5106-X

Also available:

Cats For Dummies
(0-7645-5275-9)

Chess For Dummies
(0-7645-5003-9)

Dog Training For Dummies
(0-7645-5286-4)

Labrador Retrievers For Dummies
(0-7645-5281-3)

Martial Arts For Dummies
(0-7645-5358-5)

Piano For Dummies
(0-7645-5105-1)

Pilates For Dummies
(0-7645-5397-6)

Power Yoga For Dummies
(0-7645-5342-9)

Puppies For Dummies
(0-7645-5255-4)

Quilting For Dummies
(0-7645-5118-3)

Rock Guitar For Dummies
(0-7645-5356-9)

Weight Training For Dummies
(0-7645-5168-X)

Available wherever books are sold.
to www.dummies.com or call 1-877-762-2974 to order direct

 WILEY

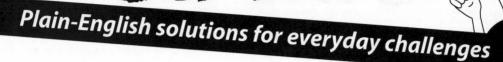

FOR DUMMIES®

Plain-English solutions for everyday challenges

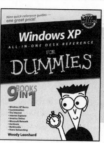